TABLE OF CONTENTS

WRITER'S MARKET

GUIDE TO GETTING
PUBLISHED

THE EDITORS OF WRITER'S DIGEST

WD

WRITER'S DIGEST
BOOKS

WritersDigest.*com*
Cincinnati, Ohio

For more resources for writers, visit www.writersdigest.com/books.

To receive a free weekly e-mail newsletter delivering tips and updates about writing and about Writer's Digest products, register directly at http://newsletters.fwpublications.com.

14 13 12 11   5 4 3 2

Distributed in Canada by Fraser Direct
100 Armstrong Avenue
Georgetown, Ontario, Canada L7G 5S4
Tel: (905) 877-4411

Distributed in the U.K. and Europe by David & Charles
Brunel House, Newton Abbot, Devon, TQ12 4PU, England
Tel: (+44) 1626-323200, Fax: (+44) 1626-323319
E-mail: postmaster@davidandcharles.co.uk

Distributed in Australia by Capricorn Link
P.O. Box 704, Windsor, NSW 2756 Australia
Tel: (02) 4577-3555

Library of Congress Cataloging-in-Publication Data
Writer's market guide to getting published / from the editors of Writer's digest. -- 3rd ed.
    p. cm.
  Includes index.
  ISBN 978-1-58297-608-2 (pbk. : alk. paper)
  1. Authorship--Marketing. 2. Authorship. I. Writer's Digest Books (Firm)
PN161.W832 2010
808'.02--dc22   2009029475

Edited by Jana Riess
Designed by Terri Woesner
Production coordinated by Mark Griffin

PART FOUR: YOUR WRITING BUSINESS

INTRODUCTION TO THE THIRD EDITION

THERE'S AN OLD chestnut in publishing that asserts there's really nothing to writing; all you have to do is sit down at a typewriter and open a vein. Although we would change "typewriter" to "keyboard" today, the sentiment still stands: Writing is difficult, and it can drain us as well as exhilarate us. And unfortunately, writing a manuscript is just the first step, since navigating the publishing process can also seem daunting and enervating.

Yet it doesn't have to be that way. *The Writer's Market Guide to Getting Published* exists to help you plot a course through the rocky shoals of the publishing process, from the first stages (Do I need an agent? How do I write a query letter?) to the last (What do I need to do to promote my book in a crowded marketplace?). This book will guide you through the first stages of your career as a writer, offering practical and up-to-date information about the many choices you'll face in the months ahead. In addition to focusing on book publishing, it also offers guidance for freelance magazine writers, corporate writers, and screenwriters.

The Writer's Market Guide to Getting Published is actually the third edition of a book by Joe Feiertag and Mary Carmen Cupito called *Writer's Market Companion*, which was last updated in 2004. There's far more to this third edition than a new title; Jana Riess, a former editor at *Publishers Weekly*, has completely overhauled and expanded the content, with the following new features:

- A stronger focus on marketing, publicity, and building your readership. Today, the writers who get published—and whose books are successful—are the ones who approach their writing like a business as well as an art. Part Three of this guide delves into how to think about marketing and publicity (which is your responsibility as much as, if not more than, it is your publisher's). We look at the rise of social networking and provide useful tips on using your blog, website, and Facebook presence to your advantage. We also offer fifty ways to get the word out about your book—some of them tried-and-true, and some of them very of the moment.

- More nuts-and-bolts discussions of what editors and agents want to see in a query letter, book proposal, and sample chapter.

- A brand-new chapter on the rise of self-publishing and print-on-demand, which have taken the writing world by storm, especially in the last five years.

- An expanded focus on contracts and the fine print, with guidance on all the major elements of book and magazine contracts, including new questions about digital rights and Kindle rights.

- More information about agents and what they can do for your career.

- New sidebars throughout that describe the personal experiences of writers who have successfully published their books and articles.

At Writer's Digest Books, our goal is to help you, the writer, understand the publishing business and capitalize on current trends so you can build a successful career. This book can be used in conjunction with the annually updated listings in *Writer's Market* to help you publish and sell your writing. *The Writer's Market Guide to Getting Published* can be read straight through in a linear fashion or in a more modular way, if you are seeking particular information about a specific topic and want to focus in on that. Whatever your needs, we're confident that the comprehensive and current information in this book will help you in your quest for success.

PART ONE

YOUR WRITING GAME PLAN

SO YOU WANT to be a writer, eh? Wonderful! Welcome to the fascinating, if complex, world of professional writing. In this opening part of this book, we'll first explore the news about what's going on at magazines and in publishing today. Just as a heads-up, it's not all great news, especially with the unforgiving economy, so it's great that we're getting any doom and gloom out of the way early. We will take a glass-half-full approach and focus on how the shifting tides of writing and publishing today may actually work in your favor, especially if you are open to new trends and hot categories.

After we dissect the state of the overall market for the written word, we'll move from macro to micro and discuss how it affects you, the writer. How should you begin thinking about a writing career? We'll talk turkey—writing is hard work. The most successful writers are often not the ones with the rawest talent but with the most discipline and the hide of a rhinoceros.

How can you create excellent writing habits, cultivate your craft, and organize your writing world? Finally, we'll take a down-and-dirty look at research—with special emphasis on how Google and other websites have radically changed writers' research lives for the better.

1

THE (BRAVE NEW)
WRITER'S WORLD

ENTERTAINMENT OPTIONS HAVE exploded in recent years with e-mail, the Internet, the Wii, smart phones, and more cable TV networks than anyone dreamed imaginable. During this media revolution, some experts have predicted that the worlds of book and magazine publishing would suffer. Who would have time for dead trees when there were so many new diversions?

It's true that publishing has faced more challenges in the digital age than ever before. In 1999, there were over 31,000 magazines tracked by *The National Directory of Magazines*; at the start of 2008 there were 22,652. As we'll see in the coming pages, it's a tough time for print magazines and newspapers. Book publishing has not been immune to current economic challenges, either: At the time this book went to print, industry reports like *Publishers Lunch* and *PW Daily* have been filled almost every weekday with news of consolidations, closings, and cutbacks. But there are also positive trends that you, as a writer, can capitalize on. In this chapter we'll discuss what's rising and what's falling so you can navigate the industry to your best advantage.

THE MAGAZINE MARKET UP CLOSE

First, the bad news. Print magazines and newspapers are in deep trouble. The Magazine Publishers of America counted 191 new magazines launched in 2008, which doesn't sound so bad until you compare it to the 271 that were launched in 2007—and the hundreds launched in each calendar year before that. Although some categories (regional interest, health, cooking, and celebrity gossip) continue to be relatively strong, the overall magazine industry has been weakened considerably by a recession-heavy economy and concomitant declines in advertising revenues and subscriptions. Who wants to start up a new magazine in this kind of environment?

If the news about so few start-up magazines doesn't scare you, consider the fact that longstanding magazine stalwarts from *The Atlantic* (f.k.a. *The Atlantic Monthly*) to *Time* have cut both jobs and pages. *U.S. News & World Report* announced in the summer of 2008 that it would cease to be a weekly newsmagazine and become instead a biweekly rag, focusing less on hard news and more on culture. Then in November, it scaled back its plans still further, declaring it would be published only monthly. Even *Playboy* had a decidedly unplayful 2008, with ad revenues down by almost a third. Plenty of specialty magazines—*Golf for Women*, *CosmoGirl!*, *Quick & Simple*, and *02138*—have simply folded altogether, while others, like *Rolling Stone*, have gone on a diet and look like slimmed-down versions of their former selves. It is becoming the norm for print magazines to be deep in debt. "Red is the new black," as one magazine industry executive put it.

What does all this doom and gloom mean for you, the writer? Well, the glass-half-empty view is that since there are fewer magazines remaining to write for, and even those magazines are slashing pages and pay, there is less work and less money for you as a freelance magazine writer. On the other hand, many magazines that have made cuts in staff are actively looking for freelancers to pick up the slack left by their laid-off employees. If you can write quickly and on a timely topic, you will find work. And if you don't require much editing, you may have more work than you know what to do with, as harried editors keep coming back for more of your turnkey copy.

Another point to be embraced by glass-half-full types is this: Most of the venerable magazines haven't died; they've just been recast as online-only publications. The earlier you learn to write for this format, the better it will go for you. More and more magazines—and even daily newspapers—are going to follow in the footsteps of *The Christian Science Monitor*, which announced in its centennial year of 2008 that it would cease its weekday print schedule and become an online-only weekly publication focusing on international coverage. Of course, we can and should mourn the loss of one of the nation's best print newspapers, which has won seven Pulitzers and countless other awards. However, it's not the end of the world—just the world as we've known it thus far. The *Monitor* will continue its valiant work and possibly even extend its international readership through its new online strategy. Other publications will no doubt follow suit.

One trend is that today's consumers are looking for more niche-friendly publications. A half a century ago, the magazine market was flooded with publications like *Life* that sought to be all things to all people, appealing to the broadest possible demographic. Today, in print publications as in television, the focus is on reaching carefully targeted audiences in terms of age, socioeconomic status, race, political leanings, and hobbies. That's why *The Daily Show with Jon Stewart* thrives with the late-night left-leaning crowd, while generic 6:30 P.M. newscasts are bleeding viewers. Today's viewers and readers don't want to waste their time wading through three news segments or magazine articles before they get to the one item that is useful or interesting to them. They want key information now, and they prefer it in an entertaining fashion.

Niche is the new buzzword. This may be bad news for magazines (and the media conglomerates that typically own them), but the trend is not necessarily bad for writers—particularly those who are just starting out and looking for a foothold. It's usually easier to break into a small, niche publication than a broad-platform national magazine. Many successful writers got their start working for niche publications. Novelist Sue Monk Kidd wrote for years for the inspirational grand dame *Guideposts* magazine before she hit the big time with her novel *The Secret Life of Bees*. The key is to find magazines in a demographic you can write for on a topic that interests both you and an editor.

Growing (and Declining) Magazine Categories

Magazine industry trends often reflect those of society. Nearly 150 years ago, as Americans were discovering bicycles, the novelty and excitement spawned an entire new genre of magazine—cycling magazines. New cyclists and those who dreamed of owning one were eager to learn all they could about these two-wheeled wonders. The phenomenon still occurs today, as trends come and go.

Once again, *The National Directory of Magazines* lends some insight into where the growth is—and isn't. First, let's look at some of the categories that had notable declines between 1999 and 2007.

TYPE OF MAGAZINE	MAGAZINES IN THAT CATEGORY IN 1999	MAGAZINES IN THAT CATEGORY IN 2007	PERCENTAGE CHANGE
Sports and sporting goods	863	339	-61%
Science fiction and fantasy	107	47	-56%
Poetry and creative writing	365	196	-46%
Newsmagazines	131	40	-69%
Antiques and fine art	106	42	-60%
Entertainment	322	108	-66%
Comics	495	154	-69%
Fanzines	142	44	-69%

These numbers seem grim, but remember what we discussed earlier: Numbers don't always tell the whole story. For example, in the case of fanzines, many publishers have discovered that the Internet is a much faster, cheaper, and more efficient way of reaching their demographic. Subscribers to fanzines don't want to wait a month or more to hear about Lindsay Lohan's latest antics, or find out the convoluted plot turns of a Syfy original series. They want regular updates as well as online interactions with other fans, if not the show's stars and creators. All this is to say that the above statistics on some categories, like fanzines, entertainment, comics, and science fiction/fantasy, may actually paint too bleak a picture. Although the print components of these categories are sometimes in trouble, the categories themselves remain viable and strong.

Moreover, there are some real bright spots even in the print magazine world. Take a look at these growing categories:

TYPE OF MAGAZINE	MAGAZINES IN THAT CATEGORY IN 1999	MAGAZINES IN THAT CATEGORY IN 2007	PERCENTAGE CHANGE
Bridal	45	130	189%
Ethnic	450	732	63%
Crossword and other puzzles	126	144	14%
Interior design and decoration	146	195	34%
Dogs	62	69	11%
College alumni	450	496	10%
Golf	98	139	42%
Guns and firearms	57	68	19%

Glancing through this table, you can see that some of these magazine trends are predictable based on larger trends in America today. We are an increasingly diverse culture, with many minority and immigrant groups searching for community and understanding. We are also a well-educated culture, with a higher-than-ever percentage graduating from college (especially among women, who tend to be more faithful magazine readers). We enjoy doing certain leisure activities such as golf and skiing, and we also like reading about them. Writers who can create stories for one of these niche categories should do very well. Writers who can take a single experience and spin it into several articles, or who can approach the same topic from multiple angles for different niche markets, will do very well indeed.

Some niche categories like interior design are still growing, but at a slower rate than just a few years ago—a trend reflected by the shuttering of decorating magazines like O *at Home* and *Cottage Living* in 2008, and *Country Home* in 2009. In addition to the growth areas, other categories are holding steady. These include travel, nursing, boating, gardening, and baby and pregnancy. Religious and inspirational magazines have lost a little ground in the last few years, but not much. Niche publications for people with disabilities (e.g., *ADDitude*, a magazine specifically about ADD/ADHD) are another area of stability, if not growth.

While the newsstand is more competitive than ever, you can break into magazines by understanding their unique position in the market. Think about the type of reader each magazine is attempting to attract, and write a query that emphasizes how your piece will make that reader buy the magazine. We'll talk more about that process in chapter six, but here's an early hint: It begins with actually reading the magazines for which you want to write.

THE WORLD OF BOOKS

If our discussion of magazines hasn't put you off, throw down a stiff drink before reading this section on book publishing. In a nutshell, the picture for the publishing industry is rather miserable right now. Sales of trade books—i.e., those nonspecialized, nonacademic books you can usually purchase at a Barnes & Noble or other commercial bookstores—have been anemic. The Book Industry Study Group, a research organization that tracks the publishing industry, projected less than a 1 percent increase in book sales in 2008, and just 1.4 percent growth for 2009 to 2012—and that was *before* the economy essentially fell apart in the fall of 2008. Since that time, many granddaddy publishing companies have fallen on very rough times. According to Nielsen BookScan, actual sales of books in 2008 were even worse than the BISG prediction, clocking in at –0.2 percent after a 5 percent rise in 2007.

Although sales of books are flat, the number of books *available* continues to increase each year, thanks in good part to the ready accessibility of self-publishing and print-on-demand technology (which we'll explore in detail in chapter eleven). Bowker noted 375,000 books published in the United States in 2007 and roughly half a million in 2008, a surge caused by the explosion in print-on-demand books. Since self-published titles have a very difficult time getting into bookstores, not all of these titles are competing for shelf space, but it's safe to say that a good 150,000 new books are being marketed to bookstores annually. And remember, that's just the hot-off-the-press titles and doesn't include classic backlist books. The bottom line for you as a writer? It's becoming more and more difficult to gain attention for any book that doesn't already have instant recognition in the marketplace—through a celebrity author, an established brand name, or a TV/movie tie-in.

Further exacerbating the problem are discount chains (e.g., Walmart, Target, Costco) that often account for more than 40 percent of a best-selling book's sales, increasing the industry's dependence on hit books. Once a book takes hold in the discounters, the independent and chain bookstores often try to offer the same discount, thus influencing what gets sold at traditional stores, according to Paul Aiken, executive director of The Authors Guild. That tends to squeeze out new authors and established midlist authors—those writers who have a modest reputation and reasonable sales, but who don't usually appear on best-seller lists.

So that's the bad news. (You can put the drink down now.) And here's the real question: How does an unknown writer break into a book publishing culture so infused with celebrity, and so driven by brands and appearances?

One area of hope is in small and independent publishers, which are growing and effectively competing with the big New York six (Random House, HarperCollins, Penguin Group, Simon & Schuster, Macmillan, and Hachette Book Group). Often small presses cater to niche audiences, and they know how to reach them outside of traditional bookstore outlets. Certainly very few of the books by small presses make the national best-seller lists. But authors who sign with independents can count on personalized attention and find themselves an important part of that publisher's catalog. It's a question to ask yourself: Would you rather be published by one of the big houses and gain the prestige of the imprint, but receive little or no marketing attention, or would you prefer to be published by a lesser-known press, but have the staff's dedication and loyalty? Going her own way with a tiny house worked wonders for Phyllis Pellman Good, whose *Fix It and Forget It* cookbooks have put the eponymous press Good Books—as well as the slow cooker—on Americans' cultural radar. Now the author is a fixture on cookbook best-seller lists and a regular on QVC, and her vanity press has grown up into a full-fledged publishing house with lines of cookbooks, children's books, and religion titles.

Where's the Growth?

Although the overall outlook for publishing is a bit unnerving, there are some bright spots. Religion books have grown robustly in the last decade, as have travel and business. Here are Bowker's top ten category figures for the period between 2002 and 2007:

BOOK CATEGORY	PERCENTAGE GROWTH BETWEEN 2002 AND 2007 (TOTAL, NOT ANNUALIZED)
Fiction	99%
Poetry and drama	79%
Literature	56%
Religion	55%
Biography	54%
Arts	43%
Philosophy and psychology	42%
Cooking	37%
Travel	34%
History	30%

Behind the Numbers: Fiction

Isn't it encouraging to look at this table and realize that fiction, literature, poetry, and drama are still thriving in this country? Clearly, there is an enduring market for good stories, including classic literature, contemporary literature, and the many genres (science fiction, romance, suspense, etc.) that readers enjoy.

2007 and 2008 were the years of *Twilight* mania, with millions of people waiting with bated breath for the next installments in Stephenie Meyer's vampire series. Another powerhouse, Jodi Picoult, sold more than two million books in 2007 alone, and had ten separate novels on *Publishers Weekly*'s end-of-year 2007 best-seller list. That success was cemented in 2009 when Picoult's novel *My Sister's Keeper* was released as a major Hollywood summer movie. In fact, movies and television are having a bigger impact on book sales than ever before and play a strong role in creating top sellers, according to *Publishers Weekly*. Other books that received a surge in sales as a result of a movie tie-in include *The Kite Runner, No Country for Old Men, Nights in Rodanthe, The Secret Life of Bees, I Am Legend*, and *Marley & Me* (which is not fiction, despite how outlandish some of Marley's exploits may appear).

But it runs the other way, too. If a book deal generates buzz before publication, Hollywood will snatch up that book's movie rights. When this happens, Hollywood executives are gambling that a particular novel will strike enough of a chord with readers to justify the expense of making and marketing a movie about it. It doesn't always play out the way they hope—in Hollywood, far more books are "optioned" than are made into films—but production companies want to secure the rights in advance just in case a book turns out to be a hit. The system works on behalf of authors and publishers as well, when a movie deal helps generate even more interest in the book—and more sales—than there might have been otherwise.

Because fiction drives so much of the publishing industry, editors are always on the lookout for the next fresh voice. This is good news for the as-yet unpublished writer. There are many success stories, such as debut novelist Syrie James's *The Lost Memoirs of Jane Austen* selling well over 100,000 copies since its publication in 2007. The novel also spawned what every publisher dreams of—a franchise of sorts—with *The Secret Diaries of Charlotte Brönte* as a sophomore effort and more expected in the future. So there's a good deal of hope for struggling novelists who are trying to break in if the work is considered "marketable."

What is marketable these days? Thrillers, such as Dan Brown's *Angels & Demons* and *The Lost Symbol*, continue to sell briskly. Vampire novels are blood-hot. Fiction geared for women does well, perhaps because women are responsible for more than 60 percent of book purchases in the United States. In 2007, romance became the largest single category for books, at 13 percent of overall sales, according to the Romance Writers of America. That's double the sales of general literary fiction, and the category shows no signs of slowing down, growing quickly in an era of stagnant sales for some other categories. "Chick lit," though a hot category in the early part of the decade, has cooled off. Such books typically feature single twentysomethings who are looking for love while trying to succeed in fast-paced careers, usually in the media. Although chick lit has not disappeared, it has declined in sales and output. Some well-established chick lit novelists, like Emily Giffin and Sophie Kinsella, continue to do well, but the category is less receptive to new voices than it was five years ago.

Just as we saw that niche magazines that appeal to a particular ethnic group are enjoying some growth, one of the strong trends in book publishing is African-American fiction, which has seen a period of sustained development in the last ten years. A number of publishers now have imprints dedicated to African-American books, such as Harlem Moon (Random House) or Dafina (Kensington). Many of these lists aren't restricted to novels, but include nonfiction (e.g., HarperCollins's Amistad imprint, which publishes African-American history, self-help, children's books, cookbooks, and memoirs all under the same umbrella).

Despite the growing openness to African-American audiences and "urban fiction," very few black authors ever hit the best-seller lists—and this will remain a challenge for the category in years to come. Latino/a publishing has been a source of growth as well, and many publishers are beginning Spanish-language efforts. In 2008, the Spanish-language publishing fair had its largest turnout ever and estimated that sales were up by 7.5 percent, primarily for books in translation. According to the U.S. Census, the Hispanic growth rate in America is more than three and a half times that of the general population—meaning that Spanish-language publishing will continue to grow to serve this emerging market.

Two of the hottest categories in fiction today are Christian fiction and erotica. As a writer you would be ill advised to attempt to combine these two categories in the same book; the former has strict rules prohibiting graphic sexual depictions (or even touching below the neck), while the latter has strict expectations that all can and must be bared. What's especially interesting is that both categories have exploded at the same time, and that both have sparked a proliferation of subgenres: erotica suspense, Christian suspense, erotica science fiction, Christian science fiction, etc. But this is great news for writers in those categories and subgenres.

Behind the Numbers: Nonfiction

On the nonfiction front, religion still leads the way. The spirituality market has become too lucrative to ignore. In 2001, for the first time, religious titles sat atop *Publishers Weekly*'s end-of-year best-seller lists for both fiction and nonfiction. Throughout the last decade, bestsellers like *The Purpose Driven Life* by Rick Warren, *Your Best Life Now* by Joel Osteen, and *The Secret* by Rhonda Byrne have become blockbusters, paving the way for such books to be given greater prominence in trade bookstores and also in warehouse stores like Sam's Club and Costco. Smaller religion presses have thrived, and large New York trade houses have started or purchased their own Christian imprints (WaterBrook Multnomah and Doubleday Religion for Random House; HarperOne and Zondervan for HarperCollins; FaithWords for Hachette Book Group; Jossey-Bass for Wiley; Howard Books for Simon & Schuster), giving today's religion writers a variety of outlets for their work.

In the nonfiction world, diet books, always a popular topic, were particularly strong in 2008 with the proliferation of *Eat This, Not That!* and the continued success of the Oprah-fueled *You: On a Diet*. Niche diet books for women, including *How to Eat Like a Hot Chick* and the edgier how-to *Skinny Bitch*, made a mark, charting a new trend away from the one-size-fits-all diet book toward future diet books that might target specific niches: fortysomething women, older people, African Americans, psychotic plumbers, or what have you. Niching is the philosophy behind the best-selling *GenoType Diet*, which assesses people's diet "type" based on their alleged genetic makeup. But this is hardly a category for a newcomer, since success often depends on a strong marketing platform and trustworthy credentials. Just calling yourself a doctor, or even playing one on television, does not make you eligible to write a diet book.

A more likely place for an unknown writer to break in is on the self-help shelf, another consistently strong category. Some of the growth in the self-help category has come from baby boomers' goal to age well—or possibly live forever. Some of the subcategories in self-help include parenting, marriage, personal growth, psychology, health and wellness, and fitness.

One key about the kinds of books that do well in this category is what the media is covering. You can be sure that whatever trend you see consistently covered on television, in magazines, and on radio will be followed up by the slower-paced book publishing industry, though of course the trick is to get your book published before the trend is yesterday's news. Pay attention to what's happening around you. Each type of media feeds into the other, and if you can pinpoint which way the trends are leaning, you might be able to pitch a nonfiction book that matches a publisher's needs.

On the other hand, you might become a successful self-help author because you can clearly identify a book that's needed that does *not* yet exist. When entertainment public relations entrepreneur Terrie Williams suffered from depression, she dutifully went to the bookstore to look for helpful books on the topic. She found dozens, but nothing specifically targeted to African Americans, addressing unique issues that blacks might have to cope with alongside depression. So she wrote *Black Pain: It Just Looks Like We're Not Hurting* and began speaking about depression to black groups around the country. "Somehow, I have found a niche within a niche—in a segment of book publishing that appeared to be saturated," she wrote in an essay in *Publishers Weekly.*

So in nonfiction, it pays to watch what's going on in the media and keep a close eye on what's already available on your topic. With fiction, it does no good to follow the trends, since by the time you have your novel ready, the trend may be on its way out. Instead, write what you're passionate about—or what you choose to read.

Less Promising Categories

We've spent a lot of time talking about positive trends and growth areas in the book market. However, we also need to spend a few moments highlighting some categories that Bowker reports have fallen into decline.

CATEGORY	PERCENTAGE DECLINE FROM 2002 TO 2007
Computers	-25%
Language	-18%
Agriculture	-8%
Juvenile	-1%
Technology	-1%

A couple of caveats on these numbers. First, just as we saw with some categories of magazines, some of the growth has moved from print media toward online outlets. Now that computers and their accompanying (and often infuriating) software are a given in our lives, most people feel comfortable enough using computers that their first line of defense when they have a computer problem is to look it up *on their computer.* The proliferation of fantastic tech support sites and (free!) Q&A discussions with experts has meant that most people don't feel they need to hop in the car and try to dig through all of the indexes of the computer books at Barnes & Noble. So long as they have a working Internet connection, they can find the answer for free from the comfort of their own home. That is, if they don't bash the computer with a sledgehammer first.

The second caveat is that after these numbers were published, the juvenile category (which encompasses everything from *Goodnight Moon* to *The Sisterhood of the Traveling Pants,* or zero to age eighteen) had a bit of a rebound. The Book Industry Study Group projects that the juvenile category will show modest growth of 2 to 3 percent a year through 2011.

Those aren't exactly boy wizard numbers, but they aren't in negative territory either, so YA novelists, picture book enthusiasts, and other writers for kids shouldn't lose hope.

CHARTING YOUR PATH: BOOKS OR MAGAZINES?

Writing for magazines and books requires different sets of work habits, and each offers distinct rewards in terms of satisfaction and compensation. Whether you will do best pursuing magazine writing or a book contract depends largely on your personal style and the goals you set for yourself. For an overview of the relative advantages of each, consider the following points.

Books pay a lot more than most magazine articles. But unless you are an established author, or are lucky enough to have two or more publishers bidding against each other, the initial compensation is usually in the range of several thousand dollars. (Take a moment and read this last sentence one or two more times. We'll talk about money in a later chapter, but in case you were thinking that your first book would provide your (a) retirement plan, (b) Tahiti fund, or (c) yacht down payment, it's never too early for a reality check.) Typically, this pay is in the form of an advance against royalties, which is paid over the course of a year while the book is being written and edited.

Depending on the initial advance, a book that sells ten thousand copies (which—another reality check!—most don't) typically earns enough to cover the writer's advance and the publisher's other expenses. For many writers, the initial advance is the only money they ever see because of poor sales. Even so, most books will probably earn you more than most magazine articles. If your book is even a modest success, the rewards can mount quickly, particularly as your book can lead to other opportunities such as paid speaking engagements.

Of course, many book authors have to share a slice of their income with the agent who got them the book deal in the first place. That's because most book editors at larger publishing houses won't look at a manuscript unless it is referred to them by an agent. A high percentage of published authors use agents, especially in fiction, which says something about the difficulty of breaking into book publishing.

In the final analysis, books provide long-term benefits beyond the direct financial rewards. The prestige of writing a book can often boost your career. The research and expertise you gain from a book project can be spun into a variety of magazine articles, or other books. Books have a way of putting writers on the map more than magazine articles do—for proof of this, think of how many book authors are interviewed on programs like *Fresh Air, Talk of the Nation,* or *The Diane Rehm Show.* Magazine writers don't have the same cachet, perhaps because people in the media know that it only takes a few days or weeks to write a magazine article. It often takes a year or more to write a book.

However, don't dismiss the magazine option just yet. The key advantage to magazine writing is that there are many more opportunities, based on the sheer number of local, regional, and national publications. Most publish anywhere from eight to twenty articles per issue. Unlike books, which have a longer shelf life, magazines continually need good articles. Additionally, magazine writing usually entails a brief commitment of a few days to a week—unlike books, which require a sustained effort. Magazine writing can be a great option when you already have a full-time job, or have small children at home, or simply enjoy the freedom of exploring many different topics instead of narrowing in on one for months on end.

Yet, depending on how you prefer to work, the transient nature of magazine writing can be a disadvantage. Every few days, or every week at most, you have to hustle to find more work. You must also juggle several projects at once. Magazine writers need to be organized, proactive, and committed.

GETTING STARTED

The way to approach a magazine editor, book publisher, or literary agent is through a query letter or a lengthier book proposal. (Both of these will be discussed in more detail in subsequent chapters.) In either case, think of your goal as not just getting your work accepted, but keeping it from being rejected. Understanding the difference can affect how well you compete in the marketplace.

Think of editors and agents with stacks of book proposals or query letters in their e-mail inboxes. They are extremely busy people with many demands on their time and creative energy. Their goal is to get through the stacks as quickly as possible—a task that may seem insurmountable at times. They are looking for clues to determine whether you have what it takes to get published. The sooner they can determine this, the easier their job becomes. In short, you are trying to keep from being rejected because that is just what the agent or editor is looking to do. In this type of environment, every sentence should give them a reason to read the next sentence. Each paragraph should make them want to read the next.

Six Keys to Success

If the task seems daunting, it really doesn't need to be. You can make yourself stand out from the stack by simply arming yourself with the right skills and the proper research. The six pieces of advice that follow are cited by many writing instructors and published authors as the secrets to success. These points can go a long way toward making you stand out from the pack.

1. Read and analyze good writing. Writing doesn't come from a vacuum. You must read to understand what good writing is all about. You must read to inspire yourself. Read as much as you can inside and outside of your chosen genre—books, articles, short stories, poetry, ad copy—anything that helps you develop a better awareness of style.

As important as reading, you must *analyze* what you see on the page. Therein lies the art of writing. Study the details: the style of language, the dialogue, the narration, the structure of sentences, paragraphs, and the story itself. Ask yourself why they are written the way they are. What might you have done differently?

2. Learn the mechanics of a strong book proposal. Grammar, spelling, punctuation, proper formats for manuscripts, queries, and proposals—all of it matters a great deal in this business. You would be amazed at the unprofessional, imprecise, error-ridden proposals that land on editors' and agents' desks. Don't let your great ideas be rejected so easily because you didn't pay attention to important details.

3. Write every day. What you learn from reading and studying, you must put into practice. "Many people want to be writers but they don't want to write. They want the name, the prestige, but they don't want the hard work—to sit down and write," author Leon Fletcher notes.

4. Study the writing markets thoroughly. It's not enough to decide that you want to write mysteries and then scan *Writer's Market* or *Literary Market Place* for a publisher who produces that kind of book. You need to know what types of mysteries a publisher wants. As we'll explore in the next chapter and elsewhere, you can do this by reading as many books as possible by the publisher you plan to approach. Use Amazon.com to easily research what already has been published so you can differentiate your book concept.

5. Make sure you mean business. As writers, we are very fortunate to be in a business that allows us to aspire to a form of art. But publishing is still very much a business. "When a publisher takes on a title, he or she is, for practical purposes, betting that this manuscript will generate enough income to pay the author, to market it, to pay for the services of the people who will be working to get this manuscript into publication, to cover the production costs, to promote it upon production, and to have enough left for a reasonable profit," notes author Patricia J. Bell.

If writing professionally is a business, successful writers must give thought to the kind of service they offer. Do you make your editor's job easier by meeting deadlines and by keeping him abreast of your progress? Are you readily available to make revisions or answer questions? Do you resist being edited, stubbornly clinging to your original wording in all instances, or do you graciously welcome your editor's guidance and expertise? These are the value-added items that make editors want to do business with you. Most editors can determine as early as the proposal process whether you are an author who resists editorial guidance—your refusal to cooperate in that early stage will be a gigantic clue to the editor that she does not want to work with you over the long term.

6. Be persistent. "Persistence is the most typical, common trait of successful, published writers—even more typical and more common than writing skill," says Leon Fletcher. If, for instance, an editor rejects your proposal, that doesn't mean he is rejecting you as a writer. What the standard issue rejection letter says could actually be true: Your idea just didn't fit his needs at that time. Try again somewhere else and keep trying until you succeed.

2

FROM IDEA
TO MARKET

THE FIRST RULE of writing has always remained the same: Write what you know. It is excellent advice. But the second rule is just as important: Write what you know so it speaks to other people. In this chapter, we'll explore how an idea can become a marketable book or article that other people will actually want to read. This will prepare you for Part Two of this book, which gives more detailed information about how to get your books and articles published and your screenplays developed. In other words, the time to think about marketing your work is before you even begin to write it. You don't want to waste your time and passion writing something that no one is going to buy.

Whether you are successful as a writer depends greatly on how you position your work. For example, a memoir about your husband's traumatic brain injury is probably not going to find a publisher, but that experience could inform a variety of other very marketable books. You might consider writing a self-help guide for family members whose loved one has suffered a traumatic brain injury and need guidance on all the accompanying medical, financial, emotional, and bioethical issues involved. You would weave in your own experiences to show the reader that you have been there too, and have done the research and understand the relevant problems and emotions, but your experience would only be the frame in which you seek to help the reader. Or, you could decide to use that experience as a plot element in a novel. Your characters' travails would have the ring of authenticity because you have navigated those waters yourself and know the genuine emotions they would be feeling.

You might find writing either of these types of books personally cathartic, but be savvy: Publishers are far less interested in authors who write to fuel their own personal growth as they are in authors who write because they know they can communicate with an audience and can sell books. Publishing is a business.

THE GREAT IDEA

When it comes to writing, coming up with a great idea that translates well into an article or book can be tricky. One of the biggest keys to finding and developing such ideas involves staying tuned into the world around you, drawing inspiration from books, magazines, news reports, friends, strangers—in short, everything and everyone. When debut novelist Michele Claire Lucas was reading through the *New York Times* travel section one day, she came across an article about a farming village in France that had been totally destroyed by the Nazis, with every man, woman, and child rounded up and killed for no obvious reason. Lucas wondered what would have happened if a girl had survived the massacre, and how that girl might deal with the lingering trauma as she grew into adulthood. The result was *A High and Hidden Place*, published by HarperSanFrancisco in 2005 to critical acclaim.

Ideas, of course, are everywhere, and writers are attuned to recognizing them. At a book signing, for example, children's writer Marcia Thornton Jones and a mother of one of her young readers named Jack were chatting about how many people they knew by that name. "Jacks are wild," the mother said. "That sounds like the name of a children's book!" Jones said, pulling out her journal and jotting it down.

Chance remarks rouse ideas as well. On the way to basketball camp with his two sons and their friends, Jim Kraft, a children's book author, noticed that suddenly all fell silent. Kraft's younger son commented, "Suddenly silence." The next minute, Kraft had an idea for a book. It became "Night Noises," a children's story about what happens when all the normal noises of the night suddenly stop.

The process isn't so very different for nonfiction writers. While you may not be inventing a new reality, you still must rely on your inner creativity to provide a fresh perspective or to spot a unique news angle. Pat Crowley, a newspaper reporter and freelance magazine writer, says ideas rush at him everywhere he goes. On the way to talk to a journalism class, the radio prompted two freelance story ideas. One was about whether lowering the legal blood alcohol limit, as lawmakers were proposing following a rash of drunken driving accidents, really makes any difference. The other idea involved the alarming side effects that advertisers calmly list in their commercials for drugs—an idea that hit him while listening to an ad for an anti-hair-loss product, which sounded great until the announcer mentioned it could cause inconveniences such as dry mouth, blackouts, or sexual dysfunction. "People would rather lose every hair they have than have sexual dysfunction," says Crowley, "and that's the way I'll sell it."

DREAMS AND VISIONS

Although it may sound far-fetched, some writers do have thunderbolt-y kinds of experiences in accessing their creativity. Novelists in particular may find that they are most creative in their sleep. Mega-selling YA novelist Stephenie Meyer, for example, has confessed on her website that she got the idea for *Twilight* in a dream after months of very sporadic, unsuccessful writing. "In my dream, two people were having an intense conversation in a meadow in the woods," Meyer recounts. "One of these people was just your average girl. The other person was fantastically beautiful, sparkly, and a vampire. They were discussing the difficulties inherent in the facts that (a) they were falling in love with each other, while (b) the vampire was particularly attracted to the scent of her blood and was having a difficult time restraining himself from killing her immediately." When she woke up, Meyer did what she needed to do to tend to her young children, and then sat down to give voice to the dream, relating the dream conversation almost verbatim in her notes. That became a pivotal scene in Twilight, which became a hit novel, which spawned a ridiculously successful franchise, which should teach us all a lesson: Don't dismiss any creative dreams you have. Keep a notebook handy and write them down before they slip away.

J.K. Rowling's story of the genesis of Harry Potter is no less dramatic. While traveling on a train to London, she conjured Harry in her head. She saw his scar, his glasses, his unruly hair. She knew that he was a wizard—and that he himself didn't know that yet. Rowling had been writing "almost continuously since the age of six," but she didn't have a working pen with her to scribble down the ideas that were coming fast and furious into her mind. Too shy to borrow one, she simply sat and thought about Harry for four hours on the train, which she later realized was a very valuable way to get started. She was elated. "I'd never felt that excited about anything to do with writing," she later told the BBC. "I'd never had an idea that gave me such a physical response."

WRITER'S MARKET GUIDE TO GETTING PUBLISHED

TO MARKET

The conventional wisdom among newbie writers is that you should first write whatever it is and *then* turn your attention to more prosaic affairs like actually getting a contract to see your work in a book or magazine. You sit in your garret with a tattered beret of some kind on your head, like Winona Ryder in the movie *Little Women*, and churn out your writing without a thought about whether said writing may actually enable you to heat said garret. And with long fiction, this is in fact the usual method: You write the novel first and then try, often for years, to get someone to take a look at it. Screenplays work that way, too, as does poetry, if you're lucky enough to sell it at all. We'll get to all that in later chapters.

However, this approach doesn't work as well for nonfiction, and may actually reduce your chances of success because most publishers of nonfiction have very specific needs that must be met in order for them to buy a book. You can do yourself a huge favor early on by ascertaining the market for your writing ideas before you've put in a lot of time, effort, and money toward researching them. Finding the right market for your work remains one of the most crucial steps in the publishing process, regardless of what you're writing. Let's take a look at the best ways to identify appropriate markets for your books (we'll deal with magazines more specifically in chapter six).

Finding a Book Market for Your Ideas

To find a publisher for your book, turn to the back of the *Writer's Market* for the Book Publishers Subject Index. There, you'll find lists of books arranged by topic, from adventure to YA for fiction, and from agriculture to world affairs for nonfiction. Then read the listing about each publisher, which will tell you such vital information as how it prefers to be approached, what percentage of books it publishes from first-time authors, and contact information. Visit the publisher's website for catalogs and submission guidelines.

There are ways to supplement this basic strategy. One route is old-fashioned, but tried-and-true: Investigate the books you like that are similar to yours. (It goes without saying that *of course* your book is unique and life changing, but surely there exist lesser creatures that are similar enough to your book to help you do some comparisons.) It is actually easier to carry out this strategy online, because Amazon.com will show you *all* of the relevant titles, whereas your local bookstore likely has only the newest and best-selling ones in stock. Take notes on which publishers consistently crop up in your subject area—a strategy that will help you down the road as you write your query letter. Then look in the acknowledgments of these books to see if there are two or three editors whose names appear consistently. (If the authors say nice things about these editors, so much the better for you if you get the privilege of working with one.)

You'll also need to browse an actual bricks-and-mortar bookstore to see what's selling, advises children's book author Debbie Dadey. What books are on the front tables, or given face-out presentation on the shelves? What books are recommended as "staff picks"? Seeing what's *not* on the bookstore shelves can be a useful marketing exercise as well, as Dadey's experience attests. "You've got to write what you want to write, what really is important to you," she says. Writing a series called *The Adventures of the Bailey School Kids* was important to her and co-author Marcia Thornton Jones. Both educators, they saw a need for books for primary school children who were reluctant readers, or who wanted to read but weren't yet ready for a novel and scorned picture books as too babyish. They realized there weren't many books filling that need, and their series became immensely popular with just those children.

As we've said, *Writer's Market* is one of the most popular books for beginning writers to use to learn about various markets. But if you can't find what you need there, more information about book publishers is contained in numerous catalogs and directories like *Books in Print*. Its *Publishers Trade List Annual*, for example, is a compilation of publishers' catalogs. Browsing through this book, available at many libraries, gives you a sense of which houses publish books like yours and provides you with an idea of the competition.

Or you can choose to do all of your research on Amazon.com, which functions almost as effectively as *Books in Print* without all of the hassle. What's more, Amazon.com lets you organize results in various ways, which can be useful. For example, sorting by publication date could show you that it's been several years since a book appeared that was similar to yours—a possible hole in the market. Or sorting by the bestsellers (the default sort method on Amazon.com) can teach you what kinds of books are performing best in the marketplace … or worst. Play around with the results and search methods to see what yields the most information.

This is just a brief overview of how to think like a marketer of your writing; we'll cover these topics more in-depth in Part Two. Now, you are ready to begin thinking about your writing life, and for that, you need a plan.

RESOURCES

Need more help finding markets for your work? Try the books and websites listed below.

BOOKS

Some of the books and directories listed below are updated annually. Always check to make sure you are looking at the most current edition.

Bacon's Internet Media Directory (Bacon) Lists online-only publications, as well as online counterparts to print publications. At around $600, though, this might be more of a library resource.

Bacon's Newspaper and Magazine Directory (Bacon). Lists more than 22,000 magazines, newsletters, newspapers, and news syndicates; also lists editors' names and beat areas. The cost is around $450, so this again might merit a good library visit.

Books in Print (R.R. Bowker). The Subject Guide to this comprehensive annual compilation describes books according to topic. Forthcoming Books, a bimonthly, lists books printed between annual publications of BIP. At www.booksinprint.com you can purchase a subscription that gives access to enhanced content such as book reviews.

The Canadian Writer's Market (McClelland & Stewart). Lists markets in Canada for books, magazine and newspaper articles, and trade journals; also lists literary agents and publishers.

Christian Writers' Market Guide (WaterBrook Press). Lists more than 1,200 markets. Includes publishers of books and periodicals, arranged by subject, as well as a host of other publishing information, including writers conferences, editorial services, and market analyses. The author also runs a useful blog at www.stuartmarket.blogspot.com.

Literary Market Place (Information Today, Inc.). This resource includes more than 15,000 entries listing names and contact information for book publishers, electronic publishers, literary agents, direct mail promoters, and more. Searchable online by subject area (for a hefty fee) at www.literarymarketplace.com. LMP's Industry Yellow Pages is a directory of names, addresses, phone numbers, and e-mails of people listed in LMP.

Market Books (Writer's Digest Books). These annually updated books include *Writer's Market* and *Writer's Market Deluxe Edition* (which provides access to www.writersmarket.com), *Children's Writer's & Illustrator's Market*, *Guide to Literary Agents*, *Poet's Market*, and *Novel & Short Story Writer's Market*. Each book includes thousands of up-to-date market listings that include submission information, market facts, etc.

WEBSITES

These days, most writers merge onto the Information Superhighway when they need information fast about writing and publishing. However, as most of us know, not all information available on the Internet was created equal. Here is a carefully vetted list of reliable, well-informed places to begin your quest for information.

www.writersdigest.com. With tips on publishing, behind-the-scenes blogs about all aspects of the industry, and comprehensive lists of writers conferences and contests, this website is a great starting point. You would also do well to subscribe to its print magazine, *Writer's Digest*, which comes out bimonthly.

www.publishersweekly.com. To learn about the business of book publishing, news, events, writers' associations, online publishers, and more, start with the industry standard.

http://guidetoliteraryagents.com/blog. Do you need an agent? If so, how do you get one? This up-to-the-minute blog provides information about trends among literary agents, and links to their own sites and blogs.

www.bookwire.com. BookWire online is a booklover's dream, with author interviews (including some on video), book reviews, news about forthcoming titles, links to publishers' home pages, and more.

www.mediabistro.com. This is a must-bookmark site for freelance journalists and writers of magazine articles. In addition to lots of media news and links, you can post your resume and links to clips so magazine editors can find you. There are also webinars on various topics about writing, publishing, and marketing; some are free and some are by subscription.

www.writerswrite.com. Although its largely text home page is bland and you may be tempted to skip this site, it offers terrific information for anyone who writes. (Don't judge a website by its cover.) It has a leg up on the competition merely in its comprehensiveness: songwriters, screenwriters, poets, and playwrights can find advice here, as well as novelists and nonfiction book writers.

3

GET OFF YOUR BUTT
AND WRITE

"SO, WHAT DO you do?" asks the fellow dad at the soccer match, glancing over at you while he keeps an eye on his daughter, the star forward.

"I'm a writer," you announce proudly.

"That's fascinating! Anything I would recognize?" he asks, while you both cheer a save by your team's goalie.

"Not yet," you admit. "I haven't had much luck yet in getting published." There is a pause while he makes a sympathetic-sounding cluck. "Actually, I haven't been writing much lately at all," you continue. "Being home with the kids takes so much of my energy that by the time they're in bed at the end of the day all I want to do is watch television. Plus, writing is so discouraging when you can't get someone to even look at your work."

There is a beat while he processes this. "But, you're a writer, right? How can you be a writer without actually *writing*?"

This scene may cause you to chuckle with recognition or possibly to hang your head in shame. Real writers *write*. Successful writers find the time every day to hone their craft and meet their writing obligations—whether those obligations are external (from editors) or internal (from an incontestable desire to write). And although some of you may be tempted to skip this chapter to get to Part Two where we discuss the "good stuff" like how to get published, hear this first: What usually separates good writers from bad ones (and often, published writers from unpublished ones) is a strong work habit. That's it. That's the big secret. Real writers work hard. In fact, most work ridiculously hard.

Professional writers know there's nothing like a looming deadline to make them focus on their work. In fact, the real problem for beginning writers is usually not scrambling to meet a deadline, but simply organizing their time efficiently enough to find time to write at a productive pace. All writers feel this way from time to time. As other commitments encroach on our days, writing is often pushed aside like an unpleasant chore.

Accomplishing your writing goals requires making a writing plan, which is a time schedule that lists what you need to do and when. This chapter explores some ideas on managing your time so you find time to write. It also gives you tips on how to best use the time you have to produce a finished piece, and includes checklists on steps that should be taken to research, write, and rewrite.

CHOOSE TO WRITE

Everybody on the planet has the same amount of time every day. How we choose to use that time makes some of us writers and others of us short-order cooks. If you are a short-order cook who wants to write, however, you could probably take a bit of time to think about how you use your time.

Sandra Felton, who has written more than a dozen books on how to get organized, including *Neat Mom*, *Messie Kids* and *The New Messies Manual*, points to prioritizing and dedication as helpful organizational tools for writers. "I think the whole answer is focus," she says. "I think what focus means is you have to decide what you want to do and lob off other stuff that you also want to do. Because you want to write more."

Note that the choice is not between writing and doing something else that you don't want to do. The choice is among a nearly overwhelming array of things that seem appealing: checking in with your friends on Facebook, reading for pleasure, or having people over for dinner. Then there's going to movies and the theater and the opera and family get-togethers and on trips and watching way too much television. Sometimes, people would rather even do laundry and dishes than write. (All writers have days like that, but if that's your constant M.O., you may wish to rethink a literary vocation.) Faced with so many options, people tend to choose too many and feel like they're short of time.

Some people actually can use stray snippets of free time to write, penning novels on the back of envelopes while waiting in the checkout line at the grocery store. If they have ten minutes between helping a child with homework and driving her to flute lessons, they use those ten precious minutes to write or polish a small chunk of prose. Such people are the envy of the rest of us and can legitimately pass over this chapter and collect $200. For the rest of us, writing for publication requires larger pieces of time to research, ponder, draft, rewrite, and polish.

MAKE WRITING A HABIT

Finding writing time requires a modicum of organization, but using it productively demands dedication. The theme of virtually every article about getting organized to write is straightforward: *Just do it*. Wanting to write and writing itself are cousins, not identical twins. Psychological research indicates that writing every day, whether your muse is whispering in your ear or has deserted you, produces not only more writing but also more ideas for future writing.

The writing habit, like the exercise habit, is its own reward. When you don't do it, you feel as if you're cheating yourself. Real writers don't sit around and wait for "inspiration" to strike before they put fingers to keyboard; they put fingers to keyboard and know that somewhere during those hours they will discover small nuggets of inspiration. The fingers-to-keyboard, butt-in-the-chair pose is like exercise for the writer. In an anaerobic way, this is just like real runners who pound the pavement or the treadmill in all weather, whether they are busy with work or on vacation. Like physical exercise, writing is often not enjoyable while you're doing it, though occasionally an endorphin or two will spark and the serotonin does its thing. Most of the time, though, writing is just a matter of discipline, plain and simple. Discipline comes more easily to some people than to others, but it is certainly a skill that can be cultivated.

"The only thing I can tell you I do that's inviolate is when I have to write, I get up in the morning and literally go straight to the typewriter," says Stephanie Culp, who has written books on organization and time management. "Any little distraction that takes me away from my desk kills it. When I'm writing something large, it takes about three fitful days, and then I'm in the rhythm of it, and I write it. I can still write a book in three weeks."

Here are some tips for getting into a writing habit.

- Start by setting aside an hour or a half hour every day to write. (See the sidebar for an even more realistic early goal.)

- Or set a goal to write a certain number of words every day.

- Try to write at the same time every day so it will feel peculiar to do something else at that time.

- Write even if you feel uninspired, even if you don't feel ready to write. If you want to be a writer, you must write. Just do it.

PERFECT PROSE ABS IN JUST MINUTES A DAY!

We've just read suggestions to set aside an hour, or at least half an hour, each day for writing. But what if even half an hour seems too daunting? What if you are either so busy or so stymied by writer's block that you just can't seem to get started?

Here's one answer: Lower your expectations about time, but keep writing. In *Writing Your Dissertation in Fifteen Minutes a Day*,

Joan Bolker teaches writers how to break down huge tasks into tiny steps—even if they can only initially handle writing for fifteen minutes each day. You don't have to be writing a dissertation or other scholarly work to appreciate the book's great advice that's applicable to all writers. Among the best nuggets is to start with a goal of only fifteen minutes of freewriting, then gradually work your way from a "zero draft" (for your eyes only) through a first draft and beyond. Bolker teaches readers to "park on the downward slope" when they write, meaning that instead of pouring out every single idea they have in a day's work, they should stop mid-idea, or even mid-sentence, to make it that much easier to get started again the next day.

YOUR WRITING PLAN

Often, getting started on a writing project is the hardest part. Most writing jobs, however, can be viewed as a sequence of doable tasks that follow the same general path from beginning to end. If you accomplish each task in order, you can follow the plan to a finished piece. The more you write, the more you will be able to anticipate how much time a particular project will take you.

The planning guidelines below are designed to help you write a non-fiction magazine article, but they can be modified to suit many writing projects. A book, for example, is made of chapters that are similar to magazine pieces. Break the book down into individual chapters, and break the chapters down into component parts. Schedule your writing project into your day at specific times, and, with a little luck but more hard work, you'll finish your pieces on time.

If you're a person who resents and resists scheduling, remember that creating a writing plan is intended to help you, not restrict you. The goal is to relieve some stress, organize your life, and make your writing process more efficient. Meeting even mini-deadlines can lift your spirits and bolster your confidence. Simply crossing items off to-do lists feels so good that the act in itself becomes a reward and keeps you writing.

Take a look at the following guidelines, which will help you better organize your writing time and finish your projects.

> **1. Set reasonable, measurable goals.** Even if you're not writing to someone else's external deadline, give yourself your own deadline and treat it seriously. Because you understand the power of the written word, write down a specific goal, with a due date: "Finish article by ___ [whatever date]." Some people even establish punishments and rewards if they meet or don't meet their self-imposed deadlines: "If I complete chapter five by Friday, I can go to see the new *Harry Potter* movie; if I don't finish on time, I will force myself to scrub the toilets as penance." Well, you don't have to clean the toilets, but a *little* self-flagellation is probably good for you.

> **2. Divide and conquer.** View your writing project not as an overwhelming monolith, but a compilation of many smaller items. The reason hard jobs get bypassed is that they often seem too daunting if they're written as one entry on your list of goals. For example, "Write a book in the next year" can be overwhelming. The scope of the project is so big, and the deadline so far away, that achieving the goal seems impossible. Instead, focus on smaller tasks to do today, tomorrow, this week, and this month to help you reach that goal. You're likelier to accomplish smaller tasks in the near future than a vague goal in the abstract faraway. The tasks help you reach that distant goal step-by-step.

3. Create a plan of ordered tasks. Writing down tasks in the order in which they should be done keeps you focused, as well as frees your mind to concentrate on the important things—rather than wasting mental energy trying to remember all the niggling details that must be done each day. Break the task down into manageable steps.

4. Select dates and stick to them. "Some day, I'm going to write a book." How many times have we all thought this? Turn your lofty dream into an actual accomplishment by adopting a workable schedule. For example, choose a date on your calendar for beginning your writing project. Make it today. You'll be surprised by how much more quickly you'll work with deadlines, especially if they come with positive and negative consequences. For example, if you miss your deadline at a major magazine, you may never be hired again and may in fact not see your piece in print, which are both negative consequences. But if you make your deadline, determine that you will give yourself a real day off, a massage, an entire chocolate cake, or what have you. Enlist other people to hold you accountable.

5. Work backward. The most important step in planning the time for your writing project is this one: On your calendar, mark the story's final due date. (If you don't have a deadline from a publisher, give yourself a reasonable one.) Then, figure out when each of the specific items, in reverse order, must be completed if you are to meet that deadline. For example, if the story needs to be e-mailed on June 30, the final fact-checking and polishing might have to be done by June 28, the second draft may have to be done by June 25, the interviews need to be completed by June 20, etc. Allow a little wiggle room in your calendar for the delays that inevitably happen: an interviewee gets the flu and has to postpone by a few days, the computer crashes, etc.

6. Make a daily to-do list to accomplish the tasks. Next to each item on your list, write the time you think it will take to accomplish it and the deadline for completing it. People commonly put far too many items on to-do lists and, as a result, feel defeated when they have to copy uncompleted items from day to day. As William James once wrote, "Nothing is so fatiguing as the eternal hanging on of an uncompleted task." So, jot down what you can reasonably expect to accomplish in a day. Some people have success using online organizational websites to help them stay on track. For example, on www.Toodledo.com, users can create goals for themselves, color-code them, assign themselves deadlines, prioritize the tasks in a "hotlist," and keep track of the time spent on each project. There are other similar sites as well, including many that are compatible with PDAs and smart phones. (Of course, the old-fashioned system of a pen and a sticky note works fine, too.)

ONE WRITER'S DAILY DISCIPLINE

Robin Lee Hatcher, a RITA-Award winning inspirational romance novelist, is one of the most focused writers around. Despite the demands of home life and interacting with readers on her website, www.robin leehatcher.com, the early-rising Idaho novelist carves out the bulk of her day for the nuts and bolts of plot, character, and dialogue.

"I try to have a disciplined order to my workdays, even though life has a way of tossing plenty of curve balls that can disrupt things. I begin with thirty minutes of exercise, followed by a time of Bible reading. Then I open my e-mail program, sort through the mail that has come in since the previous evening, and deal with anything that needs a prompt response (i.e., e-mails from my publishers and/or my agent). Afterward, I close my e-mail program, open my manuscript, and begin writing. I try to pause every hour or so to do a few stretches and get a drink of water. After a lunch break and another quick check of e-mail, I return to my office and usually write until 2:00 or 3:00. By then, the creative part of my brain is toast.

"Early in my career, I began keeping track of my word/page production each day. For many years, I wrote the information on my desk calendar. Later I tried keeping it in a computer journal program. But beginning in 2007, I have kept the information in a Journal 10+ (www.journal10.com). It's very helpful for me to be able to look back and remember that no matter what else was happening in my life, I was still able to finish a book or finish revisions or finish the line edits/copyedits/page proofs in a particular number of days. When writing a new book, I have a daily word goal that I'm shooting for. When doing revisions or edits, I have a goal of the number of existing pages that I need to get through in a day."

4 RESEARCHING YOUR IDEAS

THE LENGTHS THAT writers can go to understand their subjects may be best exemplified by James Alexander Thom, a former journalist who has written a number of acclaimed and best-selling books about the American frontier experience. When Thom decided to write the story of Mary Ingles for his book *Follow the River*, he actually retraced parts of the route Ingles followed when she escaped Indian captivity in 1755.

Following the completion of the book, Thom said he could only write Ingles's story after he had walked in her steps. Thom couldn't trace Ingles's entire six-week trek through the woods along the Ohio and Kenawha rivers, but he made five separate trips to key spots along her route. At times Thom even ate what Ingles had eaten, and at one point he fasted for a week.

For the rest of his research, Thom visited Ingles's descendants, read detailed family accounts of her life, and studied historic documents. In the long run Thom's research only made his job easier, and it made his account more believable.

This kind of dogged pursuit of authenticity can make your work stand out, whether you are writing a historical novel or an article on historic cars. To convince readers—and editors—that you know what you are talking about, you must first spend the time to understand the subject yourself.

As you outline your book or article, the idea of research may sound like drudgery, a necessary evil you must go through before you can get to your real work—the writing. Yet what many of us would consider drudgery is actually the most important step in the writing process. Consider, for a moment, that good research is what makes your finished work come alive with realism and truth. Each interview, Google session, or trip to the library adds excitement and authenticity to your finished piece. Research enlightens you and enables you to enlighten your audience. Research is nothing less than the heart and soul of what we do.

In reality, there are only so many subjects you can write from personal experience. And there are only so many subjects that you can learn firsthand, as Thom did. Fortunately, to learn everything else you can rely on others' expertise through interviews. The Internet has made millions of information sources instantly available to anyone who can afford a high-speed connection.

Whether your research is based on personal experience, interviews, document searches, the Internet, or any combination of the above, approach it with the same dogged professionalism. In the end, the quality of what you write will be based on the quality of what you know and learn. This is true whether you are writing fiction, nonfiction, or magazine articles. In all these cases, research adds the critical element of realism. This chapter provides you with the tools needed to approach research in a time-efficient and thorough manner.

The quality of what you learn is determined not just by the quality of your source material, but also by the mindset you bring to the project. Approach your research with a real desire to learn. Find enough sources to obtain as many points of view as possible. Don't just accept the things you read or hear; ask questions and make your judgments based on factual information. At the same time, challenge your own assumptions. Be willing to consider other ideas and opinions even if it means reevaluating your work or redoing what you have done so far (which is admittedly painful).

FINDING THE RIGHT INFORMATION

The task of research is somewhat like that of writing. More important than *where* to start is *the need* to start. You can't know exactly what an article or book will be until you write it. Similarly, you can't know all the information you need or where your search will lead you until it is underway. You can, however, narrow your choices with some foresight and good planning. From libraries and the Internet, to business and government sources, there's no shortage of places to find the right information on any subject. Begin with the places that will be of most benefit for your topic.

THE INTERNET

These days, your research should definitely start online. (If you haven't done this before, get someone to help you.) Hundreds of millions of Web pages are maintained by government agencies, universities, libraries, corporations, organizations, and individuals. Some experts estimate that the amount of information online is expanding at several pages per second. You can read and download government reports, newspaper and magazine articles, research studies, even the full text of books. While it can't supplant libraries and other sources of detailed information (at least not yet), using the Web for research is like shopping at a flea market. Every page is valuable to someone, but finding what is meaningful to you often requires sorting through a lot of junk. Not every source you find is reliable. Knowing a few shortcuts can save you valuable time.

Search Engines

No doubt you've already discovered the first major shortcut: search engines. Search engines help you find more specific information on a subject. They constantly scan the Web to create indexes of information. When you type in a word or phrase and hit the search button, the search engine creates a list of Web pages that relate to your subject. Some popular search engines include:

Google (www.google.com)

This is the granddaddy of them all, and the most comprehensive. When you look something up on Google, you'll find links organized from the most to least relevant. Frame your search parameters carefully: "Julia Roberts as Erin Brockovich" will find those pages that list the two names together. If you're writing an article on how Julia Roberts's starring role as Erin Brockovich transformed her image from toothsome movie star to serious actress, you don't want to have to wade through the hundreds of fan pages you'd find by just typing in "Julia Roberts."

Google's ambitious drive to be one-stop shopping for all conceivable information on the Internet has led it to create several initiatives that may also prove useful for your research:

- **Google Alerts** allow you to choose any phrase and receive a daily digest e-mail of all of the links to pages where that phrase has been used in a day. Authors may wish to put a Google Alert on a subject or individual they are currently researching to monitor any developing stories. If you're working on a profile article about an innovative Wall Street entrepreneur, for instance, you will want to put a Google Alert on her name to receive any news stories that mention her. www.google.com/alerts

- **Google Book Search** allows you to search millions of books that Google has scanned and posted online. This effort started with the classics—older, out-of-print books in the public domain—but soon mushroomed to include just about anything with printed words between two covers. This may be bad news for you as an author (Google has taken heat from The Authors Guild for potentially damaging authors' livelihood by making their content available for free, a topic we'll discuss in chapter fifteen), but it's fantastic for researchers. Can't find the quote you put into your article but know you need to give a citation for it? Try typing it verbatim into the Book Search: Google will show you a facsimile of the page where it can be found and all the bibliographic information, so you don't have to spend two hours frantically searching for the quote in every book you own. http://books.google.com

- Like Google Books, **Google Scholar** gives you access to nonbook research information, especially more academic and specialized sources like journal articles, theses, dissertations, abstracts, and the like. http://scholar.google.com

- **Google Translate** is precisely what it sounds like: an instant translator. It's not quite up to the futuristic standards of Star Trek's Universal Translator, but it's getting there, with more languages being added all the time. This can save you tremendous time and expense if you're doing historical research and some of your documents are in German, or you're writing a travel guide to Botswana and never mastered Setswana. The prose Google spits back may not be elegant (and is sometimes unintentionally funny), but you will get the basic meaning. http://translate.google.com

- **Google Maps** and **Google Earth** can help you in unexpected ways with your writing. What if you're writing a novel set in Paris, but can't quite remember the street layout from your character's hotel to the café where she first encounters her soul mate over crème brûlée? Use Google Maps (http://maps.google.com) to get your heroine from place to place and Google Earth (http://earth.google.com) to zoom in on the café, reminding yourself of the sights, buildings, and flower vendors all around it. These tools are fantastic for helping to evoke a setting.

- **Google Blog Search** allows you to search the blogs of ordinary people for your research. This is especially useful if you want to add a personal component to a story you are writing. For example, if you were doing a piece on Lyme disease for a health magazine, you would of course research your topic in science journals, medical websites, and the like. But if you also want to hear from ordinary people who are suffering from the disease, you could run a blog search on Lyme disease and hear what individual people have experienced. This can be a great way to find interview subjects, too, since people who are willing to blog publicly about a subject are often also willing to talk about it with a writer. http://blogsearch.google.com

- **Google Images** is a search engine specifically designed for jpegs, tiffs, and other art formats. This is where you go if you want to find a photograph of someone, a book or album cover, or clip art. (Remember that most of these images are copyright protected, so you will need to double-click on the picture to find out where it came from and then contact the rights holder listed.) http://images.google.com

Yahoo! Search (www.search.yahoo.com)

Yahoo may not be quite as ginormous as Google, but its boast of "twenty billion web objects" is certainly nothing to sneeze at. You can find just about anything you want to with this tool, as with Google. Yahoo also has some special tricks up its sleeve:

- **Yahoo People Search** is like the white pages and yellow pages combined in a national database. If you know the last name and state of the person you're seeking, you will probably be able to find him. But what makes the Yahoo tool particularly helpful (and different from www.yellowpages.com, which is another good resource) is the e-mail search feature. If your quarry has an e-mail address that is publicly listed anywhere (e.g., at the university where he teaches or the law firm where she practices), Yahoo People Search will come up trumps. http://people.yahoo.com

- **Yahoo Video**, like Google Images, is a specialized search engine—in this case, one that is designed specifically to trawl through streaming video. Want to find an interview with an author or celebrity? A clip of the President giving the State of the Union Address? This is where you want to be. http://video.search.yahoo.com

Exalead (www.exalead.com/search)

Although it's probably less than half the size of Yahoo and a fraction of the size of Google, some people swear by Exalead, especially since it provides thumbnail page previews of the pages churned out by your search. Exalead has more advanced options for making sophisticated searches, better than either Google or Yahoo. Unlike Google and Yahoo, your searches will turn up thumbnail facsimiles of the relevant pages, and your search parameters can be easily narrowed using Boolean search techniques (e.g., "Seattle NOT travel" or "Masterpiece Mystery NOT Masterpiece Classics").

Specialized Search Engines

In addition to the general, big-picture searches you can do with Google and other engines, there are also subject-specific search engines. They can help you hone in on Web pages more likely to cover your topic in detail. Some popular specialized search engines and directories include:

> **Academic Info** (www.academicinfo.net). This site provides educational information, online courses, and comprehensive subject guides on an enormous range of topics.

> **Infomine** (http://infomine.ucr.edu). Like Academic Info, this emphasizes scholarly resources like journal articles, but also includes government documents and more.

> **LawCrawler** (www.lawcrawler.com). Does your mystery novel have characters embroiled in a last-will-and-testament court battle? Find legal precedents, case briefs, and even expert witnesses at this site.

> **U.S. National Library of Medicine** (www.nlm.nih.gov). Run by the National Institutes of Health, this site offers comprehensive medical information, including fascinating details on the history of medicine in America, current research and treatments, and public health.

LIBRARIES

For most topics, a library is a great place to conduct research. After all, libraries hold the cumulative written knowledge of our entire history and civilization. Practically nothing is known that cannot be found in a library somewhere. Best of all, there are guides (research librarians and reference librarians) to point you in the right direction. Thanks to interlibrary loans, virtually no volume is beyond your reach. With directories on the Internet, searching for reference materials in the library system has never been easier.

There are three types of libraries: public libraries, college libraries, and specialized libraries maintained by industries or special interest groups. The federal government is another leading source of information, but many of its publications are also available in larger libraries.

Public Libraries

These are usually the best places for conducting research. The selection of material is unmatched by any suburban branch location (though if you know what you want you can often have it sent from the main library to the branch near you). The reference librarian at your local library is a valuable source of information. Many accept phone calls and e-mails from patrons asking research questions, so long as the questions are specific and can be answered quickly.

College Libraries

A library at a large institution will have more resources available than most branches of your public library. Colleges and public university libraries are usually open to the public, though you may not be able to withdraw a book unless you are affiliated with the school. In addition to the central campus library at most universities, many of the academic departments have their own specialized libraries, which may be open to the public.

Specialized Libraries

There are thousands of special libraries throughout the United States. While their collections may be limited to certain subjects, many offer an unparalleled amount of information on their specific subject matter, be it medicine, engineering, history, or art. Most are open to the public at least on a limited basis, though you will probably need permission in advance to gain access. Even those that aren't normally open to the public likely will allow you access if you explain the nature of your research. You can find out about special libraries in the *Directory of Special Libraries and Information Centers* or in the *Subject Directory of Special Libraries and Information Centers*. Both volumes are available at larger public libraries. The Special Libraries Association (www.sla.org) also may be of assistance.

BUSINESS AND GOVERNMENT SOURCES

Businesses

Businesses routinely make information available through their public relations offices, customer service departments, and sales staffs. Many trade associations also can provide you with valuable material, including chambers of commerce and tourism offices at the state and local level. In fact, many exist primarily to disseminate information and are often eager to provide writers with information. Don't hesitate to contact these people; they can be an enormous help. Three books that list thousands of these viable information sources include *Encyclopedia of Associations: International Organizations*, *Encyclopedia of Associations: National Organizations of the U.S.*, and *Encyclopedia of Associations: Regional, State and Local Organizations*.

Federal Government Information

There are several sources for government publications. You can contact the authoring agency directly, or use any number of government outlets that serve as information clearinghouses. In many instances, the cost to purchase government documents can be prohibitive. Fortunately, many documents are available for free viewing at public libraries or at thousands of other depositories throughout the country. *The Monthly Catalog of U.S. Government Publications*, published by the Government Printing Office, is one way to find what you need. The GPO's Subject Bibliography Index lists thousands of publications by category. To inquire about government documents, try the following agencies:

> **The Federal Citizen Information Center** (www.pueblo. gsa.gov) serves as a single point of contact for people who have questions about any federal agency. Its information specialists can also help you locate government documents and publications.

> The **U.S. Census Bureau** (www.census.gov) has thousands of reports about the U.S. population and economy. It offers statistics on such diverse subjects as fertility, education, mining, ancestry, income, migration, school enrollment, construction, and international trade. You can access data through more than two thousand libraries and other locations that serve as data centers and federal depositories.

> The **U.S. Government Accountability Office** (www.gao. gov) is the investigative arm of Congress that compiles reports on all aspects of government. All of GAO's unclassified reports are available to the public. Known as the "watchdog" of the U.S. Government, the GAO is a good place to go if you need information about government spending, fraud, legal decisions, or other controversies, from salmonella scares to aviation crash reports.

The **U.S. Government Printing Office** (www.access.gpo.gov) is the largest distributor of government documents. The GPO provides information to designated libraries and other locations throughout the country, where you can view the information for free.

The **National Technical Information Service** (www.ntis.gov) distributes scientific, technical, and engineering documents.

HOW RELIABLE IS WIKIPEDIA?

Remember when men in polyester suits used to go door-to-door selling encyclopedias, telling your parents that you and your siblings would have the edge over your peers at school if you could only have access to the entire set of *Encyclopedia Britannica* at home? Nowadays, no one sells encyclopedias in just this way, and stalwarts like *Encyclopedia Britannica*, which charge a subscription fee for online usage, are facing stiff competition from free upstarts like Wikipedia.

Online, a "wiki" (a Hawaiian word for "fast") is any collectively generated content that is the product of many individuals, who are usually unpaid. The idea of a wiki is that everyone gets the chance to be an author or an editor. On Wikipedia, for example, you could decide one day to write a page about a new hybrid of gardenia. You begin the page, contributing your own research about the gardenia. But the process doesn't end when you upload your entry. A few hours later, Bob in Ireland updates your content with information about rare gardenias in the U.K., and then Joyce in Seattle disputes something Bob has alleged. As the weeks go on, the content is refined, edited, and expanded.

Wikipedia is beloved by students and denounced by some of their professors, who abhor the concept of throwing the gates wide open to the noncredentialed *hoi polloi*. However, at least for well-established topics, Wikipedia can be surprisingly accurate. Too many cooks do not spoil the soup, but make it more precise. When using Wikipedia, be sure it's just the start of your information gathering, and not the sum of it; also watch out for disputed content (which will result in an alert at the top of the page). If you're in doubt, click on "History" at the top of the page, which will show you all the changes that have been made to the page and when. Then you can decide on its veracity for yourself.

TIPS AND TRICKS FOR EFFECTIVE RESEARCH

While it's fairly easy to write out a list of places to get information, what to do when you get there is another story. There is more than one path to the same point, and some are quicker than others. Think of unique ways to get the information you need, and think of unique ways to use the information you get. In other words, be as creative in your research as you are in your writing. Use the tips and tricks listed below to help you find the best research path possible.

- Work from the general to the specific. Look for general background information first. Use that to better define your search and begin to look for more specific information.

- Develop a rapport with the reference or research librarians at your local library. They live to help people find information. (Be sure to hit the highlights yourself first; it would be a real waste of a librarian's time if you haven't so much as Googled your topic yet. Save the librarian as your backup plan when you've exhausted your options or hit a wall with your research.)

- Scan the Table of Contents of books you think might be relevant. If you are doing this online, try using Amazon.com's "Look Inside" feature to give you a sense of the book before buying.

- To get a quick overview of a large book or document, check the index for a list of illustrations, charts, tables, or graphs. Lengthy, complicated subjects are often summarized with charts and graphs. This is especially true of government and scientific documents. If you find a graphic that is of particular interest, scan the text pages around it for related details. Also look for an executive summary or introduction at the front of the document and conclusion statements at the end of each section.

- If you have trouble finding information on your subject, it could be you are using the wrong search words. Check your words against the subject heading list in the directory you are searching.

- When retrieving your books from the library shelves, browse nearby books to see if any others might be useful. Library shelves are arranged so that nonfiction books about the same topic are generally kept near each other.

- Keep a list of what you find and where you found it. You may need to go back to it later.

- A volume number usually refers to the year that a periodical was published. Volume 10 refers to a magazine in its tenth year of publication.

- When you need facts, assume that there is a reference source that has what you need. There nearly always is.

- Most books and many articles themselves have bibliographies that list additional sources of information. By following these leads you can amass a body of information quickly.

MANAGING ALL YOUR RESEARCH NOTES ONLINE

Are you an index card person, a sticky-note-makes-a-fine-bookmark person, or a legal pad notes person? All writers have different methods for taking notes while they do research, and most of them are time-honored. However, just in the last few years, research websites have sprung up online that may make you gleefully burn your three-by-five cards once and for all.

The most advanced and promising of these is probably Zotero (www.zotero.org), a free plug-in program that you can download right onto your Internet browser. Zotero was developed by and for scholars, but anyone can use it, and did we mention it's free? What's great about Zotero is that it works right alongside common book and research sites and downloads bibliographic information at the click of a mouse. If you're on Amazon.com and you've found three books that will help you in your research, you click the Zotero button that will be in the bottom right-hand corner of your screen and it will automatically download all of the bibliographic information into your Zotero notes file, which you can organize by project, chapter, subject, or however you choose. The organization system works rather like an iPod's playlist, where you can store the same information in multiple places to make it easier to find later, and everything is automatically searchable.

Once you've downloaded the bibliographic info, you can take notes directly into that book or article's entry in your system; you can download all your notes into Microsoft Word later when you're ready to write; and you can input all the bibliographic information automatically in the style of your choosing. You can tag blog pages, websites, or other Internet research and send them directly to your notes for instant retrieval. You can find books in your public library's online catalog and automatically create Zotero entries for each with just one click. Coming soon (though possibly for a fee): automatic saves of your searches and notes, not just on your own hard drive, but on the Internet, so you always have a backup of your precious research should your latte become one with your laptop. Zotero isn't perfect yet, but it's growing more sophisticated every day. Check it out.

PART TWO

TO MARKET, TO MARKET

NOW YOU HAVE learned all the basics of mucking through research and the importance of writing every day. You're well on your way to publication … right? Well, almost. In this section—the longest in the book—we're going to learn all about the various markets you may wish to write for: magazines, fiction and non-fiction books, movies and television, and corporations. Along the way, we'll talk about whether you need a literary agent and how to handle rejection, a common setback for every writer. You'll learn the difference between a query letter and a proposal, and about the exploding possibilities that exist in self-publishing.

Pay close attention to the sections that matter most to you, and always remember this key fact: Whether you are a poet or a freelance journalist, a suspense novelist or a science writer, you are not only writing for yourself. You are writing for readers—the more the better. If you want a publishing house or a Hollywood studio to pay attention to your writing, you have to think always of who your potential audience is. This is what we mean by "the market": Who is your readership?

To market we go.

5 BEFORE YOU WRITE THAT QUERY LETTER

IN THIS CHAPTER, we're going to assume that you have either a working manuscript (a completed draft of your book), especially if you are writing fiction, or at least a few strong chapters, which is usually sufficient when you are proposing nonfiction. Congratulations! You are well on your way to publishing your book.

This chapter has been created to save you some time, heartache, and confusion as you navigate the tricky waters of book publishing. Here, we'll discuss the number one favor you can do for yourself before you write that query letter and book proposal; dissect the question of whether or not you need an agent; and help you understand the realities of rejection, a sad and near-universal fact in book publishing.

BUILDING YOUR PLATFORM: YOUR NUMBER ONE JOB

You'd think that when your brilliant and scintillating proposal lands on an editor's desk, her first act would be to tear through your writing, smile at your wit, and cry at your heartrending hospital scenes. Then she'll call you and offer you a contract, even though she doesn't know the first thing about you except that your writing positively sings.

Right? Wrong. More likely, before she reads your writing—before she decides whether it's worth her time to even *glance* at your writing—she is scrutinizing your author platform. The author platform is the first major test of your book proposal. Fail here, and your writing will not even get a fair hearing.

What is an author platform? Think of the good old days in nineteenth-century Hyde Park in London. That is where Londoners would go when they wanted to see a spectacle: dozens of people setting up platforms on soapboxes so they could shout their messages to the masses. Londoners would stroll among those platforms, hearing the street preachers and evangelists, the cough syrup hawkers and quack doctors, all proclaiming their messages as loudly as they could. The bigger a speaker's soapbox and the louder his voice, the greater his following.

Authors don't use literal soapboxes and platforms anymore to sell their books, but they certainly need the twenty-first century equivalents. An author's *platform* is her influence over a particular audience or readership, which often translates into an ability to sell a book. And if there's one thing you need to take away from this chapter, it's this: *It is primarily the authors' responsibility to sell their books, not their publishers'*. Authors tend to imagine that all they have to do is write the book and the publisher will take care of the rest, hopefully by promoting the book with splashy and expensive advertising in, say, *The New York Times*. If this is your expectation, you need to have your eyes opened a little bit. The reality in publishing is that authors who promote their books well and unself-consciously have a huge leg up in an editor's eyes. When you're approaching a publisher with your book proposal, you want to come to the table with the complete meal: great writing, naturally, but also a built-in audience of readers who will pay twenty dollars or more apiece to hear what you have to say.

The A-List Platform

What does a platform look like? Let's start with the ideal, and work our way down from there. Obviously, if you are lucky enough to have an A-List platform, you will be way ahead of your competitors (fellow writers who are competing for an editor's attention). However, very few new authors have an A-List platform, so don't panic. Here are some of the expected qualities of an A-List Platform:

- It is national, covering the whole of the United States. The A-List author is someone who speaks at least once a month (and usually more) all around the nation to audiences in the hundreds or even thousands.

- It involves a national media component. An A-List author could host an NPR show, appear regularly on a decorating show on HGTV, or have created a highly popular cooking segment on YouTube.

- The author's name is recognized by hundreds of thousands, or even millions, of people.

- The author has connections at major national media outlets, and/or will use private resources to hire an outside book publicist.

Okay, are you terrified? Don't be. Almost nobody fits into the A-List, but we put it here to give you an idea of what all publishers dream about: an author who comes into their office with a ready-made package for selling a particular book. Believe us, a publisher is going to take a book on parenting written by Katie Couric any day over one by an unknown author, even if that unknown happens to be a better writer or have a Ph.D. in child psychology. At the end of the day, platform is potentially more important than the writing itself—as depressing as that is.

The B-List Platform

If the A-List Platform is a publisher's secret dream, many of them would fall over themselves to work with authors with a B-List platform. This kind of platform:

- Is regional or national, often covering one area of the United States very thoroughly. A classic example would be a Southern novelist who has built a following in Southern literary magazines with her Faulkneresque short stories, and has readers clamoring for a full-length novel.

- The B-List author is someone who speaks at least once a month (and usually more) around the region or the nation to audiences in the dozens or hundreds.

- It involves a media component. A B-List author could have a history of being interviewed on local, regional, and national radio and TV programs, or writing for print publications. Perhaps he is a geriatrician in clinical practice who is a regular columnist on health and aging in *AARP The Magazine*.

- The author's name is recognized by thousands of people. The author is credentialed in her field and has all the relevant education to be considered an expert.

- The author has a website or blog that helps him connect with readers in his target market. For the geriatrician above, for example, the website could be an "Ask the Doctor" Q&A where he responds weekly or even daily to readers' health queries.

The C-List Platform

Most likely, the C-list is where most first-time authors will find themselves. Believe us when we say that even coming to a publisher with a small platform is far, far better than coming in with no platform at all. It's like arriving at a party covered by a well-placed loincloth as opposed to those writers who crash the scene stark naked, looking to mooch some food from their hosts. A C-list author might:

- Have a local or regional following.

- Speak regularly to small or medium-sized audiences at libraries, synagogues, community centers, colleges, churches, or the like.

- Have some media experience, either as a guest on a local radio or TV program or as a contributor to a local or regional newspaper.

- Be credentialed in a particular field, with enough education and expertise to be considered highly knowledgable.

- Have a website or blog that helps her connect with readers in her target market.

There are a couple of key reasons why you need some kind of platform before you come to a publisher. The most important is because it shows you're a team player. Having a platform and writing about it in your proposal demonstrates that you see it primarily as *your* job, not the publisher's, to sell your book. It shows that you expect to be a full and proactive participant in the journey of promoting and speaking about your book. This is music to your editor's ears. Another key reason you need a platform is that you really are the expert when it comes to your topic, especially in nonfiction. You can't expect that publisher to be able to promote the book to niche audiences as effectively as you, the expert.

We'll talk about book proposals and marketing plans more in chapters seven and eight, but for now just remember that the proposal needs to be as specific as possible about all the ways you as an author plan to reach your target market. If you are writing a book on fandom and *Battlestar Galactica*, you will do yourself a huge favor if your proposal includes a marketing plan that includes you selling your book at the huge annual Comic-Con show and promoting it on fan websites with weekly giveaways that drive traffic to your book's website. If you're a gardening expert, you get the edge if your proposal includes a schedule of the gardening shows, whether local, regional, or national, that have invited you to speak over the next two years. Think creatively about how to build your platform. Your excitement and willingness to think like a marketer will do wonders in helping you snag an editor or agent.

WHEN SHOULD I BEGIN BUILDING MY PLATFORM?

In *The Right Way to Write, Publish and Sell Your Book*, Patricia Fry suggests that it's not enough to start building your author platform before you write the book proposal; ideally, you need to begin building the platform before you even begin writing the *book*.

This is true even if you're writing fiction. Authors should choose a setting that will spark discussion and that is a source of pride for residents of that area, who often can be some of the most vocal advocates for selling a novel by word-of-mouth. Also, Fry advises novelists to include hot topics in their stories, because those are potential media hooks down the road when you are trying to get interviews. Some controversial topics are here today and gone tomorrow, but others appear to be perennial, and novelists who offer a thoughtful take on them can stand out. For example, if your novel deals with an issue like euthanasia or a disability, you or your publicist may be able to get you interviewed about how your book might relate to those issues if they should be in the news. Think now about how you can publicize your book when it is published, and let that help you shape your writing.

DO I NEED A LITERARY AGENT?

While many publishers, especially smaller ones, accept material from writers who don't have agents, editors often prefer to work with agents who understand the house's needs and the editor's tastes.

"I think there's always a way for a talented writer to get published," says Tracy Carns, publishing director of Overlook Press. But she advises beginning writers—especially those interested in working with a larger publishing house—to first find an agent. "This is a business of relationships," she says, "and agents have a relationship with the editor and publisher. They know what we like." She says she is far more likely to read a proposal sent by a trusted agent than a cold submission. "I'll obviously look at everything, but not all submissions are created equal. Selling a manuscript is a specialized skill. That's what agents do. Why should a writer be expected to do that? You don't take out your own appendix. If you're a writer, you should write."

Although this is terrific advice, and most writers could benefit from having an agent, the fact is that most working authors *don't* have one, especially if they're just starting out. Since agents work on commission—usually 15 percent of whatever their authors make—they are often reluctant to take on brand-new authors with no publishing experience. (You can do the math: If most first-time authors' advances are just a few thousand dollars, if that, it would be awfully hard for an agent to make a living from

15 percent of that unless the agent had dozens of prolific clients.) If you are going it alone, you'll want to pay particular attention to chapter fifteen, which deals with contracts and the legal end of publishing, but know that good literary agents do far more than help you negotiate fair terms.

What Does a Literary Agent Do?

Many writers have heard that they need a literary agent, but they are in the dark about what the agent is expected to do. Agents are, in a word, brokers between authors and publishers. The best agents are very familiar with the lists of many different publishing houses, and even the personal preferences of various editors within those houses. They have become gatekeepers for the major publishers for whom they are now essential. Some of the functions of a literary agent include:

- Matching a book proposal or manuscript with the right publishing house, often by sifting through the proverbial "slush pile" that publishers don't have time to touch

- Negotiating a favorable contract for the author, with competitive terms of advance, royalty, subsidiary rights, and marketing

- Being familiar with publishing law and changing terms for author contracts

- Acting as a mediator between the author and the publisher during the writing and production processes, while weighing in on business questions of cover art, title, publicity decisions, and regular royalty statements

- Staying abreast of hot topics and trends in publishing

- Traveling to book fairs and trade shows to sell international rights

- Helping an author map out a long-term strategy and a career, rather than just place a single book

Some agents are more involved with the actual editing than others. There are agents who will go back and forth with an author about a book proposal several times before the agent feels satisfied that it's ready to send out to publishers. Other agents—who are not necessarily worse agents—are less involved with the editorial process, preferring to focus more on the business end of things.

You Definitely Need an Agent If ...

- You are adamant that you want to sell your book only to one of the largest, most prestigious New York houses. Many of them will only look at proposals that come in through literary agents.

- It matters a great deal to you to get the highest possible advance for your book.

- You can't imagine trying to negotiate your own book contracts or think seriously about the business aspects of your writing.

- You are already an established writer with several books to your name, but would like to take your career to the next level.

You Probably Don't Need an Agent If ...

- You are open to working with many different kinds of publishing houses—large and prestigious, small and independent.

- You are expecting a relatively low advance and are just beginning your writing career.

- You don't mind taking care of the business end of things yourself.

OK, SO HOW DO I GET ONE?

There's an old joke in publishing that an agent is like a loan from the bank: You can only get one if you can demonstrate that you don't need one. Agents are looking for motivated, experienced authors who are experts in their fields and have a platform for selling their books. You'll notice that these are the exact same qualifications that editors are looking for, as outlined above in the section on author platform. Are you beginning to sense a theme here? That's right: Agents are seeking the same qualities as publishers. Here's how to find one.

The Basics of Contacting Literary Agents

Once you and your manuscript are thoroughly prepared, the time is right to contact an agent. Finding an agent can often be as difficult as finding a publisher—or even more so. One agent interviewed for this book estimated that top literary agents choose to represent fewer than 1 percent of the writers who want to work with them. Nevertheless, there are many ways to maximize your chances of finding the right agent.

> **1. Referrals.** The best way to get your foot in an agent's door is to be referred by one of his clients, or by an editor or another agent he has worked with in the past. Because an agent trusts his clients, he will usually read referred work before over-the-transom submissions. (Over-the-transom is a nice way of saying "unsolicited," dating back to the day when writers would deposit their manuscripts in the one

window of a publisher's office that was left open overnight for airflow.) If you are friends with anyone in the publishing business who has connections with agents, ask politely for a referral.

2. Conferences. Going to a conference is your best bet for meeting an agent in person. Many conferences invite agents to either give a speech or simply be available for meetings with authors. This is especially true for fiction, but you can find conferences that work for nonfiction writers as well. Agents view conferences as a way to find writers. Often agents set aside time for one-on-one discussions with writers, and occasionally they may even look at material writers bring to the conference. If an agent is impressed with you and your work, she may ask for writing samples after the conference. When you send your query, be sure to mention the specific conference where you met and remind her that she asked to see your work.

3. Submissions. The most common way to contact an agent is by a query letter or a proposal package. Most agents will accept unsolicited queries. Some will also look at outlines and sample chapters. Almost none want unsolicited complete manuscripts (yet they receive them all the time from oblivious authors). Check the agent's online submission guidelines to learn exactly how an agent prefers to be solicited. Never call—let the writing in your query letter speak for itself.

Agents agree to be listed in directories such as *Guide to Literary Agents* to indicate to writers what they want to see and how they wish to receive submissions. As you start to query agents, make sure you follow their individual submission directions. This, too, shows an agent you've done your research. Like publishers, agencies have specialties. Some are only interested in novel-length works of fiction, or they may specialize in specific types of genre fiction (romance, mystery, science-fiction, etc.). Others may focus on nonfiction books in science, medicine, and technology, or on juvenile literature. Others are open to a wide variety of subjects and may actually have member agents within the agency who specialize in only a handful of the topics covered by the entire agency. Whatever the case, do your homework, because the quickest way for your query to end up in an agent's recycling bin is to send a type of material that the agency does not represent.

4. Your platform. Since agents work entirely on commission, their bread and butter depends on whether authors have viable platforms to sell their books. If Anna Agent wants to be eating filet mignon in retirement and not Alpo, she will want to ensure that all of her authors have a platform. So here's a quiz. Which is easier for Anna: (a) helping her authors painstakingly build a platform nail by board, or (b) piggybacking on to the as-yet-unagented college professor she heard this morning on NPR? Yep, the answer is (b): Anna wants authors who already have a platform, and she'll contact them out of the blue to get it. (Wouldn't it be a nice change of pace to be courted by an agent, rather than chasing one down and hoping, like a spurned lover, that maybe one will answer your e-mail?) As Christina Katz says in *Get Known Before the*

Book Deal, "Publishing professionals already know that publishing success isn't about how talented you are; rather, it's about what you do with how talented you are." Agents want authors who have already demonstrated that they are "full-in" in their commitment to getting their name and expertise recognized. You want to be one of those authors, not the kind just sitting around waiting to be discovered. If you are assertive about building your platform, you may be surprised at how many agents are willing to work with you or even seek you out.

5. Publishing credits. Some agents read magazines or journals to find writers to represent. If you have had an outstanding piece published in a periodical, you may be contacted by an agent wishing to represent you. In such cases, make sure the agent has read your work. Some agents send form letters to writers, and such agents often make their living entirely from charging reading fees, not from commissions on sales.

However, many reputable and respected agents also contact potential clients in this way. For them, you already possess some of the attributes of a good client: You have publishing credits, and an editor has validated your work. To receive a letter from a reputable agent who has read your material and wants to represent you is an honor.

Occasionally, writers who have self-published or who have had their work published electronically may attract an agent's attention, especially if the self-published book has sold well or received a lot of positive reviews. We'll discuss this route in greater detail in chapter eleven.

HOW CAN YOU TELL A GOOD AGENT
FROM A BAD ONE?

One of the sad facts in the publishing business is that while agents have a remarkable amount of power in vetting authors, authors have far less control when it comes to vetting agents. Agents don't go to "agent school" or get a degree in agenting. Most did not set out to become literary agents back when they had Career Day in junior high. So how can you evaluate an agent's experience and education?

In general, you want to stay away from agencies that advertise heavily. Many of these agencies charge a reading fee just to look at your work. Although there are exceptions, very few reputable agents charge a reading fee, a marketing fee, or a "submission fee." Real agents don't make a dime until they actually sell your work to a publishing house. Also, be wary of a literary agency that refers you to a specific editorial service for an overhaul of your book; chances are the agent is getting a kickback for that referral.

If the worst-case scenario is to find an agent who is a literary scam artist, the more common scenario is to hook up with a bona fide agent who is simply inexperienced, overcommitted, or incompetent. There is no licensing vehicle for literary agents, so just about anyone can hang out a shingle and claim that job title. You want to be careful. If you are sending your work to an agent, be sure to check the agency out beforehand. For example, is the agent a member of the Association of Authors' Representatives? (www.aaronline.org) That is the premier organization of literary and dramatic agents who have to have at least two years of experience and adhere to a code of ethics before joining.

If you are lucky enough to get positive feedback from an agent who wants to represent you, don't sign an agreement right away. Ask the agent to send you copies of some books he has represented, and to provide you with the contact information of authors whose work he has placed successfully. Reputable agents expect this and will not be offended that you are checking up on their work. If the agent *is* offended, or does not provide you with that information, consider it a red flag that the agent is inexperienced or does not feel secure that his own clients would provide him with a good evaluation.

When you speak to the agent's authors, ask about the agent's strengths and weaknesses, special skills, contacts at publishing houses, and assertiveness in selling international rights. Don't ask directly about how much money or what kind of royalty rate the agent was able to get the author, though the author may volunteer this information. Do ask questions about the agent's responsiveness. Was the agent available for brainstorming, helping with book revisions, and running interference with a publisher over cover art or titling? Or did the agent take the money and run? Does the agent charge extra for things like copying, or is that included in the percentage? Would the author recommend this agent to her friends who are writers?

PREPARING YOURSELF FOR A WALL OF REJECTION

Nobody likes rejection, but it's a fact of life in publishing. For some writers, rejection letters become a perverse point of pride, and you can find some websites entirely devoted to them (with some very entertaining entries).

And a California-based literary journal has chosen as its title *The Rejected Quarterly, Featuring Fine Literature Rejected at Least Five Times*.

When (not if) you are rejected, know that you are joining the ranks of some of the best writers of all time. Hemingway, Alcott, Austen, Orwell—all found their brilliance falling on deaf ears. Popular writers like J.K. Rowling have known their share of rejection—more than a dozen publishers rejected *Harry Potter and the Philosopher's Stone* before Bloomsbury signed the author for a modest advance of £1,500, a little less than $2,500. Rewards come to those who are patient and persistent.

Step 1: Try to Learn From the Rejection Letter

The most helpful letters are from editors and agents who have (a) actually read your material, and (b) taken the time to tell you why it's not a good fit for them. If you get such a letter, don't waste your energy fighting the advice or information it contains. One first-time novelist heard from several editors and one agent that the ending of his otherwise promising debut did not make sense and seemed to come out of nowhere. Rather than changing the ending and trying again, however, he refused to listen and kept insisting that the ending was perfect as it was. As of this writing, he has been trying for ten years and his novel remains unpublished. Don't be that stubborn.

Try to decode what the rejection letter or e-mail is telling you. Does the editor worry that you don't have enough of a platform? If so, go and build one and try again in a year. Does the agent feel there are too many books on the shelves that address your topic? If so, make sure you improve the "competitive books" section of your proposal by evaluating the other books available and explaining why yours is unique and necessary. Or, if you determine after careful study that your book isn't unique enough yet, revise your proposal, title, and marketing plan so your book *will* offer something that its competition does not.

Occasionally, an editor or agent will refer you to another publishing house or agent. If this happens to you, be grateful! This person is going out of her way to help you find the right outlet for your work. Be sure to follow up on any and all contacts you receive through a thoughtful rejection letter.

Take any personal, specific comments as encouragement—editors rarely have time to pen such notes, and if they have taken the time to do so, that's a positive sign that they think you are a promising writer, even if this particular project doesn't fit their needs. It can also be helpful to include the editor's comments in a submission log so you can keep track of where you submitted and how the house or agency responded.

What's harder to learn from are boilerplate rejection letters that don't give you any information about why your work has not been chosen. Don't write back demanding more information; just send a quick thank-you e-mail to the person in question. Appreciate the fact that she at least let you know one way or the other—some publishers never respond at all, and just keep authors guessing.

Step 2: Try to Laugh About It

Rejection is very difficult, but it helps to share the misery with other writers and maintain a sense of humor. Here are a couple of websites to help you laugh off the sting:

- At www.inkygirl.com/writers-and-rejection-dont-give-up/, authors can read other writers' rejections, including Shannon Hale, Ray Bradbury, Judy Blume, and Ursula LeGuin. There's healthy camaraderie in realizing that rejection happens to everyone … multiple times.

- In case your can-do attitude takes a serious hit from receiving one rejection after another, however, take heart. One company has come through with a revolutionary new way to, ahem, put it behind you. At Lulu (www.lulu.com), authors can upload the text of their rejection letters and have them printed on custom-made toilet paper. Yes, really.

Many of the publishing industry's happiest endings began badly, with a lot of rejection. Almost all authors have been through it. In fact, console yourself for a moment by looking at the *New York Times* best-seller list and reminding yourself that at one time, every author on that list was unpublished, uncertain, and untried, just like you. Many of their routes to success began with an avalanche of rejection—and so might yours. Each rejection brings you that much closer to zeroing in on the publisher or agent who is right for you.

FROM REJECTION TO TRIUMPH

When children's novelist Madeleine L'Engle wrote *A Wrinkle in Time* in the late 1950s, many publishing houses rejected it. For ten years, L'Engle wrote steadily and raised her family, but did not publish so much as a poem or a short story. Those were difficult years, filled with personal joy and a house full of children, along with professional doubt and the sting of rejection. Some publishers responded that *A Wrinkle in Time* was too dark, that it had witches, and that children would be frightened by the novel's scarier themes. Others complained that its exalted vocabulary and edgy scientific ideas were too demanding for middle-grade readers. Maddeningly, one editor confessed in a rejection letter that he personally loved the book, "but didn't quite dare do it, as it isn't really classifiable." It didn't fit into any known category for children. Finally, one publisher (Farrar, Straus and Giroux) gave L'Engle a contract, and the book won a Newbery Medal and has become a modern classic. L'Engle was so delighted with her publisher that she published her fiction with FSG faithfully for four decades until her death. That in itself is a lesson: Although you may be rejected more times than you care to count, it only takes one "yes" to make it all worthwhile.

RESOURCES

BUILDING YOUR PLATFORM

Get Known Before the Book Deal by Christina Katz (Writer's Digest Books). "Writer Mama" Katz discusses why you need an author platform and how to build one.

Self-Promotion for the Creative Person: Get the Word Out About Who You Are and What You Do by Lee Silber (Three Rivers Press). This book teaches authors, artists, and other creative types how to begin thinking like marketers and publicity professionals.

LITERARY AGENTS

Literary Agents: What They Do, How They Do it, and How to Find and Work With the Right One for You by Michael Larsen (Wiley). As a nonfiction literary agent and author, Larsen shares his expertise on the ins and outs of getting an agent.

Guide to Literary Agents **edited by Chuck Sambuchino** (Writer's Digest Books). This annual book provides listings, guidelines, and contact information for more than a thousand literary agents.

Literary Agents: The Essential Guide for Writers by **Debby Mayer** (Penguin). This book explains the agent's role in some detail, discusses money and subsidiary rights, and gives advice on market trends.

REJECTION LETTERS

Rotten Rejections: The Letters That Publishers Wish They'd Never Sent **by André Bernard** (Robson Books). This collection will soothe the heart of any rejected writer, providing actual examples of rejections of now-famous works of literature. One of the more famous mistakes is one editor's rejection of George Orwell's *Animal Farm*, declaring that it was impossible to sell animal stories. Indeed.

6

SELLING YOUR
ARTICLES

THE WONDERFUL THING about magazines is that there are just so many of them. Even in a recessed economy, when print magazines are folding every month, having thousands of magazines means there are thousands of potential markets for a writer's work.

The terrible thing about magazines is that there are just so many of them. Those thousands of magazines all have different audiences, different styles, and different voices—and different requirements of their writers.

The trick to selling your short nonfiction to any of these magazines is matching the article to the magazine. In other words, to sell an article to a magazine, writers have to do a little marketing. Now, before you argue that you are a writer and not a marketing professional, go back and read the first two chapters, which discuss the market in general. Then consider: The skills you use in marketing your story are not so different from those you use in everyday life.

Say you're seated at a dinner party next to a woman in an evening gown, high heels, pearls, and a coiffure of perfection. Would you initiate a conversation by leaning her way and inquiring, "Hey, what'dja think about that boxing match on TV last night?" Rather than assuming she's a boxing fan, you'd probably invest a bit of time to learn her interests before plunging into such a conversation.

Yet would-be writers commit such gaffes with magazines every day. They try to sell stories on canoeing to backpacking magazines. They offer fiction to magazines that publish nonfiction. They view themselves as writers whose work will be appreciated by whoever reads it, rather than as someone whose job is to figure out who their audience is and to tell those people a story they'd be interested in hearing.

Professional magazine writers recognize that magazines are as individual as people are. They hold conversations with their readers every month, discussing their topics of mutual interest in their own style of language. Magazine editors know the people who read their magazines. They know their ages, their sexes, and their incomes. They know what stirs their interests and what bores them. So if you go to the trouble of learning about the magazine and its audience, you improve your chances of joining in its conversation with its readers.

AVOIDING REJECTION

Most editors expect to be approached professionally by writers. And professional writers do not write 2,000-word feature articles and blindly ship them off to random magazines. Most professionals (at least when they were getting started) first write a letter that proposes a story idea and that proffers themselves as the perfect person to write it—the query letter.

Queries are letters of introduction and sales pitches combined. While your query must explain in some detail what your story will be about, it also must be concise. Editors are busy people, and many figure that if you can't boil the story idea down to a page or so, it probably doesn't have a point.

In theory, querying doesn't sound so hard. But ask editors to describe the actual queries they receive, and you'll most likely hear sorrowful sighs. Many say they often receive what they delicately call "inappropriate" queries. And the single biggest reason for the inappropriateness is a writer's ignorance of their publications. Again and again editors complain that most people who write queries haven't even bothered to read the magazine.

BUILDING YOUR NETWORK OF
EDITORIAL CONTACTS

Success in magazine writing, as in most any kind of job, is often a case of "who you know." There are so many talented writers that assignments tend to go to people that editors know personally and have worked with in the past. Freelance writer Michael Joseph Gross, who has written for *Vanity Fair*, *The Atlantic Monthly*, and *The New York Times Magazine*, among other publications, got his foot in the door when he took a break from seminary to intern at *Esquire*. While learning the business, he would send out faxes with his story ideas on *Esquire* stationery. His first successful pitch was for *The New York Observer*. "As soon as you have one clip, then you've shown that you can do something, and you send that along with your next pitch," Gross says. Connections are very important. "If you're trying to write for print magazines, which is what I've mostly done, print remains a pretty small old-fashioned business. Most people live in New York, and a lot of them know each other. After I wrote the piece for *The New York Observer*, I had an idea for *The New Republic* and my editor knew someone there, and I was able to say, 'Bob sent me.'" That led to another assignment, which was for a major story, but to Gross's disappointment the story was subsequently killed. Although that was not the ending he'd been hoping for, the editor felt bad about having to kill it, so he gave Gross some valuable introductions to other editors. "Apparent failures can be very useful," Gross explains. "I think that's something that people don't realize. They get discouraged very early, as perhaps they should, because this is not a good job to have unless you're dying to do it." Perseverance and professionalism are key. He advises writers to "take nothing personally" and remember that magazine editors are trapped under "an absolute avalanche of information."

FINDING MAGAZINE MARKETS FOR YOUR IDEAS

To get the nod to write for a magazine, you must match your idea to a specific market. This requires you to *read the magazine* (see sidebar) before pitching an idea. In fact, many writers start with the magazine rather than the idea. Here are some steps to follow:

> **1. Find the right magazine(s).** If you don't already have a magazine in mind, try consulting a directory like *Writer's Market* to help you narrow your search. For example, in the table of contents of *Writer's Market*, look for the category of magazine that matches your idea (Retirement? Travel? Regional?), and then flip to the individual listings to find publications that seem to be suited to the idea. You'll be amazed by the diversity there, from *The Magazine of Fantasy and Science Fiction* through *AntiqueWeek* to more traditional outlets like *Good Housekeeping*. The listings have icons that give a sense of the different periodicals' pay range, article length, and so forth.

READ THE MAGAZINE ... AND ITS COMPETITORS

One of the most common complaints from magazine editors is that they get blanket pitches from writers who have no idea of what kinds of stories their magazines actually publish. Most authors are smart enough to know that they shouldn't send an article about saving money on taxes to *Dog Fancy* or *Gourmet*, but unless they read the finance magazines carefully, they're not always going to know the differences between *Money*, *Kiplinger's Personal Finance*, *SmartMoney*, or *Bloomberg Personal Finance*, which are the major players in the personal finance world.

Set yourself apart by doing additional homework. Be like that really annoying student in your college classes who not only read the assignment, but all the recommended reading as well and became the darling of the professor. Here's how: If you're going to write for a particular market, you need to educate yourself on not only the magazine you are pitching to, but also its direct competitors. The differences among them may seem subtle to you, but they are major to the editors you are pitching. If you write to *Money* and pitch an article about how fiftysomething employees can help boost their job security by making themselves indispensable at the office, you're showing that you have done your homework about *Money*'s target demographic and typical articles. If you can pitch that same story and also note that although direct rival *Kiplinger's Personal Finance* ran a similar story last quarter, it missed three important strategies as outlined by Finance Gurus X and Y, you get a gold star. And possibly a contract.

2. Research the heck out of that magazine. Read it from cover to cover. Ask yourself whether your writing style is a good fit. Are you breezy and personal while the magazine's style is formal and reserved? Will the topic that interests you also interest an editor at this magazine? Are there regular departments that would be good vehicles for breaking in with an editor there?

We're not kidding about actually reading at least one issue of the magazine. Don't cheat here. In order to truly get to know a publication, you'll need to do more than just check out the table of contents. You'll also need to scan several months' worth to get an accurate idea of what stories the magazine's editors prefer. Reading through the letters to the editor also can generate ideas targeted to readers' concerns. When you read the articles, take note of the tone, sourcing, style, slant, and organization of each so you'll know how to write yours. Finally, taking a look at the ads will give you a good picture of who reads the magazine.

3. Fire up your search engine. Once you've identified a specific magazine, take some time to study its writers' guidelines, which are usually posted on its website. These are often found when you click on "Contact Us" at a magazine's website, but you can also usually find them by typing "submissions" in a search box on the site itself. Sometimes, a magazine will only have the most basic information about where to send a query and sample clips, but sometimes it will have very detailed instructions about content, format, and the like. If it *does* have detailed instructions and you did not take the time to find and follow them, you are unlikely to impress an editor, so be sure not to skip this step.

One of your other goals in doing online research at this stage is to find out as much as you can about your editor. Using the masthead of the magazine (the list, buried amid the advertisements, of who covers what subject areas and departments), you can usually get the name of the editor you want to pitch. But don't stop there. Let technology work for you. Google the life out of that editor! Does she have a work-related blog, as many editors do? This could be a gold mine if the editor talks about current trends (e.g., a food magazine editor dishes on the hottest cooking shows, or a travel editor uploads photos from his recent travels to Bhutan). Even if the editor doesn't have a website or blog, you can often find out a lot about that person's professional interests through Google (where she was quoted by an industry trade magazine, for example). Leave no cyber-stone unturned in your quest for information.

Once you're armed with the guidelines and a knowledge of the publication, think about how your idea can work within the magazine and how you can slant your idea so it matches the tone and style of the magazine. If the magazine's recently covered a topic similar to the one you'd like to propose, think about new ways you can frame your story to make it different.

BREAK INTO MAGAZINES THROUGH
A BACK DOOR: WRITE ONLINE

One of the great changes of the last decade is the explosion of possible writing avenues for online work. You are probably already familiar with some of the websites that are online-only (no print component), but did you also know that most major print magazines have an online presence with additional content that is only available on the Internet?

This is wonderful news for you as a writer. Magazine editors are often more willing to take a chance with a green, untried writer in their online content than they are with their print content. There are several reasons for this. First, magazines sometimes don't pay quite as well for online-only content as they do for what goes in the print magazine. (Hopefully, this will change as online writing edges out print writing over the next few years.) Because of the lower fee structure, publications are out less money if you don't knock their socks off with your prose. Along those same lines, online pieces are often shorter and therefore less of a challenge for breaking in new writers.

Finally—and perhaps most importantly—the magazine's risk is significantly decreased if you screw up online. If a brand-new writer doesn't meet a deadline for online content, for example, it's not usually a crisis because there are not predetermined page counts, budgets, printing schedules, and shipping costs to be considered. And if a new writer makes a mistake, like misattributing a quote or misunderstanding a statistic, it's fairly easy for an online editor to go back to the article, fix the problem, and run a fine-print correction at the bottom stating that the original version has been slightly altered. Compare that to the *Sturm und Drang* of a mistake that is discovered in a print magazine once it's already gone to press: The magazine has gone out and cannot be recalled. It's every editor's nightmare. You have made the editor look bad, and possibly cost the publication money and advertisers, so you can pretty much count on the fact that you will not be hired by that magazine again.

STRINGING FOR NEWSPAPERS

Although the newspaper industry is in financial trouble, with declining circulation, increasing reliance on wire news, and shrinking pages, there is still a place for freelance writers, or "stringers." Newspapers almost never have enough reporters to cover the stories in their areas and many, particularly smaller papers, welcome freelancers. This is especially true in the depressed economy—as newspapers lay off more of their own full-time reporters, they are looking to the cheap labor routinely provided by stringers.

Stringers may write feature stories, but they often begin by reporting on official meetings—school board meetings, town commission meetings, and the like. Some papers publish special sections, written by stringers, and some use feature stories from freelancers. If you want to string for a paper, it helps to have taken at least one journalism course to understand how to report accurately and write fast. A journalism degree will help you be even more qualified and marketable to string for newspapers.

Weekly community newspapers are often the easiest places to begin. But larger metropolitan daily papers also are traditionally understaffed and hire stringers. To find such a job, write a simple business letter to the managing editor of a larger paper or the editor of a smaller one, asking if they need stringers. You may not have to come up with story ideas yourself, but include one or two if you know the paper hasn't covered them. Mention any writing experience you have and include clips, along with a resume, and tell them you'll follow up if you don't hear anything within a month or so. It's better to use e-mail than it is to call, since the newspaper business is extremely time-sensitive and the editor may be on a tight deadline.

While it may be easier to win a newspaper assignment than one from a magazine, the financial rewards are usually far less. The range is from about $25 per story for small papers to $150 or more at larger ones. But you get more than money by working for a paper. You get published, and your clips can help you land bigger jobs. And if you're lucky, you'll also get a good editor who will work with you and with your copy.

CRAFTING A QUERY LETTER

Reading the magazine or newspaper and studying the writer's guidelines are the two biggest favors you can do for yourself before trying to write a story for any publication. Once you've done those crucial steps, you're ready to craft a query letter. We cover query letters pretty extensively in the next chapter on pitching books, but here is some basic advice about writing query letters for magazine submissions.

Queries are one or two pages—editors are notoriously overworked and sensitive to demands on their time, so one page is ideal. They are at once brief and comprehensive—try to give the editor an idea of the breadth of your story, the sources you plan to utilize, and the angle you plan to take. Above all, they need to be interesting.

Put yourself in the editor's place. It's hard for him to take a chance on an unknown writer, particularly following multiple reports of journalists making up sources or entire stories. And even if a story is accurate, sometimes editors have to work hard to salvage a weak story, creating instead a mediocre story—and missing a chance to get a great story.

That's why your query letter must be an example of your best work. Your writing should be flawless—don't let little errors like spelling or weak sentence structure get in your way. Hook the editor with a strong lead that arouses interest in the story you're proposing—make the editor want to know more. More importantly, make sure your query letter succinctly explains your idea. Nothing's worse than a query letter that loses focus midway through and inadvertently proposes an entirely different topic.

Finally, don't forget to give your article a strong title, something that successfully communicates your unique angle or hook. This will give editors something to hold onto as they consider giving you the assignment.

SHOULD LONG-FORM ARTICLES HAVE LONG-FORM QUERIES?

Standard advice for magazine writers stipulates that magazine queries should be short—no more than a page—and very much to the point. This is certainly how you should start out, especially when you are pitching short features to smaller publications. However, once you've built up a reputation and are ready to tackle some harder assignments, consider the merits of a query that is much like the article itself.

"My advice for writing pitches: Write long," says Jeff Sharlet, a contributing editor for major national magazines. "Conventional wisdom holds pitches should be short and pithy, two or three paragraphs containing an anecdote, a dubious sociological claim, and a few words about your unique access to the story. I don't doubt that such a formula works for many magazines. But if you want to write long, challenging narrative features, start by writing long, challenging narrative pitches." Sharlet has successfully pitched his work to *Harper's*, *Rolling Stone*, *New York*, and other publications, and he's rarely written a pitch less than 1,000 words. "My 'pitch' is the beginning of the story. If you can't start writing the story, you won't be able to finish it, either," he says. In one case, Sharlet says, that 1,000-word pitch became the first quarter of a 4,500-word story for *Rolling Stone*, and in another, part of a book he was writing called *The Family: The Secret Fundamentalism at the Heart of American Power*. That book went on to be a national bestseller and Sharlet was featured on *The Daily Show with Jon Stewart* and NPR. And it all started with a pitch.

To cut down on your chances of rejection, you might want to study a book on writing query letters, including *The Writer's Digest Guide to Query Letters*. But certainly consider the following tips:

Focus Your Idea

Think long and think hard about your idea. Perhaps because they lack experience in knowing just how many words it takes to tell stories, some beginning writers have trouble narrowing an idea into a workable notion. This can result in a scattered query that touches on five or six different story ideas without developing any of them, and can leave an editor scratching his head.

Focus is key. It's not enough to say you want to write an article about divorce. When devising your ideas, slice and dice a topic. Focus on an angle, one person in the news, one aspect of a larger debate. What unique angle will you take? What will make your article on divorce different from all those that have come before it? Will it be about surviving divorce? Deciding to get a divorce? Helping children cope with divorce? Understanding the divorce process from a legal perspective? How will this article help readers? Why should they bother to read it? If there's no benefit, the odds of the article getting accepted are slim.

Prove You've Done Some Homework

No one expects freelancers to research an entire feature before asking an editor if she would be interested in buying it. But you have to know enough to convince an editor you've got a story. Read what your target magazine and similar publications have printed on your topic before querying, and look for a fresh angle. You also might name some of the sources you plan to contact, or at least give their occupations. Including relevant statistics is another way to prove you're well versed in your subject matter. For example: "Recent studies indicate that more than x *(insert statistic)* million children in the United States come from divorced families. I plan to talk with at least two noted child psychiatrists in order to learn about the challenges these children face and what parents can do to help them."

Write to the Right Person

Writer's Market lists the names of editors to query at thousands of publications, but people change jobs frequently. Look online to see who should get your query. If you can't find what you're looking for, telephone and ask the receptionist (if you are lucky enough to get a human being), "Who should receive a query for a piece in your Parenting Department?" Be sure to ask how to spell the editor's name. Or, check the magazine's masthead to stay current on changing positions.

Even if an editor doesn't care if you addressed your query to the wrong person, sending it to the right person makes querying more efficient—the letter or e-mail is less likely to spend days bouncing from inbox to inbox.

Be careful if you're sending the same query to several magazines. No two magazines are exactly the same. Make sure that even if you're submitting the same idea to multiple magazines, you've tailored your query to make it specific for each publication.

Show Your Style

A query letter must convince the editor that you know how to write for the publication. Pitch the story with grace and verve. If a magazine adopts a particular tone of voice with its readers—a he-man voice for outdoor adventure magazines, for example—use that voice in your query. If the magazine allows different voices in its pages, let your own personality show through. If you've got a great anecdote or a quote, include it. Other writers could probably write the piece, but they might not be able to dig up your golden nuggets.

Sound Confident

If you've done your homework and you know your stuff, you will sound sure of yourself. Sounding confident and professional is a far better way to garner a sale than sounding like a beginner pleading for a break. Tell the editor, "I'll write [not "I hope to write"] about five ways mothers can help their daughters make and keep friends."

If you have any other nonwriting qualifications to write a particular story, note them. For a profile on a bookstore owner, for example, mention that you worked your way through college at a Barnes & Noble. If you don't have any relevant experience, don't dwell on it. There's no need to include lines like, "I've never published anything before, but I know I can do it." Let your query letter speak for itself.

Include Clips When Specified

Be sure to check a publication's guidelines for writers before sending clips. Some magazines want them with the query, and some don't. A safe bet is to include a short line at the end of your query saying, "Clips are available upon request."

If the magazine does ask for clips, be sure to use your very best. Some editors recommend sending only those clips that are similar to the article you're proposing. Thus, send clips from a children's publication if you want to write for a publication like *Highlights*. But others want to see what you've written, regardless of the subject matter. This gives editors a feel for your writing style and signals to them that you can start and finish the job.

Nowadays, most writers "send clips" by just including links to their publications when they query by e-mail. This method is fast, uncluttered, and environmentally friendly, so use it if you can. If your clips aren't online, however (which is sometimes the case for small newspapers or niche magazines), you will want to go the old-fashioned route. If you send clips by snail mail and want them back after consideration, don't forget to include a self-addressed, stamped envelope so the editor can return the clips if she rejects your idea.

Choose Wisely

In the beginning, it may help to aim for small victories as you build your writing resume. Once you've established yourself as a "published writer" by honing your craft with smaller or regional publications, you'll have an easier time cracking into national magazines.

It's also important to take into consideration that longer feature stories more often go to writers with a long-established working relationship with the publication, simply because a magazine is reluctant to risk three thousand dollars on an unknown.

So examine the shorter pieces in the magazines that you enjoy reading, and think about what you can offer. The pay will be smaller, the glory is less splendiferous, but it may be the easiest way to break in. Besides, you may be able to complete smaller pieces more quickly and do more of them than longer articles.

Wait Patiently

Waiting for a response can seem like an eternity. And sometimes it is. Writer's guidelines usually specify a standard response time, as well as indicate periods when the publication is closed to submissions. It's usually safe to add an extra month to the specified response time. This allows for any number of delays, such a backlog at the assigning editor's desk, a sudden staff change that's slowed everything down, an intense debate about whether to buy your piece, etc. Don't get overeager or personally offended if you don't get an immediate response. And don't call the editor angrily demanding an on-the-spot decision about your query—the decision won't be in your favor. If you don't hear back, it's usually best to just move on to another publication. If your curiosity gets the best of you, a short, professional e-mail or letter is the best way to go.

Move Past Rejection

If you do get a rejection letter now and again, don't let it hold you back. Learn from it—even a form rejection can reveal a lot about what a publication wants and needs. If it's a subject you're passionate about, reshape your query letter and send it to a different publication. (Don't, however, try sending the same letter to a different editor at the publication that just rejected you—you'll get a reputation all right, but not the one you want.) Every writer gets rejected throughout his or her career; it's the nature of the business. But you shouldn't let it discourage you.

The Contract

Congratulations. You've written a query that has earned you an assignment to write for a magazine. Before you start dialing for your first interview, do one final bit of preparation: Read the contract before you sign it.

Good contracts delineate the story idea, the rights you're selling the publisher, the pay, the electronic rights, the kill fee—if any—and the due date. Not all magazines use contracts, and those that do may not give so many breaks to the writer.

For more on contracts and protecting your rights, see chapter fifteen.

RESOURCES

Writer's Digest Handbook of Magazine Article Writing **edited by Michelle Ruberg** (Writer's Digest Books). This is the gold standard advice book for magazine writers, including information on pitches, market research, interviews, contracts, reprint rights, and working with an editor.

Writing Feature Stories: How to Research and Write Newspaper and Magazine Articles **by Matthew Ricketson** (Allen & Unwin).

This guide focuses more on the actual planning and writing of magazine and newspaper articles, rather than getting them published.

***The Art and Craft of Feature Writing* by William E. Blundell** (Plume). Based on *The Wall Street Journal Guide* to feature writing, this how-to book gives step-by-step instructions on reporting and writing.

SAMPLE QUERY LETTER TO *KENTUCKY MONTHLY*

Mr. Michael Embry
Executive Editor
Kentucky Monthly
P.O. Box 559
Frankfort, KY 40602-0559

Dear Mr. Embry,

Phantoms Don't Drive Sports Cars. Zombies Don't Play Soccer. Most third-grade kids know that these are some titles in a popular children's book series, The Adventures of the Bailey School Kids. Yet even some of her students and fellow teachers in Lexington don't recognize the name of Marcia Thornton Jones as the author of the popular series.

Jones and fellow teacher, Debbie Dadey, created The Bailey School Kids after a frustrating day in the classroom. Jones said to make her students pay attention, she'd have to grow ten feet tall, sprout horns, and blow smoke out her nose. So they wrote the first Bailey School Kids' book, *Vampires Don't Wear Polka Dots.* It quickly sold 250,000 copies.

The story I propose is a profile about Jones, who is a consultant for gifted and talented students, but who still writes a book a month with Dadey, using e-mail. The authors also write two other series, and Jones travels the region as a teacher and speaker about writing.

Could you please let me know if you are interested in this article? I'm including a SASE and some clips. A former medical reporter, I have written articles for a wide variety of other magazines, including *American Health for Women* and *Curriculum Administrator.* I also teach journalism at Northern Kentucky University.

Thank you for your consideration.

Sincerely,

Name
Address
Telephone Number
E-mail Address

SAMPLE QUERY LETTER TO *CINCINNATI MAGAZINE*

Linda Vaccariello
Cincinnati Magazine
One Centennial Plaza
705 Central Ave., Ste. 175
Cincinnati, OH 45202

Dear Ms. Vaccariello,

Have you been to Oldenburg, Indiana? I'll take you there. In a proposed 800–1,000 word *Weekend* article, I'll be your readers' guide to this old-fashioned German hamlet a little over an hour's drive from Cincinnati. Settled in 1837 by German Catholic immigrants, Oldenburg retains much of the old country atmosphere and charm, with today's residents still adhering to a founding philosophy of religion, family, and home.

There is such a proliferation of churches the community is often identified as the village of spires. The graceful, Gothic church steeples that thrust up through the trees and dominate the landscape will be the focus of my article. Oldenburg is a fun-loving community that hosts a number of bazaars and festivals throughout the year. Streets still designated by their original German names reflect the town's pride in their Teutonic heritage. These features will make good sidebars for the article.

I believe *Cincinnati Magazine* readers would like to be taken to "this old little town in the valley" in the hills of southeastern Indiana, for there they can find a day's respite from the citified chaos that all too often makes us weary, worried, and longing to escape.

I have published several pieces in *Cincinnati Magazine* under "Ann Herold." Expenses for this article would be $25.00.

Very truly yours,

Name
Address
Telephone Number
E-mail Address

7

SELLING YOUR NONFICTION BOOK

AN ADAGE AMONG writers is that you do your best work when you're writing what you love. It remains as true today as ever. But there is another truth about writing books today: If you want to find a publisher for your manuscript, you have to understand what will sell, and how to sell it. Simply having an idea you love is the first step among many that must be taken before your wonderful notion is transformed into a book. This chapter will help you understand the steps to take to bring about that transformation.

Here we'll discuss winning book proposals that help connect authors with the publishers that are right for their nonfiction books. Although it is difficult to get a publisher, indulge for just a moment in some well-deserved schadenfreude: It is much easier for first-time nonfiction writers to find one than it is for first-time novelists. Whenever you become discouraged, cheer up by reminding yourself that at least you're not trying to sell fiction like those poor sods in the chapter that follows.

FINDING A PUBLISHER

Because there are so many publishers, it's essential for writers to research a publishing house before sending in a proposal. Many smaller publishers specialize in certain topics, so they are limited in what they can accept and publish. Many houses—especially smaller ones—possess a deeply held philosophy of what they will publish, and you, as a potential author, are expected to know it. This is true even for university presses, which, in the face of shrinking budgets and declining library dollars for books, have become more sensitive to bottom-line issues and marketing.

"For writers, it means that they need to study their publishers and know what kind of a book they have," says Henry Y.K. Tom, executive editor of the social sciences division at Johns Hopkins University Press. "They need to do their homework and be familiar with the lists of different publishers, so they can identify a short list of possible publishers that are actively publishing the author's subject area."

Other editors have echoed this notion. "Every time I get a fiction proposal, I don't bother to open it," says Kirsty Melville, publisher of Ten Speed Press. Her company publishes only nonfiction, and often "offbeat and quirky" nonfiction at that (some of its titles are *How to Be Happy, Dammit* and *What Color Is Your Parachute?*). Writers who clearly are familiar with the types of books Ten Speed publishes and can state how their proposed titles fit within the existing line definitely improve their chances of acceptance.

Five Useful Steps in Narrowing Your Search

The good news is that it's not at all difficult to do the research necessary to find the right publisher. Here are five valuable steps to follow.

> **1. Once you've chosen a topic, start looking for existing books similar to yours.** Which houses are publishing these books? Start a list. If you are writing a conservative political book, you'll start to notice that several publishers specialize in that, including Regnery Publishing; if your book consists of humorous stories of famous technological hacks throughout history, you'll begin seeing that The MIT Press might be a good candidate. Do some strong research.

2. Take a look at a directory like *Writer's Market* to help you as you narrow your search. Use the Subject Index in the back of the book. For example, if your book has a strong regional angle, focus on "Regional" publishers like Coastal Carolina Press, Bright Mountain Books, or Minnesota Historical Society Press. If you want to write a book that focuses on the environment, look under "Nature/Environment" for a publishing house that specializes in that subject. By directly targeting publishing houses you know publish your subject, you'll greatly enhance your chances of acceptance.

3. Once you've identified a specific house, take a look at its current line of books by checking the house's website, where you can see current and backlist (older) titles. Compare your idea to the house's current line—have they recently covered your topic? If so, how will be yours be different and better? Take a look at who the authors are, too—does the catalog feature books by first-time authors, or do all the authors have multiple books already under their belts?

4. Sign up to receive the house's catalog and any e-mail newsletters about new titles, discounts, and promotions. This way, you'll learn about both the preferred content of that house's books and also something about the publisher's effectiveness in direct marketing. Look on the website to see what the press is doing to help its authors get the message out. Does the publishing house have a podcast program with author interviews? Links to authors' own websites? A presence on Faccbook?

5. Carefully read the house's submission guidelines for new writers, which should be available on the website. Assume that if the press took the time to create these specific guidelines, take the time to follow them.

Now, it's time to prepare your submission package.

MAKE YOUR BOOK COMPETITIVE

It is crucial for you to research titles similar to the one you plan to write. Doing this type of research before you actually start writing can help you decide what your book needs to cover in order to make it stand out. For example, take a look at the best-selling competing titles, and ask yourself how your book will be different—specifically, how it will be better. If you can't answer this question, it might be time to ask yourself why you're writing the book at all. Eventually, all of this research will end up in the Competitive Analysis section of your book proposal. (We'll discuss the parts of a proposal starting on page 118.)

Such research used to require going to a bookstore or library, seeing what was shelved near a competing book, and hoping that what you discovered was comprehensive. Now it's easy to visit an online bookstore like Amazon.com, type in the title of a competitive book, and sit back and watch the computer pull up similar books. This will allow you to see how the other titles rank in sales (at least insofar as Amazon.com rankings are reliable sales data), read commentaries from other readers, and see whether the book was reviewed in major newspapers or magazines. You can check out the Table of Contents using the "Search Inside This Book" feature and closely examine the cover art, though if you want to really peruse the book you'll need to head to a bookstore or library. You can even chat with bookstore owners about how books on the subject are selling or with the librarian about how often people check out similar titles.

If your topic is weighted down by a whole shelf full of books, don't despair. That may well be a good thing—it proves that editors believe many people are interested in reading about that topic.

When author Janice Papolos was preparing her book proposal for *The Virgin Homeowner,* she researched in *Books in Print,* Bowker's comprehensive data listings of books available in print. She found that other books for new homeowners were massive door-stoppers that advised readers how to haul out expensive tools to fix everything from the basement floor to the roof. Each had been reprinted multiple times. That, she believed, proved there was a strong market, an ever-renewing, reading populace.

She also knew her book would be different from other books on the market because it wasn't designed to show people how to fix things. Instead, it would be a fun and humorous book about her experiences learning about tending her house after living in apartments, her discovery of the meaning of such peculiar terminology as "flashing" and "flange," and her realization of why it's important to know such things.

"I like to say there are 3,000 components to a house and I was clueless about 2,999 of them," she says. "I thought my boiler had a higher IQ than I did." But she learned important things about owning a house and worked this notion into a theme of her book that would appeal to readers: What you don't know *can* hurt you. Her proposal worked—*The Virgin Homeowner* was published by W.W. Norton & Company and hailed by *The Wall Street Journal* as one of the books "most useful to homeowners."

CRAFTING A BOOK QUERY LETTER

Editors are extremely busy people. Some joke with a sort of gallows humor that between marketing meetings, strategy meetings, Kindle initiatives, conferences, and publishing board meetings, they hope to find five minutes a day to do what they are paid to do for a living: read. That's an exaggeration, or at least we hope it is, but it is certainly true that most editors don't have a lot of free time to read unpublished writers.

Rarely will an editor read an entire unsolicited manuscript—and unless an editor actually requested to see yours, it is considered unsolicited. In fact, many won't accept unsolicited material of any kind, especially at the larger trade publishing houses. Even if a publisher does, it's often an editorial assistant or an intern who wades into the "slush pile" to read it. Agents can smooth the way for writers by contacting editors they have worked with and whose tastes they understand, transforming the material from unsolicited to solicited. But if you don't have an agent, your query letter is your primary calling card. Let's make it a good one: one that demonstrates a fresh idea, provides evidence that you know your material, and indicates that you are the right person to write this book.

As we learned earlier, queries are brief letters selling your idea and yourself. Aim for *one page* that piques the reader's interest. Mention the title of your book and explain what it is about, who its audience would be, and why they'd be interested in reading it. Also include a paragraph of your writing credentials and your expertise, making it clear that you have a platform for vigorously selling your book.

A word about voice: Allow your voice in the letter to display the same enthusiasm as it does when you're talking with friends about your book. Agents and editors like writers who believe their books are wonderful, but they dislike being told, "This will be a bestseller." Impart your ardor for your work more subtly.

WHAT NOT TO DO: FIVE THINGS NEVER TO SAY IN A NONFICTION QUERY LETTER

1. **"This book is destined to be an Oprah pick/*New York Times* bestseller/ageless classic."** Don't exaggerate the sales claims of your book. Publishers have very reliable information on the sales of similar or competing titles, so they will know when your pie-in-the-sky projections are unrealistic. Unless you know Oprah Winfrey personally, don't assume that yours will be among the elite handful of titles that she features on her show.

2. **"There are no other books at all like mine."** According to former publisher Debra Farrington, this actually means, "I don't know the literature in my field." Don't be lazy about doing the research on competing titles. What deals with a similar topic? If it addresses a unique topic, are you employing a style that has been successful elsewhere? Mention specific titles if they are relevant. Explaining that your book is like the exposé *Fast Food Nation*, but for the gambling industry instead, is a lot more compelling than a generic sales pitch for a book about the growth of casinos.

3. **"God told me to contact you about publishing this book he dictated to me."** You'd be surprised at how many writers invoke the Almighty in their queries. (One exasperated publisher responded, "If God ordered you to write this book, why didn't he also tell you to run spell check?") Keep any claims

to divine inspiration between you and your Maker, even if your book is about religion.

4. **"I'm not sure if there's a book here. Can you take a look at my ramblings and give me some free advice?"** It's not a publisher's job to do your work for you. If you aren't certain that you're a real writer, with a book that thousands of people would pay good money to buy, why should an editor waste even five minutes on you?

5. **"My family members say my book is great."** It's terrific to include endorsements in your query letter if they are by leaders in your field, well-known authors, or other important people. But let's face it: Your family's imprimatur isn't going to convince an editor that your writing is superb or that you have a viable author platform. Keep it professional. So while it's lovely to have an endorsement from Malcolm Gladwell saying that your book on first impressions is going to be even bigger than *Blink*, it's absolutely not helpful to mention that your family or friends think you've got a winner on your hands.

The Opening Sentences

If you decide to query an editor, remember that query letters that are informed and personal tend to make it to the top of the pile. Instead of addressing your e-mailed query letter to "Dear Editor" and submitting it through the house's generic submissions button on the website (which you should also do as backup), try to find out who would be the right person for your kind of book. Even at small publishing houses, editors have specific areas of expertise, and you want your project to fall on sympathetic ears. Here are some ways to get a name:

- Check the website to see if the publishing house lists editors by areas of specialization. If you can't find that information on the website, call the publisher's publicity department to find out who edits books on your topic.

- Scan *Writer's Market* and read publications like *Writer's Digest* for mentions of specific editors.

- Read the acknowledgments in similar books. Authors often thank their editors there.

Next, carefully research each possibility by learning more about the individual publishing houses. Check their websites for author lists and forthcoming titles. Google all the editors on your list to learn more about their acquisition interests. After your research is complete, follow each publishing house's submission guidelines (available online, by calling, or in a directory like *Writer's Market*), and submit your query letter.

E-MAIL OR SNAIL MAIL?

Many people wonder nowadays about whether it is acceptable to submit a query letter by e-mail. This is increasingly the wrong question; the right question is whether it is advisable any longer to query by snail mail. E-mail is fast, efficient, and wonderfully direct.

"Paper proposals show that you don't really know anything about how things work now," says Sheryl Fullerton, executive editor at Jossey-Bass (a Wiley imprint), and author of *You Can Write! The Inside Scoop on Publishing Your Nonfiction Book*. "It just shows how clueless you are." Remember that you are selling not only your book but your ability to *promote* the book. With this in mind, it just doesn't send the right message to use a paper proposal. A big part of your job as an author is going to be to publicize your book, especially online (see chapter thirteen). If you look like you're barely comfortable with e-mail, how will a publisher trust that you have the expertise and confidence to run a successful blog, Facebook fan group, and Twitter account?

If you're still not convinced about why it's better to use e-mail, consider this: It vastly increases your chances of catching the attention of an actual editor at the other end of the wire, rather than whatever summer intern has been tapped with the unfortunate job of slogging through all the unsolicited materials in the slush pile. E-mail also makes it much easier for a publisher to respond quickly—with a yes, she would like to see more, or a no, he doesn't think this book will fit the house's list. Even if you are being rejected, it's better to hear the news quickly. If you are in doubt about using e-mail exclusively, do it both ways—a belt-and-suspenders approach. But don't shy away from e-mail altogether.

The subject line of your e-mail should say "Query," followed by a colon and your book title or topic. This helps a busy editor understand a bit about your project even before clicking to open the e-mail.

Your opener might go something like this:

Dear Ms. Anderson,

Devery Cox, my colleague in the economics department at Prestige College, had such a wonderful experience working with you on his book *From Bust to Boom* that he suggested I contact you about publishing my book on a similar topic. *Bricks and Mortar Is Still the Best Investment* teaches homeowners about long-term wealth building through real estate, even in an economic downturn. I have discussed these ideas on the National Public Radio program *The Motley Fool* in my capacity as President of the National Association of Microeconomics, and the hosts would like to have me back on the show once my book is published.

You can see why this letter would catch an editor's attention. It comes through the recommendation of a mutual acquaintance who is an expert in the field; it is about a timely and useful topic; the author is familiar with the house's publishing program; and the author has already begun building a national platform. The opening paragraph is short and to the point. It does not make grandiose assertions ("this is going to be the hottest econ book since *Predictably Irrational!*"), but it quietly establishes the author as a leading expert.

It should go without saying that the query letter should be free of errors, clean, and polite—but editors and agents agree that this, nevertheless, must be said. Whether you're submitting the query by e-mail or snail mail, such details matter. So check, double-check, proofread, and have your spouse or best friend proofread to make sure the letter or e-mail is perfect before you send it out. Otherwise, it will be a waste of your time.

Here's one thing to check out before you craft the opening paragraph of your query letter. In 2009, a group of literary agents started a Twitter feed called Queryfail with the worst opening lines they'd had the misfortune of reading. Among the worst offenders were these openers: "My book is differentiated from *Twilight* because the vampires have wings, and are half-breed angels" and "My book is about a friendship based on mutual vomiting practices in high school." Although the agents of Queryfail rightly came under fire for holding these authors' mistakes up for public ridicule, they countered that they were educating writers about the importance of following posted guidelines about how to write a query letter. Your take-home lesson? Don't let your query wind up on someone's annual Worst-Dressed List. Do your homework.

The Body of Your Query Letter

Generally, an entire query letter is just one page: one paragraph of introduction, one to two paragraphs about the book, one paragraph about the author's experience and platform, and a concluding paragraph. Every sentence needs to entice the editor to read further.

For the example above, the middle two paragraphs of the query letter might proceed as follows:

> I wrote *Bricks and Mortar Is Still the Best Investment* after I observed middle-class Americans occupying two extremes where their homes were concerned: either they expected that their homes would increase in value by double digits, or they abandoned real estate when the bottom fell out of the housing market back in 2008. Unfortunately, many of the personal finance books available careen between those extremes as well. From the standpoint of microeconomics, however, the truth lies in the middle. The first part of my

book traces the disastrous housing crisis brought on by sub-prime lenders and overzealous home valuations, while the second part teaches homeowners what they need to do to recover financially. I offer important strategies for utilizing real estate as a reliable wealth-building strategy, while encouraging readers to keep their expectations about home valuations realistic.

I have written two specialized economics books with university presses, but now that I have tenure, I am eager to publish for a popular audience. This book is pitched at a general audience through the use of a more journalistic style, which seems like an excellent fit for your list. A model for me in the writing has been Daniel McGinn's bestseller *House Lust*, though my book is more of a prescriptive personal finance guide than his. In addition to the promise of a spotlight on NPR's financial program *The Motley Fool*, I also know a producer at MSNBC who has read the book and agreed to endorse it. I have begun setting up real estate workshops throughout the Northeast where I can sell the book. You can see a list of my upcoming speaking engagements, and some op-ed pieces I have written about real estate for *The Boston Globe* and *The New York Times*, at www.davidrheinekker.com.

There's a whole lot to like about this author's query letter. He knows where his book is poised to fit into the market, is specific about the target audience, and reveals that he has been working to build his author platform. (Note that he has a website, has published op-ed articles, has radio and TV contacts, *and* is a tenured college professor. Too bad we only made him up for this book.)

Wrapping Up Your Query Letter

End your query by asking the agent or editor if he would be interested in seeing more. Remember that the query letter is an introduction, an invitation to dance at the ball. It's foreplay. Don't send off a query letter unless you are ready to roll if the agent or editor gives you a happy answer: "We love it. Send in the full proposal." For nonfiction, that means you have written your book proposal and at least two very good sample chapters. If someone nibbles at your query letter, be ready immediately with the main course: your book proposal.

Here's what our fictional Dr. Heinekker said at the end of his exemplary query letter:

> I have crafted a full book proposal according to the specifications on your company's website. If you would like to read it, I can send you the proposal as well as the first two chapters. (Please let me know if you would prefer these documents by e-mail or in a printed copy mailed to your work address.) The completed manuscript will be 70,000 words and will be finished in December, after my sabbatical from teaching this fall.
>
> It would a great honor to work with you on this project, and I look forward to hearing from you soon.
>
> Sincerely,
>
> Dr. David R. Heinekker

Again, this author has prepared well, and it shows. He has all the necessary materials ready in the wings, and a plan for the book's completion. He is willing to submit those materials in whatever way Ms. Anderson would like to see them: e-mail, snail mail, owl post, what have you.

A Word About Simultaneous Submissions

Many authors wonder about the etiquette of simultaneous submissions. Is it kosher to send your query out to more than one publisher or agent at a time? Is it advisable?

The answer is complicated. Generally, publishers don't like simultaneous submissions and authors do, for precisely the same reason: they give authors more options and publishers less time to respond. In the old days, when everything was done by snail mail, Author X would send her manila envelope exclusively to Publisher A, then wait for the obligatory two months before inquiring about her book's fate. (It has been rejected, but no one has bothered to let her know.) Eventually, Author X goes on to Publisher B, then some months later to Publisher C, and so on. Two years pass before she is finally able to sell her book to Publisher J. Though grateful to be published, she mutters that surely there must be a better way.

Nowadays, most (but not all) publishers are more amenable to simultaneous submissions, which is good news for authors. However, be sure to do these two things if you opt for simultaneous submissions:

- Check the publisher's website or listing in *Writer's Digest* to make sure that simultaneous submissions are acceptable.

- Indicate in the last paragraph of your query letter that it is a simultaneous submission.

In general, the smaller the publishing house, the more willing its editors are to take simultaneous submissions. Be aware that if you're seeking an agent, the rules can be different for agents than they are for editors at publishing houses. Many agents want a guaranteed period of time to look at your proposal exclusively.

Good luck with your query letter, and remember that all editors and agents are individuals. What strikes one as tired and derivative may strike another as a perfect entrant for a hot market. So if your query is rejected but you believe in it, don't hesitate to send it to someone else on your list. You can't consider one editor's opinion the only valid one.

CRAFTING A BOOK PROPOSAL

Book proposals usually aren't something to dash off in a day or two. They can take months to write if you do a thorough job of researching. Some beginners might find it easier to simply write the book first, then use it to prepare a proposal—which editors say is not a bad notion since they want to be assured an unknown writer can produce an entire book before committing their house to the manuscript. However, writing the proposal first can give you a better idea of what your book needs to include in order to make it stand apart from other similar titles.

There isn't one right way to write a nonfiction book proposal, just as there is no one right way to write a book. That said, here are some guidelines: A proposal usually averages twenty-five pages or more. It contains a table of contents, an overview with a breakdown of potential markets, a competitive analysis section, an about the author section, a promotional plan, a detailed outline of what will be in each chapter, and two or three sample chapters. But keep in mind, the organization sometimes varies. Regardless, it should be concise, written in the active voice, and well researched.

An excellent resource is the classic *How to Write a Book Proposal* by literary agent Michael Larsen. He discusses the basic parts of a book proposal (which we'll highlight more concisely below), crafting a "hook" for your book, obtaining endorsements, building a platform, researching competitive titles and sales, and many other things you'll need to know.

The Table of Contents

The table of contents for your proposal should list what you've included in your submission. Each section of your proposal should start on its own page, so it's fairly easy to draft a useful table of contents for an agent or editor to follow as she reads through your proposal. Just so we're clear, this is a TOC for the proposal itself, and not the book—that will come later.

The Overview

The overview includes a strong title, a detailed description of what you plan to write, why it's important, who would want to read it, how it differs from other books on the market, how you'll research it, an estimated length of the finished book, how long you'll take to write it (usually a year or less), and a description of illustrations, appendices, and other back matter.

Spend time thinking of a good title for your book. It should intrigue and inform. Of course, if your book is accepted for publication, there is every chance in the world that the publisher will change the title further down the road. (Publishers actually have "titling meetings" where they carefully discuss each book and the pros and cons of various book titles.) So while you should be aware that your title is a "working," or provisional, title, also come up with the best, most descriptive, most memorable working title you can.

The Competitive Analysis

While it's important for you to know what competition you are facing and how you can make your book unique, you also must convince an agent, an editor, and a publishing house of the same. This argument takes up the competitive analysis section of your book proposal.

You basically are trying to allay an editor's fears about the inevitable competition your book will face in the marketplace. You want him to be comfortable about bringing your title to print. Your skill at assessing the competition should show the editor you are an expert in your chosen subject, you are professional in your approach, and you've found a fresh angle on the subject.

Many authors make the mistake of thinking that the competitive analysis section of the proposal is only about content: If they can show that every other book in the field is inadequate, out of date, or inferior, they will help their book idea shine in an editor's eyes. This is wrongheaded for two reasons. First, authors who come across as overly snarky about their colleagues are not necessarily authors an editor wants to work with, so don't overdo the criticism. It's fine to point out holes in arguments, outdated materials, etc., but keep an upbeat tone. More importantly, know that content is only one half of the "competitive books" analysis; the publisher is also going to want to know *how those other books have sold*. For example, will your book on fibromyalgia face a crowded shelf of titles on that subject, only one or two of which have performed consistently? Or have sales been strong across the board, even for the books that are a little subpar or outdated? For more information about how to get sales information about books, see the sidebar on page 121.

Begin with a short overview of the genre or category into which your book will fit. Show how the category is performing in general. Next, analyze no more than five leading competitors, looking at how those books have sold and why your title will sell. Don't bother to analyze out-of-print titles, self-published books, scholarly tomes, or professional books. Editors are only concerned about the titles that will compete with your book in the consumer marketplace.

Formatting is similar to the rest of your proposal. Write concisely so this section is no more than a couple pages. You want to focus on how your book will be timelier, more comprehensive, and more up-to-date than those that have come before. Remember, all of this has to be backed up by the rest of your proposal. If you think your book will be better written or have more commercial appeal, your proposal must show how.

HOW CAN I FIND SALES INFORMATION ABOUT THE COMPETITION?

One of the problems with book proposals is that publishers generally have access to more sales information than authors do, but they want authors to take first crack at doing the research. Think of it as a challenge and a learning opportunity. There are several ways to access sales information.

Unfortunately, the very best way is probably blocked for you. Unless you're independently wealthy or work for a large publishing house, you probably won't have access to Nielsen BookScan, which is a gold mine of information for publishers. But we mention it here anyway because you need to understand that whatever you say about book sales in your proposal will be confirmed or invalidated by what a publisher finds in looking up the competition on BookScan, so *don't make stuff up*. BookScan is typically thought to represent about 70 percent of book sales, including chain stores, Amazon.com, airport stores, and many independents. It gives hard numbers of what publishers call "sell through"—books that have actually sold through to a consumer rather than just books that are sitting on the shelves in stores. One thing you should know, though, is that there are some retail channels that BookScan doesn't canvas. If you are pitching a religion book, for instance, you might want to remind your publisher that most religion stores are not included in BookScan's calculations, so the sales of the competition may appear far lower than they actually are. Also, if your book exists in a subject area where most books are sold at conferences or workshops, well, that's not included in BookScan either.

Here are some things you *can* find out fairly easily without using a tool like BookScan:

> You can learn whether a book ever made a national bestseller list just by Googling it. (The publisher will also probably trumpet this important information on the front or back cover.)

> You can read author interviews and media stories online to see what kind of publicity a book generated. If you can't get hard sales data, it still makes an impact to say, "The author appeared on *Good Morning America* and *The Colbert Report* to discuss the book." National media attention shows that the topic is a marketable one.

> You can get Amazon.com sales rankings—an overall ranking, and a ranking by category. Amazon.com rankings are not comprehensive, but they're better than nothing.

> You can talk to booksellers. Real, live booksellers can be a font of information about book sales, author tours, etc.

> You can check the copyright page of the books in question and see how many times they have been reprinted.

The About the Author Section

The "about the author" section of your proposal should tell an agent or editor why you're the right person to write this book. Go into detail about your experience and training, and stress any professional connections that may help you write and promote the book—for example, you're the leader of an organization that deals in some way with your subject matter. Also, even though you're writing about yourself here, this section should still be written in the third person.

The Promotional Plan

The promotional plan is the place to list what you plan to do to promote your book and ensure that it sells. For example, are you planning to speak at trade shows or conferences? Can you hold workshops that will help sell the book? This is where you strut your stuff and show your publisher all the great things you have been doing and still plan to do to build your platform. Emphasize what *you* are doing, not what you hope a publisher will do. Don't write that you hope for full-page ads in *Publishers Weekly* or would be available to go on an all-expenses-paid book tour. (Dream on.) For ideas, look at Part Three of this book, on building your readership.

The Outline

The outline should be like a detailed table of contents of the book. You want to keep this relatively short, even though it is thorough. Michael Larsen, an agent and author of *How to Write a Book Proposal*, recommends a line of outline for every page of text in each chapter, so a twenty-page chapter would get twenty lines of summation.

The Sample Chapters

Finally, sample chapters should prove that you know how to research and write. These are critically important, so don't send rough drafts, and choose chapters that are representative of the content and style of the whole book. (Keep in mind that in most cases, it's best to send the first two or three chapters, so make sure those are especially strong.) Editors and agents will be looking for good writing, evidence of research, and your ability to keep readers interested. Be sure to have these chapters vetted by outside readers in your field before sending them to a publishing house.

Before You Send It Out

Before you send your proposal, keep in mind that agents and editors read all day. Anything you can do to make your letters and manuscripts easier on the eyes makes them more appealing.

- Do use standard fonts like Times New Roman.

- Do use wide margins of about 1½ inches.

- Do number the pages.

- Do start each section of your proposal on a new page.

- Do double-space the chapters, but single-space the other parts of the proposal.

- Do triple-check the spelling of the editor or agent's name one last time.

If you are submitting by snail mail instead of electronically, add these two no-nos to your list:

- Don't type on both sides of the page.

- Don't bind anything in your proposal.

Remember one last cliché about the publishing business: Even brilliant writers are rejected by publishers; some of them are even rejected several times. Some writers learn to appreciate rejection. If an editor tells you why she rejects your book proposal, don't let it crush you—let it teach you how to make it better. Then send it out to the next person on your list. Remember as you send it off that as much as you hope to find a publisher for your beloved book, publishers are hoping to find a book they would love to publish.

RESOURCES

Use the following books, organizations, and websites (many of which are referred to within this chapter) to help you put together a dynamic and salable book proposal.

BOOKS

The following books can help you concept and develop the different aspects of your nonfiction book proposal:

> ***Formatting & Submitting Your Manuscript*, third edition by Chuck Sambuchino** (Writer's Digest Books). Not sure how to put together your proposal package? Using dozens of real-life examples, this book tells you how.

Guide to Literary Agents **edited by Chuck Sambuchino** (Writer's Digest Books). This annual book provides the most up-to-date information on literary agents, including their contact information, response time, submission guidelines, etc.

How to Write a Book Proposal, **third edition by Michael Larsen** (Writer's Digest Books). This book covers every aspect of researching, writing, and submitting a nonfiction book proposal. Several sample proposals also are included and explained.

Thinking Like Your Editor: How to Write Great Serious Nonfiction—and Get It Published **by Susan Rabiner and Alfred Fortunato** (W.W. Norton & Company). This book is especially helpful for academics and other professionals who want to write for a more popular audience.

Write the Perfect Book Proposal: 10 That Sold and Why **by Jeff Herman and Deborah Levine Herman** (Wiley). In addition to helping authors craft the different parts of a book proposal, this guide dissects ten successful proposals and explains why they worked.

The Writer's Digest Guide to Query Letters **by Wendy Burt-Thomas** (Writer's Digest Books). Burt-Thomas, a successful freelance writer, gives advice about book proposals and magazine pitches and includes twenty-five examples of successful query letters. This book also has a special section on the best way to query a literary agent.

ORGANIZATIONS

The following organizations can provide you with additional guidance and resources as you prepare your proposal:

Association of American University Presses (www.aaupnet.org). This organization offers multiple resources about scholarly publishing including online discussion lists and a directory of presses.

Association of Authors' Representatives (www.aaronline.org). Authors looking for an agent can search its member database. It also offers suggestions for topics you may want to discuss once you have found an agent.

WEBSITES

The websites listed here all include helpful information on crafting proposals.

BookWire (www.bookwire.com). A comprehensive site about book publishing with good links to other useful sites.

Publishers' Catalogues (www.lights.ca/publisher). Lists catalogs of publishers everywhere.

Writers' Federation of Nova Scotia (www.writers.ns.ca). Advice on writing a nonfiction book proposal.

WritersNet (www.writers.net). Offers an online directory of literary agents along with advice for writers.

8 SELLING YOUR FICTION

AFTER TEN YEARS of writing, Janet Evanovich decided to get serious about getting published. She had three novels written, all of which "had been sent to and rejected by a seemingly endless round of publishing houses and agents," she says. So she decided to abandon those projects—"big, bizarre books"—and try her hand at genre writing. Her first effort was rejected, but the second manuscript was accepted, and she was on her way to becoming the best-selling author of the Stephanie Plum mystery series. Rather than viewing the similarities of genre fiction as restrictions against creativity, Evanovich saw them more as the parameters of publication, and now her books regularly debut at the top of the best-seller lists.

Science fiction writer Walter C. Hunt waited fourteen years for his novel, *The Dark Wing*, to see publication. Written in the late 1980s, the book was sent to several speculative fiction houses—Ace, Baen, Warner, and others—and rejected, usually because the timing was wrong. "We like the book, but it isn't what we're doing right now," was a frequent comment from editors. But Hunt's patience paid off. "I waited fourteen years for the same editor to get a position at science fiction publisher Tor Books," he says. *The Dark Wing* was published in 2001, followed by *The Dark Path*, *The Dark Ascent*, and *The Dark Crusade*. Hunt has finally found his readership.

As both Evanovich's and Hunt's experiences demonstrate, there are few straight paths to getting your fiction published. The process is fraught with circumstances a writer cannot control. Editors change publishing houses or get laid off. A short story from the slush pile too closely resembles another one just acquired. Imprints fold. Editorial focus changes. All of these circumstances and more can conspire to keep a manuscript from finding an editorial home. To increase your likelihood of success (publication!), it is important that you focus on the elements of the process a writer *can* control—the mechanics of fiction submission.

SELLING YOUR SHORT STORIES

As you probably know, the competition for publishing short fiction is fierce, and the days when a fiction writer could earn a respectable living writing short stories are long gone. Only a select few "slick" magazines today even publish literary short fiction (think *The New Yorker, Harper's, GQ, Esquire, Playboy*, and *The Atlantic*), and to get an acceptance letter from one of these publications you'll need to be writing at the level of the late John Updike. Traditional markets for more mainstream short fiction—swamped by a heavy volume of submissions—either do not accept unsolicited submissions or have quit publishing short stories altogether.

On the other hand, magazines that do publish fiction are always hungry for new voices, and if you're willing to investigate the field, you'll find there are still healthy markets out there for all types of short fiction, including short shorts and the interactive fiction called hypertext. Another encouraging development in the field is the proliferation of online magazines and journals. Finding paper costs high and subscription numbers too low to sustain production, many periodicals have either developed websites to complement their print publications or moved online all together (see the sidebar on page 90 for more information on online markets).

Research

One main key to selling to magazines and literary journals is reading them. You can tell a lot about an editor's sensibility by spending time reading the short stories she chooses to publish, and in so doing discern whether or not your work is a good fit for that publication. It saves postage and time, and it'll increase your chances of publication because you'll end up targeting the right publications. Doing your research also gives you an opportunity to personally connect with an editor in your cover letter. Mentioning that you've taken the time to read a particular magazine or journal, and have found your work similar to the types of fiction they publish, will give you a definite edge over your competition in the slush pile.

It's also important to read several back issues of a publication you want to submit to, and keep track of editorial changes. Sometimes, a venerable literary publication can undergo a changing of editorial guard, and an incoming editor significantly changes the tone and feel of that magazine.

Find out what a magazine is looking for in fiction by checking its website. In addition, you can find detailed guidelines in market directories such as the annual *Novel & Short Story Writer's Market*. But your work is not finished once you've determined whether a publication wants romance, mystery, or literary short stories. It's not just what but how. With competition as fierce as in today's market, editors need methods for shrinking the slush pile, and one quick way is to reject outright any submission that doesn't follow guidelines. Writers are creative spirits, but in the submission process it's best to be an utter conformist and follow to the letter what an editor asks for in submissions. There are no bonus points for clever, attention-getting gimmicks. Pay attention to the details: What is the maximum word count? Does a publication accept multiple or simultaneous submissions, or neither? Will a journal accept electronic submissions? If not, does the editor want a disposable copy of the manuscript, or will she return yours? Do you need to enclose a self-addressed stamped envelope? The full list of particulars is long and important.

Jill Adams, editor of *The Barcelona Review*, says, "The best advice I can give is to read the guidelines carefully and take them seriously." Adams said she gets frustrated when writers ignore her electronic literary review's maximum word length of 4,000 words and send 10,000-word manuscripts, saying that they couldn't possibly cut the piece and retain its integrity. "Maybe not," Adams says. "But then it's not the story for our review, and my time—and the writer's—has been wasted."

Revise

Another major key to getting your short fiction published is remembering to revise. It can be easy in the afterglow of a finished story to want to rush it out into the world, to share your enthusiasm for your creation with readers. This is never a good idea. Phil Wagner, editor of the literary journal *The Iconoclast*, says, "Do all rewrites before sending a story out. Few editors have time to work with writers on promising stories; only polished."

Know that once you've finished your short story, what you have is a first draft, which Michael Seidman in *The Complete Guide to Editing Your Fiction* calls "your attempt to quarry a stone." A story can require an unlimited number of revisions to reach its full potential. Joyce Carol Oates is known to revise work of her own that has *already been published*. Give the manuscript time to become as polished as you can make it. Joining a writers' critique group can also be helpful. Also, entering contests is a good way to get feedback on your writing. In addition to honors (and often cash prizes), contests offer writers the opportunity to be judged on the basis of quality alone, without the outside factors that sometimes influence publishing decisions. New writers who win contests may be published for the first time, while more experienced writers may gain recognition for an entire body of work. For more on contests, see chapter seventeen.

Submit

When the story is ready and you've targeted a publication, it's time to submit. If you are submitting by e-mail, send a cover letter to the editor in question and note that you can send the story as an attachment if the editor requests it. This is now the standard method of submission, even for small publications, though there are some editors (particularly of a more established generation) who still prefer an old-fashioned submission.

If that is the case, clip a brief cover letter to your short story and mail it to a specific editor, making sure your submission is addressed to the appropriate person. Because reading a flat page is simpler than one that's been folded in thirds and squashed into a business envelope, send submissions in a manila envelope, with a stamped, self-addressed return envelope. If the publication accepts e-mail submissions, follow the instructions carefully; sending an unreadable file is, obviously, self-defeating.

Cover letters are polite pieces of business correspondence, simply acting as an introduction to your story. They should include the name of the story, a sentence or two on what it's about, its word count, a mention of why you're sending it to a particular magazine, and a paragraph about who you are. The cover letter won't make the sale. That depends on your story. But a sloppy or typo-ridden one can easily kill it.

Be prepared to be persistent, because magazines, online and on paper, report being inundated with submissions for fiction. At *The Barcelona Review*, only about one of the two hundred submissions it receives each month is accepted, and sometimes not that many. If your short story is sent back, send it out again. Always keep a copy for yourself and a record of where and when you sent it. A submission log can help you keep a record of where and when stories were sent, which were returned, editors' comments, and other pertinent information.

SELLING YOUR NOVEL

Finding a publisher for a novel is in many ways like finding a home for your short fiction—it's a matter of persistence, talent, and luck. Be aware that success is not easy in fiction. According to Donald Maass, literary agent and author of *Writing the Breakout Novel*, the discouraging fact is that "roughly two-thirds of all fiction purchases are made because the consumer is already familiar with the author." Fiction readers gravitate toward novelists they already know and like, and it can be hard for a first-timer to get a foot in the door.

Success may not be easy, but it is certainly not impossible. It involves first writing well, then researching publishers and agents, and then sending and resending material until it reaches someone who appreciates it as much as you do.

IT'S NO MYSTERY: ONE NOVELIST'S SUCCESS STORY

Novelist Jeanne M. Dams is an example of how persistence can pay off in selling your fiction. Dams is now the author of more than a dozen mysteries, including the Dorothy Martin series, but it took drive and determination to get there. Frustrated in her job in education, Dams took up writing because "I had some silly idea there was an easier way to make a living than what I was doing." It took five years to finish her first novel, about an American woman and her cat who solve a murder mystery. Eventually, Dams quit her job and devoted herself to finishing and then selling the novel. "Everybody tells you not to do that, and everybody's right," Dams said. "There were times I really wasn't sure how we were going to pay the electric bill."

It would be two years before she found a publisher for her novel *The Body in the Transept*, a "cozy" mystery (so named because it's an Agatha Christie type of book, one to cuddle up with in an armchair on a rainy day with a cup of tea). "I obeyed the rules and sent it to one publisher at a time," she said. "Then I got sick of the time lag." So she began sending queries, synopses, and/or sample chapters to several publishers and agents at once.

Dams attended writers conferences to learn her craft and to make contacts. She submitted the manuscript for critiques. Eventually, she attended a Mystery Writers of America conference called "Of Dark and Stormy Nights" because her work could be critiqued by an agent or editor rather than other writers. Her manuscript landed in the hands of Michael Seidman, who was then an editor of mysteries at Walker & Company.

Knowing that Seidman had a reputation for disliking cozies, Dams determined that she would simply have to steel herself and learn from the experience. But she was flabbergasted when Seidman simply looked at her and asked, "Why hasn't this already been published?" It soon was. Armed with Seidman's comments, Dams found an agent. *The Body in the Transept* was the first of her Dorothy Martin series, and won the Agatha Award for best first mystery novel of 1995.

The Outlook

First-time novelists are well advised to learn what they can about changes in the publishing industry to understand how such changes might affect them. Before the book publishing industry became consolidated in the later part of the last century, editors established relationships with writers and cultivated their work. An editor had the time to recognize potential and coax out of the writer the best book he could produce. The writer-editor relationship was usually a long-term proposition, with the publishing company looking for its payoff later in the arc of a writer's career—on the third or fourth novel, say, when the writer began to fully realize his talent and develop a following.

Since that time, publishing houses have consolidated into roughly half a dozen major trade houses, including Simon & Schuster, Random House, HarperCollins, Macmillan, Penguin Group, and Hachette Book Group—all of which have numerous specialized imprints under their umbrellas. (Random House actually gives its sales reps a color flow chart explaining all of the different imprints like Bantam, Doubleday, Dell, Knopf, Harmony, WaterBrook, and so on.) Lots of analysis has been devoted to how these changes have altered the face of publishing, and to the reasons behind these changes, but one thing is certain: At these houses, profit is king, and that has far-reaching ramifications for writers.

Editors at major houses do not have nearly the amount of time to spend with their writers as they used to. The result is what you may have heard called "the death of the midlist author," or a phenomenon in which blockbuster novelists continue to publish, and first-time authors are highly sought after as the next "big thing," but an author with a modestly selling first novel may well not get a second chance, at least not with her original publishing house. The publisher may want to make room in the list for a new author with breakout potential. This is actually good news for debut novelists, at least in the beginning of their careers. There is opportunity for writers with talent, determination, and no track record, who at least have the potential for a hit.

With an Agent

That said, it is increasingly difficult for a first-time writer to get a reading at one of the major New York houses without an agent. Unwieldy slush piles have caused the majority to decline unsolicited, unagented submissions, so in many cases you have to have an agent to even get in the door. As we saw in chapter five, there are obvious advantages to working with an agent. First, she will give you a leg up on finding the right editor for your manuscript. Agents are industry insiders who know the tastes of editors at both independent publishers and imprints of the big houses. Acting as business manager, an agent also handles contracts, rights negotiations, and royalties, which frees an author's time for writing. But of course it's a service you'll pay for—the average contract stipulates the agent earns 15 percent of your book's domestic sales, and the foreign sales percentage may be higher.

And Without

Many authors choose to work without an agent, and even with the closed nature of New York City's publishing houses, they can still succeed in going this route. Best-selling author Janet Fitch (*White Oleander*) chose to go it alone, and sold her manuscript to the first editor she approached at Little, Brown. So it can happen either way. If you do choose not to work with an agent, remember you are your own business manager. You'll want to distance yourself from the passion of your writing and approach the submission process as completely different from the creative. You will need to precisely meet the submission specifications of each publisher you're sending your work to. This will accomplish the first and most important goal—it will increase your odds of getting your manuscript read. Don't make the novice's mistake of believing an editor will overlook sloppiness or inattention to detail to find the author is actually the creative heir to James Joyce. It just doesn't happen.

THE CONTEST ROUTE TO SUCCESS

Louise Penny, a British mystery novelist who endured many rejection letters and discouraging moments, shares the story of her route to success.

"This is how I got a leading London literary agent and three book deals with Hodder Headline in the United Kingdom and St. Martin's Minotaur in the United States. Ready?

"I entered a contest.

"I was surfing the Web and came across the Crime Writers' Association in Great Britain and noticed their Debut Dagger contest ... There were eight hundred entries worldwide in my year (2004). They short-listed fourteen, and I was one. I knew then my life had changed. As a reward for being short-listed, we were all invited to the awards lunch in London. My husband Michael and I went. I came in second—and networked like mad. I cannot overstate the importance that award has had on my career. I met my agent Teresa a couple of nights later, at a private party—but she knew my name and my submission. All good London agents who deal with mysteries read all the short-listed CWA submissions.

"Now—I did something else that was crucial to my success. Before the awards I did my homework and found out who were considered the top agents in London. When Teresa introduced herself at the party, I was able to look her in the eyes and truthfully tell her I'd heard of her and she was considered a top agent. I think that made an impression. If nothing else, it showed a degree of work and commitment on my part. In my experience you get out what you put in. The harder you work, the more research you do, the more knowledge you have, the better your chances of success."

Research

When selling your novel, it is imperative that you research the markets thoroughly. Make a point to familiarize yourself with the industry by getting closer to it. Here are some ideas for educating yourself about the fiction publishing world.

- Regularly visit publishers' websites and review what titles are currently on their list, what titles are upcoming, and whether or not there is news of a new imprint, folding imprint—any changes that may affect how you submit your work.

- Visit your public library and regularly read *Publishers Weekly*. You'll want to pay special attention to PW's First Fiction feature story every year, which highlights the success stories of debut novelists just like you. Who were their agents? Why did their novel hook an editor or agent?

- Check out the editors' blogs on www.writersdigest.com. These can be a great way to educate yourself, as the editors link to publishing news, discuss trends, and interview editors and agents.

- Sign up for the free version of *Publishers Lunch*, delivered every weekday to your e-mail inbox. (If you want more detail, you can also pay for a subscription to the full version of Publishers Lunch.)

- Bookstores also hold a wealth of information. Browse the stacks and familiarize yourself with the fiction being published today. What are you seeing a lot of? What is consistently popular? What trends are emerging?

- Booksellers can be wonderful resources for information about publishing trends. As you gradually become more familiar with the industry, you'll develop a sense of the sorts of fiction different publishing houses are looking for—their publishing "personalities"—and discover new opportunities as well.

Submit

Some book publishers want to see only a query first, but many want a letter with sample chapters, an outline, or sometimes even the complete manuscript. As we saw earlier (on page 92), a query letter is the introduction of writer to editor or agent, but it is also a sales pitch. It tells enough about the book to intrigue the reader, mentions the title, offers the author's credentials and expertise, and asks for a chance to send in more of the manuscript.

Editors and agents say they look to the query not only for the idea but also for a sense of how a writer uses words, and they say they usually can tell if a person cannot write simply by reading their letters or e-mails. When writers send an interesting query, Judith Shepard, editor-in-chief of The

Permanent Press, says she also asks them to send the first twenty pages of the manuscript. "If someone wants to send me a query with the first twenty pages, that's more practical," she says. "What I prefer not to have, but what I get, are full manuscripts."

Before mailing or e-mailing anything, put yourself in the place of an editor. The Permanent Press, which publishes about twelve books a year, receives about seven thousand submissions annually. "We get so many submissions I almost hate to see the postman come," Shepard says. "But if someone is completely unknown, it's the letter that gets me. I'm very taken by the words that people use … how people express themselves. I'm not as interested in the story line."

CRAFTING A FICTION PROPOSAL

As with nonfiction, there are several key elements to any strong fiction proposal.

Your Query Letter

Before you send the proposal, a query letter is your letter of inquiry. It serves two functions: to tell editors what you have to offer, and to ask if they're interested in seeing it. Many editors prefer that you send the query letter either by itself or with a synopsis and a few sample pages from your novel (not more than twenty). This is called a blind query or a proposal query, because you're sending it without having been asked to send it. No matter what you call it, it's your three-minute chance to hook the editor on your novel. If he likes your query, he'll e-mail back and ask for either specific parts of your novel proposal (a synopsis and sample chapters, for example) or the entire manuscript. Then he will make his decision.

Remember, your query letter is vital. You must make it compelling and interesting enough to hook your reader. Although every winning query works its own magic, all good queries should contain the following:

- A "grabber" or hook sentence that makes the reader want to get her hands on the actual novel.

- One to three paragraphs about your novel.

- A short paragraph about you and your publishing credentials (if you have any).

- A good reason why you're soliciting the person you're soliciting. Why this publisher instead of another?

- The length of the novel.

- A sentence or two about its intended audience.

- An indication that an SASE is enclosed, if you are not using e-mail.

Your Synopsis

If the publisher asks for a synopsis along with the query, you're lucky—you have another opportunity to hook an editor. The synopsis supplies key information about your novel (plot, theme, characterization, setting), while also showing how all these coalesce to form the big picture (your novel). You want to quickly tell what your novel is about without making the editor read the manuscript in its entirety. Remember what we have been emphasizing throughout this book: Editors are extremely busy people. They are not going to want to read your entire manuscript, and you will get in their good graces by saving them valuable time.

There are no hard-and-fast rules about the synopsis. Some editors look at it as a one-page sales pitch, while others expect it to be a comprehensive summary of the entire novel. Many editors prefer a short synopsis that runs from one to two single-spaced pages, or three to five double-spaced pages. On the other hand, some plot-heavy fiction, such as thrillers and mysteries, may require more space, and can run from ten to twenty-five double-spaced pages, depending on the length of the manuscript and the number of plot shifts. If you opt for a longer synopsis, aim for one synopsis page for every twenty-five manuscript pages. But try to keep it as short as possible.

When compiling your synopsis, be sure to include the following:

- A strong lead sentence.

- Logical paragraph organization.

- A concise expression of ideas with no repetition.

- An introduction of your main characters and their core conflicts.

- Plot high points.

- Narrative (third-person) writing in the present tense.

- Transitions between ideas.

- Strong verbs and minimal use of adjectives and adverbs.

- Correct punctuation and spelling.

- The story's conclusion. (Yes, you do need to give away the ending. It's pivotal to a publisher's decision about your book, because so many promising novels fall apart in the last pages.)

Your Outline

An outline is often used interchangeably with a synopsis. For most editors, however, there is a distinction. While a synopsis is a brief, encapsulated version of the novel at large, an outline makes each chapter its own story, usually containing a few paragraphs per chapter. In short, you're breaking down the novel and synopsizing each chapter individually. Try to keep each chapter to about a page, and begin each new chapter on a different page.

Never submit an outline unless an editor asks for it. Fewer and fewer agents and editors want outlines these days. Most just request a cover or query letter, a few sample chapters, and a short synopsis. Outlines are most often requested by genre fiction editors, because genre books run for many pages and have numerous plot shifts.

In compiling your outline, keep in mind:

- Your outline is an extended, more detailed and structural version of your synopsis.

- Remember to explain the how the plot and character development unfold in the chapter.

- Write in the present tense.

- Reveal how the chapter opens and ends.

- Make sure the chapters follow sequentially.

- Do not include dialogue or extended description.

A NOTE ON PROMOTION

Today more than ever an author needs to be ready to take a very active role in selling her book. Some authors report being surprised by a lack of promotion and publicity for their new books, but increasingly this is the norm in book publishing. Best-selling author Terry McMillan (*Waiting to Exhale, How Stella Got Her Groove Back*) sold her first novel, *Mama*, to Houghton Mifflin in 1987, and was largely responsible for its success. "As soon as I found out the publicity department wasn't going to do anything other than send out the standard releases, and I wasn't going on a book tour, I said, 'What is going on here?'" she says. McMillan wrote bookstores, colleges, and universities, setting up readings and promoting the book, and sent her publicist her itinerary. She ended up selling about ten thousand books.

Keep in mind that some of the traditional methods of promoting books just aren't working anymore. We'll discuss this more in chapters twelve through fourteen, but for now just know that if you are harboring any expectations that your publishing house is going to drop a fortune on advertising and a traditional book tour, you will probably be disappointed. In *Writing the Breakout Novel*, Donald Maass unpacks the traditional book tour and does the math. Imagine that you go on an old-fashioned twenty-city book tour and have the good fortune of getting a hundred people at each book signing. (Which never happens, by the way.) Maybe you sell two thousand copies of your novel on the tour. But when you factor in the travel expenses of sending an author on the road, and the in-house expenses of having a publicist plan all those appearances, you can begin to see that the books sold on a tour don't even begin to cover the financial outlay of getting an author out and about. Book tours make authors feel important, just as high-profile advertising makes authors feel important, but they don't actually go very far in selling books. So you will have to get creative.

Although it's less important for a novelist to have a platform than for a nonfiction author to have one, it can certainly help. Some publishers will be interested in your level of willingness to promote your book before a contract is signed, and it's important that you as an author know going into the process what may be required of you once your book is published.

RESOURCES

The books, magazines, and websites listed here can provide you with additional information on all aspects of writing and selling your fiction.

BOOKS

Most of the books listed below come from top literary agents, respected authors, and noted editors. Let their years of experience give you the extra edge you need to get ahead.

Beginning Writer's Answer Book **edited by Jane Friedman** (Writer's Digest Books). Updated in 2006, this Q&A book offers answers to a thousand questions about writing and publishing, for both fiction and nonfiction.

The Complete Handbook of Novel Writing **edited by Meg Leder, Jack Heffron, and the editors of Writer's Digest** (Writer's Digest Books). This four-hundred-page book offers writing instruction, submission tips, author interviews, and more.

Fiction: The Art and Craft of Writing and Getting Published **by Michael Seidman** (Pomegranate Press). This author and editor tells you what the common submission stumbling blocks are and how to avoid them. He also offers writing tips and exercises to help you improve your work.

The First Five Pages: A Writer's Guide to Staying Out of the Rejection Pile **by Noah Lukeman** (Fireside). The author draws on his experience as a literary agent to show you how to identify and correct bad writing and get your novel read.

How to Write a Damn Good Novel **by James N. Frey** (St. Martin's Press). (No, not that James Frey, who wrote the disputed "memoir" *A Million Little Pieces*.) For beginners and experienced writers, this book focuses on the basics of storytelling and shows you how to improve and correct your work. There's also a sequel; pay particular attention to chapter eight of the second book, in which Frey uncovers the Seven Deadly Mistakes that keep novelists from being their best.

How to Write & Sell Your First Novel, **revised edition by Oscar Collier with Frances Spatz Leighton** (Writer's Digest Books). This guide uses case studies to reveal the keys to writing and publishing a successful novel.

Novel & Short Story Writer's Market **by Alice Pope** (Writer's Digest Books). This annually updated resource directory provides listings, writing guidelines, and contact information for more than a thousand book and magazine publishers.

The Marshall Plan for Novel Writing **by Evan Marshall** (Writer's Digest Books). This book covers all aspects of novel writing. Other books in The Marshall Plan series include *The Marshall Plan Workbook* (Writer's Digest Books), which offers detailed worksheets to take you through the entire process, and *The Marshall Plan for Getting Your Novel Published* (Writer's Digest Books), which focuses mostly on the submission process, including detailed instruction for putting together a winning synopsis package.

The Plot Thickens: 8 Ways to Bring Fiction to Life **by Noah Lukeman** (St. Martin's Press). In this follow-up to *The First*

Five Pages, Lukeman teaches you how to correct common plot problems and improve your novel.

***Some Writers Deserve to Starve! 31 Brutal Truths About the Publishing Industry* by Elaura Niles** (Writer's Digest Books). With a take-no-prisoners approach and terrific humor, this book helps authors to wise up about the realities of book publishing. No whining allowed.

***The Writer's Digest Writing Clinic* edited by Kelly Nickell** (Writer's Digest Books). Learn how to edit and revise your novels, short stories, query letters, and synopses through real-life examples of critiques by professional editors.

***Writing & Selling the YA Novel* by K.L. Going** (Writer's Digest Books). Specifically for authors who want to write for teens, this book navigates the ever-expanding waters of YA fiction.

***Writing the Breakout Novel* by Donald Maass** (Writer's Digest Books). This experienced literary agent and author shares to the secrets to crafting a great novel. *Writing the Breakout Novel Workbook* (Writer's Digest Books) expands on the principles behind the first book by taking you step-by-step through the fiction writing process and teaching you how to read like a writer.

MAGAZINES

Use the following publications to stay ahead of what's happening in the publishing industry, learn about your craft, and more.

Locus: The Magazine of the Science Fiction & Fantasy Field. This monthly magazine includes news, interviews, book reviews, market listings, convention coverage, etc. www.locusmag.com

Publishers Weekly. This weekly magazine provides the latest on the industry news. www.publishersweekly.com

Writer's Digest. This monthly magazine features interviews with authors, writing instruction, market information, etc. www.writersdigest.com

WEBSITES

The websites listed here can provide you with additional information on fiction publishing and preparing your synopsis.

Authorlink (www.authorlink.com). An excellent site for news about publishing and articles about writing.

Booktalk (www.booktalk.com). Promising "all the buzz about books," this site offers connections to publishers and agents, and some news about the industry.

Poets & Writers (www.pw.org). Offers links to workshops, services, and publications of interest to writers.

Sisters in Crime (www.sinc-ic.org). A good site for mystery writers, male and female.

Writer's Digest (www.writersdigest.com). In addition to its own excellent information, this site also links to the 101 Best Sites for writers of all kinds.

Writer's Market (www.writersmarket.com) Like its print companion, *Writer's Market*, this site provides up-to-date listings of publishers and agents, with a tool that helps you keep track of where you've submitted and when.

Writers Weekly (www.writersweekly.com). Offers articles, markets, and more.

Writers Write (www.writerswrite.com). Offers reviews, interviews, and articles on craft.

SAMPLE NOVEL QUERY LETTER

Dear (agent's name):

I've written a mystery novel, the first of a projected series, that I'd like to submit for your consideration. The enclosed synopsis will outline the basics; let me say here why I believe *Sounding Brass* could succeed in today's market:

(1) The book is in the classic "cozy" tradition, involving pleasant people in an attractive English setting.

(2) The protagonist is a sixtyish American woman with whom many mystery readers will be able to identify.

(3) The bright, upbeat tone is refreshing for a genre that is growing ever more grim and gritty.

(4) The cat is an appealing creature who helps solve the mystery without ever behaving like anything but a cat.

There are no gimmicks, no nonsense, just careful, literate writing and a strongly individual voice.

Although this is my first book, I've published in national (*Guideposts, Woman's World, Military History*) and local markets. I was a feature writer for over a year for a local newspaper. In addition to the second and third novels of the series, I'm working at present on a small guidebook to London's little museums.

I hope you will agree to read the manuscript of *Sounding Brass*. (Although I am querying several agents at once, I will of course send the manuscript to only one at a time. I realize that no one—including me—has time to waste.)

I look forward to hearing from you.

Sincerely,

Jeanne M. Dams

SAMPLE NOVEL COVER LETTER

Dear (agent #2):

The enclosed sample of my mystery novel *Sounding Brass* comes with Michael Seidman's recommendation. He critiqued the first chapter for this year's "Of Dark and Stormy Nights" conference in Chicago and was enthusiastic about it. (I enclose his comments.) Since he won't have time to look at it for a while, and I've already taken an unsuccessful shot at the Malice Domestic contest, I asked him about agents; he named you "one of the few agents I trust."

Sounding Brass is a traditional mystery (which is why I was surprised as well as pleased when Seidman liked it so much). It is my first novel, although I've published shorter stuff. I am at work on the second and third books of the series, and planning another series set in the Midwest. I have, also at Seidman's suggestion, sent the full MS of *Sounding Brass* to Ruth Cavin at St. Martin's, but I don't expect to hear from her any time soon. I doubt that the slush pile is her first concern. No one else is reading the book.

As a beginner in this peculiar business I am aware that I badly need a literary agent, and hope very much that you will consider representing me and my work. I look forward to your reply.

Cordially,

(Mrs.) Jeanne M. Dams

SAMPLE RESPONSE TO COVER LETTER

To: Jeanne Dams

From: Michael Seidman

I enjoyed reading this very much … I don't think I made a mark on a page. Your voice, your story, your characters … everything just comes together.

I guess the only question is why it hasn't been published yet. I'd recommend starting the novel on its rounds immediately … and if nothing happens by October, get in touch with me, because that's when I expect to be looking for more manuscripts.

My first shot would be St. Martin's Malice Domestic contest; this seems far better than anything I've read from it so far.

Editor's Note: Jeanne Dams wrote this cover letter after showing her work to editor and author Michael Seidman, whom she met at a writers conference. Notice in the cover letter how the author successfully references Seidman's comments.

SAMPLE SHORT SYNOPSIS

SOUNDING BRASS

By JEANNE M. DAMS

Dorothy Martin is American, sixtyish, recently widowed and living in the small English cathedral and university town of Sherebury. On Christmas Eve, after attending Midnight Mass at the cathedral, she literally stumbles over a body in one of the side chapels.

The body turns out to be that of Canon Billings, the cathedral's librarian, a cold, judgmental man heartily disliked by almost everyone who knew him. He was considered to be an excellent scholar (he was a lecturer at Sherebury University as well) but a poor priest. Although the list of suspects is nearly limitless, because of Billings' unpopularity and because of the thousands of people in the cathedral that night, a few individuals surface as likely. One of these is a university student, Nigel Evans, to whom Dorothy's neighbor Jane has taken a liking. Jane, an old maid with a way with kids, is sure Nigel is innocent, although he worked for the canon and hated him more than most. Dorothy begins nosing around partly to help clear Nigel, but also because the loneliness and depression of her widowed and expatriate state is too much to bear without something to occupy her time.

She makes a new friend, Alan Nesbitt, the Chief Constable of the county. Alan, though unenthusiastic about Dorothy's meddling, is strongly attracted to her (he is a widower), and somewhat grudgingly cooperates. She learns, through gossip and her own observation, that there are at least three excellent suspects besides Nigel: A verger at the cathedral, the cathedral's organist/choirmaster, and an ambitious businessman. The canon represented a threat of one kind or another to all three. Dorothy's favorite is the verger until he also turns up dead, burnt nearly beyond recognition in an arson-caused fire at the late canon's house.

After a conversation with a friend at the British Museum, Dorothy becomes curious about the canon's last research project; he seems to have been closemouthed about its topic. Dorothy asks everyone; Nigel doesn't know, the Dean of the cathedral thinks it had to do with St. Paul, and George Chambers, Billings' colleague at the university and an old friend of Dorothy and her late husband, says it was about Nero.

Dorothy is distressed after she visits George and catches him in a compromising situation with a coed, because she thinks he might have had reason to kill the censorious canon. When her beloved cat, Emmy, is poisoned in a way that points to George, Dorothy is sure he is the murderer. Emmy recovers, though, and the Chief Constable proves that George's motive is a washout.

When Dorothy finally figures out what the canon was working on, she realizes that George is the villain after all, for academic motives: Billings' research would have ruined George's reputation and chances for advancement. In a slow-motion chase through the shadowy reaches of the medieval cathedral, Dorothy is nearly killed, a priceless ancient document is destroyed, and George dies in a fall to the cathedral floor.

SAMPLE LONG SYNOPSIS

SOUNDING BRASS

BY JEANNE M. DAMS

Dorothy Martin, a sixtyish American, recently widowed, has rented a house in the small English cathedral and university town of Sherebury, as she and her husband had long planned to do. At Christmas time, a rainy, blustery Christmas entirely unlike Dorothy's idea of the way the holiday should be, she is beginning to regret her move. She feels isolated among people who, though friendly, are essentially strangers and "don't speak her language," in more ways than one. Perhaps she was foolish to leave the familiar in her search for a new life.

On Christmas Eve, at midnight Mass in the cathedral, she makes the acquaintance of Alan Nesbitt, a pleasant man who happens to be Chief Constable for the county. When the service ends well after midnight, Nesbitt offers to see Dorothy home, but as they are making their way through a darkened passage she stumbles over a body.

The deceased turns out to be one Jonathan Billings, Canon and Librarian of the cathedral. Billings, a distinguished scholar, was also a cold, judgmental man heartily disliked by almost everyone. Although the death appears to be accidental, the police must still investigate, and since Nesbitt is on the spot and a good friend, the Dean of the cathedral asks him to take charge of matters. By Christmas afternoon the police have established the fact that Billings did not die where he was found, and that the severe wound to his head was caused neither by his fall nor by the heavy altar candlestick found near the body. Verdict: murder.

The TV report of the findings does nothing to cheer Dorothy's Christmas, nor does her tea the next day with George and Alice Chambers, old friends from the days when Dorothy's late husband spent a sabbatical year at Sherebury University. George, under the guise of comforting Dorothy, really wants to gossip about possible murderers, especially young Nigel Evans, whom Dorothy has seen in the cathedral with her best friend and next-door neighbor, Jane Langland. Dorothy, retorting that given Billings' character, almost anyone might have done him in, changes the subject to George's book on an obscure biblical topic, now nearing completion and, according to Alice, destined for great academic distinction.

On the way home from George's, Dorothy, depressed and wet through from the penetrating fog, calls on Jane, a redoubtable spinster. There she receives comfort and a warming glass of whiskey, but also learns that Nigel worked for Billings in the Cathedral Library, had a terrible fight with him and was fired, and has a minor criminal record. Jane, who makes a habit of adopting stray dogs and students, is strongly partisan in his favor and convinced of his innocence, but realizes the police will consider him a prime suspect. Dorothy is distressed, while privately thinking that Nigel does, in fact, sound like a possible murderer.

She is not at all reassured by a conversation with Alan Nesbitt, who shows up at her door exuding charm underlain by faint menace. A little skillful conversation extracts her suspicions of Nigel, her interest in the classic English mystery, and her half-formed intent to do some poking around on her own. His warning that murder investigation is a dangerous business, best left to professionals, serves if anything to strengthen her desire to become further involved.

Two important things transpire at church the next day. Dorothy learns from Jeremy Sayers, the quirky, acid-tongued cathedral organist, that there are two other excellent suspects: a verger who has been stealing from the collection (although no one has been able to prove it), and Sayers himself! Apparently, Billings was about to get the goods on the verger, Robert Wallingford, and Wallingford might have killed to protect himself. And Sayers, who quarreled bitterly with Billings about cathedral music, was in danger of being fired. Dorothy, eager to talk over new developments with Jane, has the wind taken out of her sails when Jane already knows all about cathedral gossip and scandal and doesn't much care because Nigel has been arrested.

Nigel is freed on Monday for lack of solid evidence, and Dorothy, exasperated with the whole situation, keeps a date with friends for shopping, sightseeing, and tea in London. Even in the metropolis, though, she can't get away from the murder. A chance-met acquaintance in the British Museum knew Billings, and hints that there was something mysterious about the piece of research engaging the scholarly cleric at the time of his death.

The continued rain, mist, and general dreariness make Dorothy long, for the tenth time, for some proper Dickensian snow. Even the cat Esmeralda is irritable. On Tuesday Billings' memorial service provides further gloom. Stopping at Jane's before the funeral to cheer herself up, Dorothy meets Nigel for the first time and is charmed, but even more apprehensive. Nigel's temper seems quite hot enough for murder, and he's not talking much about his activities Christmas Eve. After the service Dorothy is captured by Alan (Nesbitt—they're on first-name terms by this time) and taken to tea. She's jollied into a better mood, but can't get Alan to talk about police progress into the investigation.

Dinner that night at an inn owned by Dorothy's old friends, the Endicotts, makes matters much worse. Although the Endicotts mention an ambitious developer who is delighted Billings is dead, it turns out that the whole Endicott family had good reason to wish the clergyman ill. Not only was he, in his capacity as town councilman, obstructing vital plans for expansion of the inn, but young Inga Endicott is all-but-engaged to Nigel Evans and mightily resented Billings' treatment of him.

A strained conversation with Nigel reveals that he was actually at the cathedral on Christmas Eve, some hours before Midnight Mass. He's sure Billings' body wasn't in the side chapel then, but he did see Inga, apparently coming out of Billings' house in the Cathedral Close. If the two have each been suspecting the other, both are innocent, but are they both telling the truth? Dorothy goes to the cathedral for some answers and learns that Wallingford, the verger, was missing for much of Christmas Eve when he should have been working, and that Sayers, the organist, was at the organ practicing most of the early evening. Good—Dorothy likes Sayers much better than Wallingford, and the case against the verger is getting better and better. She also learns that the Dean's wife placidly accepts the presence of the ghost-monk Dorothy thinks she's seen once or twice in the cathedral.

The next day is New Year's Eve. Before going to a party at Jane's, Dorothy learns from the Dean of the cathedral that Billings' research may have involved the writings of St. Paul, but the canon was very secretive about his work. Her curiosity grows. Could his work have something to do with his murder? At the party an increasingly attentive Alan gives Dorothy the interesting information that George Chambers is a skirt-chaser, but before she can digest what that might mean, the party is interrupted by a fire in the Cathedral Close just down the street. Canon Billings' house is burning! The investigators find that the fire was set; they also find the body of Wallingford, the verger, in the burned house. He was not the culprit, however, since he was dead before the fire started. There goes Dorothy's favorite suspect. And the rest were, at the time of the fire, either at Jane's party or, in the case of the Endicotts, working in plain view of several dozen people. Dorothy becomes even more eager to know about Billings' research project.

The next day Dorothy drags herself, after very little sleep, to see George. If anyone knows about Billings' work, it will be his colleague at the University. She finds him heading—on New Year's Day—for his office, and with him a very pretty female student. Not just with him, either, but obviously together. Suddenly Dorothy sees a motive for George. What if Billings had threatened to tell Alice, who has the money in the family? She tries to calm down and ask George about the canon's work, but George isn't sure—thinks it had to do with Nero. Billings had just returned from a trip to Corinth, which flourished during Nero's reign. She can make nothing of that, and after a little awkward conversation about the dead plant in the dented pot, she escapes.

A call from her London friends is most welcome. She is invited to join them for dinner at a charming country pub, and is able to relax more than she has since the murder. On her return home, however, she finds that someone has tried to murder her beloved cat, Esmeralda, by giving her antifreeze to drink. By the time, hours later, she's sure the cat is going to be all right, she's worked out that it must have been George who did the poisoning. George, who knows little about cars, wouldn't know that there would be no antifreeze in the garage of a Volkswagen Beetle, and would think the poisoning might be taken for an accident. He also knows how devoted Dorothy and Emmy are; Emmy's death would keep Dorothy out of the way for a while. He must have decided she was getting too near the truth when she saw him with the girl. He has to be the murderer!

When she tells Alan and he investigates, however, she is once more out of suspects. It's true enough that George is carrying on with the girl, and makes a habit of it, but Alice has known for years, and puts up with it. There was nothing for Billings to reveal. Dorothy, grimly determined to avenge Emmy, thinks the whole thing through from the beginning, and finally comes up with the truth.

Going to the cathedral to verify her conclusions in the library, she finds George there dressed up like a monk. George, the "ghost" who has been haunting the cathedral lately. He has in his hands the ancient manuscript Billings was working on when he died, a priceless "lost" letter from St. Paul. Its very existence makes George's book—and his academic future—worthless. It is for this that George has killed twice. In a slow-motion chase through the shadowy reaches of the medieval cathedral, Dorothy is nearly made a third victim to George's ambition, the ancient scroll is destroyed, and George dies in a fall to the cathedral floor.

When it's all over and the police have finished with her, Dorothy leaves, alone. She thinks she sees a monkish figure, but is too numb and exhausted to notice anything for sure except that the snow she has longed for is finally falling, pure and cleansing.

9

SELLING
YOUR SCRIPT

SO YOU WANT to make it in Hollywood. Writing for television and film remains the dream of millions. Although books and how-to articles devoted to writing and selling abound, selling a first script remains one of the most elusive dreams for many writers. That's in part because the road to Hollywood is actually many roads. "There's no track," says sitcom writer David Chambers (*The Wonder Years, Frank's Place, Hangin' With Mr. Cooper*). "Everybody has to find his own way. There's a premium on hustling and selling. You're always selling yourself. It's a constant matter of being in sales."

As Jared Rappaport (*Blindness*), who became a screenwriter after studying directing at the American Film Institute, puts it, "Everybody absolutely manufactures his own way in."

That may sound daunting, but it's actually an opportunity: Almost everybody who has made it as a writer in Hollywood did so through hard work, creativity, and perseverance. Which means that you can, too—read on to find out how.

WRITE YOUR OWN CALLING CARD

As obvious as it may seem, the first step to selling your script is writing it. There are plenty of urban legends of screenwriters who make fortunes in Hollywood simply by selling "ideas." The reality is that there is no such thing as screen*writers* who don't *write* scripts, especially when they're just starting out.

A script serves as your calling card as a screenwriter. You can have the most impressive resume in the business with a list of film and TV credits as long as your arm, but if you don't have a good script no one is going to hire you as a screenwriter. Ideas, no matter how wonderful they sound to you, are a dime a dozen. If you give the same idea to a dozen writers, you'll get a dozen completely different scripts. What matters in this business is the execution of that idea, the specific character traits, dialogue, and plot turns that make a good (or even great) script.

WHAT IF SOMEONE STEALS MY SCRIPT IDEA?

Every year, hundreds of amateur screenwriters attempt to sue production companies, studios, and networks claiming that someone stole their "idea" for a film or TV show. What most people don't know is that most of these cases are thrown out of court before trial because they just aren't true. There are thousands of professional screenwriters and tens of thousands of aspiring writers throwing out ideas every year. With those kinds of numbers, similarity of ideas is inevitable. In Hollywood legal terms, it's called "simultaneous creation." We all watch the same TV shows, movies, news broadcasts, and plays. We all read the same books, magazines, and newspapers. When multiple people are exposed to the same stimuli, they develop very similar ideas. Your friends and family might think you have an original idea, but there are tens of thousands of other creative souls out there, and at least one of them has had the same idea.

> This also explains why you cannot copyright ideas. Copyright does not protect ideas or concepts. Copyright protects you from someone stealing your story, but you need to be able to prove three things in court: (1) You created the story before the other person, (2) the other person had access to your story before they created their version of the story, and (3) there are unique elements to your story that have been used in the other person's story.
>
> New scriptwriters worry about having their ideas stolen all the time. Since you cannot copyright your idea and can only copyright the way in which you tell the story, it's best to write a complete script before you hand over the idea. Your script is your key to the front door of Hollywood.

No matter what genre you choose, before trying to sell your script, you must work prodigiously on the writing. Hollywood is awash in scripts sent in on speculation by would-be writers and from professional writers whose shows have been cancelled and are looking for work. A highly rated TV show, for example, may receive two thousand to four thousand such scripts—called spec scripts—every year, excluding several thousand more from agents.

So your spec script must stand out from the rest. It must be polished until each line of dialogue sparkles and each scene progresses both the characters and the plot. Why do you have to work so hard on your script? Because the one thing people in Hollywood agree on is that a good script will find its way in. Your spec script (or scripts) prove to the Hollywood establishment that you know how to tell a story through dialogue, how to format properly, how to write for existing characters or invent entertaining ones of your own, how to make people laugh or cry, how to craft a compelling plot—in short, how to write.

FORM AND FORMAT

A mark of a serious writer is attention to detail. Paying attention to the way scripts should be written on the page marks you as serious about the craft. But simply studying scripts—analyzing which lines are capitalized, how large the margins are, and whether lines are single- or double-spaced—is also necessary.

When it comes to writing a script, form is function. A properly formatted script allows a trained reader to quickly and accurately gauge its running time, while also making it easy to identify key requirements such as talent, locations, and props. The challenge for writers is that so many different elements (scenes, headings, dialogue, character names, etc.) have separate formatting requirements. Since proper formatting is the first sign that a script has been professionally written, writers have two choices: They can study the rules (there are a number of books listed on page 175 to help with this), or they can invest about $150 to $200 in scriptwriting software programs. The two most common are Final Draft (www.finaldraft.com) and Movie Magic Screenwriter (www.screenplay.com), and both have been endorsed by some big names in the entertainment industry. Both function similarly to standard writing programs except they have extra features to handle the technical details automatically. Character names are indented properly. Smart drag-and-drop features adjust the formatting when you move text. Other features alert you to formatting errors and inconsistencies. Templates from actual TV scripts offer a glimpse into the real world of TV scriptwriting. For those writers who would rather focus their attention on crafting great dialogue and plot twists rather than line spacing and capitalization, these script-formatting programs make for an ideal solution.

FINDING AN AGENT

Once you've made your script as good as it can be, finding someone in the business to read it is the next step. Fortunately, there are agents who can help get your scripts into the right hands. Although it's often said that getting an agent to represent you is harder than getting your first film produced, the fact is that people do it every day, and it's not impossible for a talented and thick-skinned writer.

A good agent is essential, says Richard Walter, professor and chairman of the UCLA Film and Television Writing Program. "Anybody who receives a script direct from an author has got to wonder why this isn't submitted by an agent," he says. "If you want to be a professional, you must treat yourself like a professional—and professionals have professional representation."

Of course, there's a paradox here, too. Agents need to read what you've written to decide if they'll represent you. And even though agents are always looking for the next hot property, many say they won't read scripts sent in cold. They will usually read a query letter. Think of a query letter as "a seduction, a tease, a preview of coming attractions," Walter says. Imagine it as a literary form of the movie trailer. It is usually one page and has a brief description of your idea, a brief summation of your accomplishments, and a brief request for the agent to read the script. It's also the place for you to sell your experience (if you have such) and connections in the industry. Don't go into deep detail about your script in your query, he advises, because it simply makes a "bigger target to shoot at."

Your first step is to find an agent who's willing to read your script. One of the best methods of accomplishing this is to have a friend who is already represented recommend you and your script to his agent (see the section on networking on page 165). If a current client recommends you, the agent is already more interested in you than any of the other unsolicited scripts in his "slush pile." The biggest agencies (Creative Artists Agency, International

Creative Management, Inc., and William Morris Endeavor Entertainment) won't even accept unsolicited scripts unless you're recommended by one of their current clients. So, find someone to recommend you. It doesn't need to be a family member or best friend—just someone who has an agent. Get her to read your script or listen to your pitch, and then ask her to put in a good word for you. It's all about networking.

Another common way to find an agent is to "cold call" or to submit query letters to agents listed in either *Guide to Literary Agents* or the list of agents published by the Writers Guild of America, West. Keep in mind that not all agents are open to new writers, and some agents are very specific about the kind of writers they work with (only TV drama writers, only feature film comedy writers, only sitcom writers, etc.). Pay attention and don't call or send queries to agents who won't handle your kind of material. If an agent likes your query, he'll call and either ask for the complete script or ask for a more detailed pitch (see the section on pitching on page 170).

A CRASH COURSE IN NETWORKING

In the small town of Hollywood, knowing somebody—or knowing somebody who knows somebody—is a big help in breaking into the industry.

Justin Adler's story is as typical as anything ever is in Hollywood. Adler wanted to write scripts, so right after college he got a job as a production assistant, an entry-level job, on *The Larry Sanders Show.* "I got it through family connections, which seems to be the way everything works out here," Adler says.

Between getting coffee for his bosses and answering the phones, Adler kept writing. He also learned by watching staff writers write and rewrite scripts. Eventually, he wrote a spec script and showed it to writers he had met on the job. A couple liked it enough to show it to their own agents. From those contacts, he got calls to meet with agents—and learned that one good script isn't enough. All asked if he had another. "I lied and said I was writing one," he said. "So I frantically went and wrote an *Everybody Loves Raymond* show, a show I had never seen."

After watching tapes of the show again and again, he banged out a script in four days. It was enough to get him an agent with the powerful William Morris Agency (now William Morris Endeavor Entertainment). And the agent helped him find a job as a writer on other shows.

The lesson: Use contacts and networks, but keep writing. Even if your first script is a pearl, you'll be expected to write more.

If you don't live in Hollywood, find a connection to someone who does. Ask your friends if they know anyone in the business. Ask your neighbors. Take a course at a local college from someone who has worked in television or film. Remember, every successful person in Hollywood was a beginner once, and many remember how it feels.

MARKET THE SCRIPT ON YOUR OWN: TELEVISION

If you don't have an agent, and have no contacts in the business, you can still market your script on your own. Before you try, however, take one preparatory step: Register your script with the Writers Guild of America.

Registration provides a dated record of the writer's claim to authorship and can be used as evidence in legal disputes about authorship. Note the number the Guild assigns you on the title page.

Registering the script is the easy part; getting an influential Hollywood producer to read it is something else. If you want to break into television, it's generally not a good idea to write scripts for a series of your own invention. Full-time, experienced, professional writers earn monumental salaries doing just that; why compete with folks like J.J. Abrams (*Lost*), Joss Whedon (*Buffy the Vampire Slayer; Dollhouse*), and Tina Fey (*30 Rock*)? Instead, here's your fun homework assignment: Tape several shows of an existing series. Watch them repeatedly. Learn who the characters are and how they would behave in any situation. One writer even advised typing up the script as you watch an episode to help you understand the flow of the dialogue. You can also try writing a little fan fiction anonymously on-line and gauge the reaction from other fans: If they like it, chances are the Powers That Be will dig it, too. Also watch the credits of a show you enjoy, noting the names of the producers. You can write to them, asking them to read your script. While the number of scripts bought from freelancers in television is small, it does happen.

"I've never met a producer who wouldn't kill to get a great script out of the blue sky one morning," J. Michael Straczynski writes in *The Complete Book of Scriptwriting*. After targeting a show, Straczynski recommends writing polite query letters to producers or story editors (usually they're the people who rewrite scripts and deal with freelancers), explaining your fondness for and familiarity with the show and that you want to send in a spec script.

At any given time, certain shows are hot markets for spec scripts. If you have a friend who knows anyone working in television, you can try to find out which shows "everybody" is writing spec scripts for. Many suggest that it's better to pick a show that you enjoy, that is climbing in the ratings, but that isn't a hit.

Once you write a script, remember another Hollywood paradox: Rarely is a spec script for a show ever bought and produced by that particular show. In fact, many writers advise against even trying to show it to anyone involved with the show. Why? Because the writers of that show know their characters better than anyone else ever could, and rarely can an outsider create a script better than they. So, if you want to write for *CSI: Crime Scene Investigation*, you need to write a script for one of the *Law & Order* spin-offs or another police drama and submit that as your spec script to the producers of *CSI*. This approach shows that you're familiar with the genre of the series (legal drama, medical soap, family-friendly sitcom) and can adapt its specifications to a particular setting and group of characters.

Then, even if your script isn't the right fit for the show, if your writing is strong, the producer might invite you to pitch other ideas.

MARKET THE SCRIPT ON YOUR OWN: FILM

To sell a film script, you need to match your script with the appropriate market. The best bet for a beginning writer is a "little" movie, not a big-budget, special-effects-laden extravaganza, says Ronald Tobias, the TV and documentary writer and author of *The Insider's Guide to Writing for Screen and Television*. "A friend of mine just sold a script to Bill Pullman's production company (Big Town Productions) in which Pullman is slated to star," Tobias says. "Its budget is under $10 million. There's no question that the film wouldn't have made it as far as it has if it had been written as a $30-million to $50-million picture."

Whatever type of movies you enjoy writing, remember to study films and film credits. Note what types of movies a producer, director, or actor typically makes, because you can pitch your script to any of them.

Straczynski recommends going to the websites of smaller production companies that might be interested in a script similar to yours, then finding the telephone number for the story department and getting the name of the story editor. Write this person a one-page query letter and hope it will grab his attention. Demonstrate that you are familiar with the kinds of movies the company does: For example, Drew Barrymore's production company, Flower Films, has had great success with chick flicks and romantic comedies (*Fever Pitch, Charlie's Angels, 50 First Dates, He's Just Not That Into You*), but would probably not be the place to pitch your testosterone-driven action movie.

Sending scripts to actors' agents is the worst thing to do, he said, because these agents are "trained to turn people and material away"—they deal with actors, not writers. But it's possible to ask an actor directly to read your script, and sometimes this can lead to a life-changing introduction to a producer the actor knows and has worked with. In his hometown of Bozeman, Montana, for example, Tobias said he can contact at least fifty well-known actors, producers, and directors who pass through the city. Although people believe actors are unapproachable, with the exception of the biggest names, some are receptive if you are friendly, ask politely for help, and defer to their judgment.

The book *Opening the Doors to Hollywood* recounts how David Permut, who later produced *Dragnet* and *Blind Date*, started his career by sending hundreds of letters around Hollywood, asking for "any advice you might have that might further my career." He received hundreds of form letter responses, but also some personal ones. One from writer Sidney Sheldon said, "I can think of nothing that would offer you as much future security, with the possible exception of going over Niagara Falls in a leaky raft. But if you are really interested in pursuing this endeavor, please call me."

While many experts caution against sending the full script to anyone unasked, doing so has, paradoxically, worked. When Cynthia Whitcomb, a former columnist for *Writer's Digest*, was starting out, her first scripts accumulated 120 consecutive rejections. Then, she read a *Los Angeles Times* article that said Tony Bill, who had produced *The Sting*, was starting a new production company. She got his address from the Producers Guild of America and dropped off her script—a period piece similar to *The Sting*—cold. He called and told her, among other things, that her script was too expensive, but asked her to work with him on another project. That began a career that has since included the sale of sixty scripts for movies, TV movies, and miniseries.

One last paradox to keep in mind: Even if someone in Hollywood adores your script and buys it, chances are it will be rewritten—if not by you, by others. The rewriting that goes on in Hollywood can be very different from the revising that happens with books and articles; even the basic content can change dramatically. (For proof of this, think of all the novels you've seen adapted into screenplays and how often they deviated drastically from the original.) Film and television are collaborative media, and writers must learn to expect changes to the script, including such things as cherished characters, plot twists, and even the all-important ending. If you are harboring illusions about your script remaining in the pristine state in which you first conceived it, it would be well to begin thinking of your script less as a magnum opus than as a wiki—an open source, collaborative endeavor with many fingers in the pie.

MAKING THE PITCH

Even if a producer rejects your script, he still may like your writing style and invite you to pitch more ideas—but in person this time.

It seems paradoxical that someone who is good at writing would be asked to explain her ideas orally. But there's a reason for it: The Writers Guild won't allow writers to be asked to write something without being paid, so you have to tell people your ideas before getting a contract to write them.

Your "pitch" is essentially a short (one- to three-sentence) description of your script that you can expand upon to add detailed information as you generate interest from an agent or producer. From that starting point, the writer can provide more information about the story, characters, and plot twists, focusing on whatever elements seem to spark the interest of the agent or producer.

Many people have a mortal fear of speaking in public, especially when their careers are on the line. Like most difficult things, pitching gets easier with practice. Practice pitching in front of a mirror, to your friends, to your dog. Be enthusiastic. Remember how much you love your story. Recount the big picture, but expect to be asked questions about details. Above all else, be brief. If you need some inspiration, watch the *Times* contest winners for The Perfect Screenplay at http://entertainment.timesonline.co.uk/tol/arts_and_entertainment/film/article3416294.ece Each year, contestants have just three minutes to pitch their screenplay ideas to a panel of expert judges, including producers and directors from the British entertainment industry. A live audience votes, *American Idol*-style, and the winners and runners-up get prizes and some much-needed attention for their projects. It's a great education in what to do—and what not to do.

When you pitch, it's your chance to shine. Remember to relax. As Heidi Wall, founder of the Flash Forward Institute, a coaching center for the entertainment industry, once told a WGA writer: "Everyone already knows how to pitch. We do it all the time. Whenever you try to convince someone to go to a movie with you, you're pitching."

A pitch can last from a few seconds to maybe as much as fifteen minutes if the producer is interested and keeps asking for more information. Just be sure to go to a pitch meeting armed with several ideas. If the first one doesn't fly, you'll have something to say if the executive's eyes roll back and he and asks, "So what else are you working on?"

GETTING IN THROUGH THE BACK DOOR: ONE NEW SCREENWRITER'S EXPERIENCE

Cincinnati attorney Bill Mikita started writing after a midlife wake-up call: His mother died suddenly of a brain tumor when he was half her age. "And I thought, *what if half my life is over? What do I really want to do with my life?* I had always wanted to write, but I never expressed it to anyone." It was time to pursue that dream.

Mikita capitalized on a personal friendship with a business colleague who had left Cincinnati to work for Disney in Los Angeles. "I flew out, spent some time with Rick, and I realized through meeting some producers that I could probably sell something. If I had something that they really wanted, an unknown writer could still sell something in Hollywood."

Mikita began to mine his experiences for ideas: "What did I have that no one else had? And it became apparent to me that it was my family, and growing up with a disabled brother, Steve." Mikita crafted a rough screenplay based on the true story of his brother, who was born with a rare form of muscular dystrophy. Steve Mikita was the first wheelchair student at Duke University and is now an attorney.

"Even though that first screenplay I wrote wasn't very good and maybe crudely written, I almost sold it," says Mikita. "And it gave me inspiration to keep writing. I wrote four or five other screenplays. I eventually went back to the original story, and I crafted it into something I entitled *Chasing 3000*." The story tracks two brothers who take off across the country in a race against time to see their hero, Roberto Clemente, get his three thousandth hit. "Along the way, this road trip becomes a personal odyssey where the brothers discover the importance of being brothers. So it's a feel-good movie, and it's a movie about the love that I have for my brother and he has for me," says Mikita.

Chasing 3000 became an independent production starring Ray Liotta, with Trevor Morgan and Rory Culkin playing the two brothers. Mikita enjoyed being a part of the whole process, from the writing to the revising to the long-awaited distribution deal. There have been disappointments and delays along the way, but Mikita says it has been a tremendous experience—and proof that it is still possible for an unknown screenwriter to live a dream in Hollywood.

UNDERSTAND THE BUSINESS

Reading industry publications helps beginning writers procure some marketing savvy: You will learn who makes what types of films—and you won't make the mistake of sending the wrong idea to the wrong people. Since smaller budget movies are more salable for beginners, when reading industry news you'll learn how much things cost to produce. (In 2004, the average studio movie cost over $102 million to make and market, with costs rising every year—sometimes into double-digit annual increases. By 2007, the marketing costs alone were an eye-popping $36 million, on average.) You will learn whether a film studio already is working on a movie that you thought was your very own idea. You will learn which producers make movies or shows similar to your own. Learning about the business of television and film can help you sell your scripts.

Read newspapers, such as *The New York Times* or the *Los Angeles Times*, that offer useful information about film and TV production. Peruse trade publications, such as *Variety* or *The Hollywood Reporter*, available online. These not only report what types of deals are being made, but they also list movies and shows in production, along with contact information of some key players.

One of the more useful trade publications for writers, however, is *Written By*, the magazine of the Writers Guild of America, West (www.wga.org). This magazine includes interviews with writers about writing, stories about how writers broke in to the business, and a section listing TV shows, with the name and phone number for writers to contact.

Many publications offer the contact information of people who may be interested in your script, including *Screenwriter's & Playwright's Market*, published annually by Writer's Digest Books. You can find the address for a writer or her agent from the Writers Guild, for an actor's agent or production company from the Screen Actors Guild, for directors through the Directors Guild of America, and for producers from the Producers Guild of America. The Directors Guild and Writers Guild also publish directories of their members. The *Hollywood Creative Directory*, published online and three times a year in paper form, also includes detailed staff lists for studios production companies (www.hcdonline.com).

Books also can help you target the right market for selling and finding agents. *Opening the Doors to Hollywood*, for example, includes a reference section that lists guilds/unions, libraries, sample contracts, seminars and workshops, trade publications, and writers' organizations. *Guide to Literary Agents* lists agencies according to their interests in handling ten categories of movies and of TV programs, from animation to variety shows, and also according to subject matter, from action/adventure to Westerns/frontier.

RESOURCES

Use the following books, magazines and trade publications, organizations, seminars and workshops, and websites to learn more about scriptwriting and how to sell your script.

BOOKS

Adventures in the Screen Trade: A Personal View of Hollywood and Screenwriting by **William Goldman** (Warner Books). This book offers insider advice and instruction on how to be successful in Hollywood—by the author of *The Princess Bride! Inconceivable!*

The Complete Book of Scriptwriting by **J. Michael Straczynski** (Writer's Digest Books). This book teaches you how to write and sell your scripts for television, movies, animation, radio, and the theater.

The Connected Screenwriter: A Comprehensive Guide to the U.S. and International Studios, Networks, Production Companies, and Filmmakers That Want to Buy Your Screenplay

by Barry Turner (St. Martin's Griffin). An up-to-date guide to agents, production companies, screenwriting courses, writers' festivals, prizes, and the business of screenwriting.

From Script to Screen: The Collaborative Art of Filmmaking, **second edition by Linda Seger and Edward J. Whetmore** (Lone Eagle). This book provides a careful look at the movie-making process, from the first idea, to the final music score.

The Hollywood Standard: The Complete and Authoritative Guide to Script Format and Style **by Christopher Riley** (Michael Wiese Productions). This book, written by a script proofreader, offers hundreds of examples of what to do and what not to do in formatting your screenplay or teleplay.

The Perfect Pitch: How to Sell Yourself and Your Movie Idea to Hollywood, **second edition by Ken Rotcop** (Michael Wiese Productions). How is a perfect pitch created and delivered? How can I get in to Hollywood by working at a studio?

MAGAZINES AND TRADE PUBLICATIONS

Hollywood Creative Directory. Offers up-to-date contact information for producers, TV shows, and studio and network executives (for a fee). www.hcdonline.com

The Hollywood Reporter. A daily trade paper for the entertainment industry, covering film, television, music, and more. www.hollywoodreporter.com

Hollywood Scriptwriter. This e-zine gives basic information about how to reach your goals in the film industry, and includes advice from experts. www.hollywoodscriptwriter.com

Variety. Source for entertainment news and analysis. www.variety.com

Writer's Digest. Offers basic information about writing and selling scripts. There's also a Script Notes blog at http://blog.writersdigest.com/scriptnotes. www.writersdigest.com

10
SELLING TO
CORPORATIONS

THE HEALTH CARE industry in America spends an eight-figure number every year on printed materials. The auto industry spends nearly as much. Retailers, beverage makers, computer companies, and telecommunications firms spend billions more. "Printed material" can include brochures, newsletters, catalogs, signage, instruction manuals, press releases, speeches, new home descriptions, or employee handbooks. These days it also includes website copy, online catalogs, e-mail newsletters, online tutorials, and other electronic writing—media that are fast overtaking their traditional printed counterparts. Words are everywhere we look—and someone has to write them, which gives freelance writers an endless number of markets.

Few writers set out to become corporate copywriters, technical writers, copyeditors, or ghostwriters—all tracks we will discuss in this chapter. Many fall into it as a way to supplement their spotty earnings as they await a breakthrough in their own more creative writing. Most discover that the corporate writing pays many times more, and is easier to break into, than creative writing. Many also find the work satisfying and varied as well as lucrative—and the hours can't be beat. Writers who work from home and can set their own schedule get used to the freedom and flexibility that comes from a freelance career. Once they are well established, they can work as much or as little as they want, depending on whether they need more money or more time. Corporate freelancing can be a marvelously elastic career path.

The trick is to find the right buyer for your work. Fortunately, the opportunities have never been greater. Corporations of every type are finding that hiring freelancers cuts overhead costs. They can hire freelancers only when needed instead of hiring an employee who may be idle during slow work periods. Through e-mail, videoconferencing, and other developments, technology now enables freelance writers to interact with any company regardless of location.

FINDING YOUR OWN OPPORTUNITIES

Savvy freelancers keep tabs on the local business scene to find out about new businesses in town or changes in existing businesses, such as new ownership or expansion, that may indicate a need for freelance help. As with any area of business, networking is crucial when looking for corporate assignments.

Call or e-mail all writing-related professional organizations in your area and join the active ones. The Association for Women in Communications, the Public Relations Society of America, the International Association of Business Communicators, the Society for Technical Communication— many of these national organizations may have branches in your area. Most of them publish directories of their members, often listing the member's place of employment. This gives you an automatic contact—especially if you've involved yourself in the social networking system these organizations encourage.

Take a look at the business community in your area: Who are the ten or twenty biggest employers? The website of your local community can give you this information. Keep your eyes and ears open for listings of all kinds: Search them out in business newspapers, papers by the Chamber of Commerce or tourism bureau, and directories of every type.

To get an idea of just how far you can take this game of "who needs writers?" try this exercise today: Take a conscious look around you at written copy wherever you are—a calendar that has photo captions, signs on the backs of benches or high up on billboards, corporate websites, catalogs, alumni donation appeals, even your junk mail. These were all written by someone, somewhere, who presumably collected a paycheck for his trouble. Of course, not all of these were written by freelancers, but it's safe to assume that any of them could have been. There are few communications areas left that exclude work-for-hire as a possibility. Sometimes, you will be alerted to the need for a professional writer by the *absence* of good copy. Anyone who has ever laughed at terribly written real estate listings has to wonder how much better the listing could be—and how much more quickly a house might sell—if a trained writer had been hired to play up the right features.

It's usually not practical to be a freelance generalist and hire yourself out for any kind of writing. As with most professions, specialization is the key to success. In fact, before you approach any organization, learn everything you can about its history, culture, products or services, and customer base. Only then can you find your niche and successfully sell yourself as the right person for the job.

Once you've located organizations that might need your help, send a cover letter with a good sales pitch, a short bio, and writing samples to the appropriate person in the communications, public relations, or marketing department. Make sure you send your material to a specific person and that you've spelled her name correctly. It's fine, and may actually be preferable, to use e-mail.

The person to contact at some of the larger companies and organizations may go by any number of titles. She may be a director of publications, corporate communications, or public relations. If the company has a sophisticated operation, it may have borrowed the term *creative services director* from the advertising industry, particularly if it uses both print and audiovisual media. It may also be the marketing director or the director of human services.

When you do find work, be sure to get everything in writing. The amount of detail will vary with the complexity and size of the project. At the very least, make sure the assignment, deadline, and payment terms are clearly outlined in a letter of agreement. In the business world especially, these kinds of agreements are a sign of professionalism and are appreciated on all sides.

ADVERTISING AND PR

One way to sell your writing is to target the kind of company that depends on writers and may frequently use freelance writers: advertising and public relations firms. These are the experts to whom many companies turn for help in developing their various communications-related projects. In fact, if you go to a company on your own to vie for a freelance assignment, you may compete against advertising and PR agencies. But for now, let's look at how to get an assignment from such a firm and the advantages of selecting this route.

The biggest advantage to freelancing through an advertising or PR agency is that the agency finds the clients; all you have to do is complete the work. This can be attractive if you tire of freelance hustling, especially if you can become a regular in an agency's stable of freelancers. You may assure yourself a steady source of income, and if it's a quality firm, you enhance your own reputation by association.

If you already have some experience with a specific kind of assignment (you've designed and written brochures in your last job) or you're well grounded in a certain area of expertise (you're a volunteer or a past employee in an organization that caters to senior citizens), sell yourself as an expert in this area.

There are two main reasons public relations firms might hire freelance help. Sometimes special expertise is needed, such as in writing about engineering, medicine, accounting, etc. Secondly, because they must produce a large volume of collateral material, firms sometimes find themselves in need of freelance help when the workload gets too heavy, such as during a special project, time of year, or the summer months when regular staff go on vacation. This collateral material can take the form of a postcard, a brochure, or even a direct-mail piece. Sometimes a company will be looking for someone who can creatively shepherd a project from conceptualization to production. Other times they may only need simple copywriting.

In addition to corporations, here are some other possibilities to consider:

- Hospital freelance writers. Federal cutbacks and outside competition have forced many hospitals to walk a financial tightrope— while producing even more written copy. It's no coincidence that hospitals have increased their use of freelancers to supplement or take the place of in-house employees.

- Grant writers. Some nonprofits, especially arts organizations, can no longer afford to have in-house grant writers. If you have grant writing experience and skill, you could be very marketable indeed in the nonprofit sector.

- Speechwriters. Freelancers with skill in speechwriting are especially in demand. Executives don't hire speechwriters the way a politician does. Someone from the public relations department is usually assigned the job on top of her normal duties. As a freelancer, speechwriting may be something you can do a few times a year, along with numerous other assignments. So if you have a particular knack for speechwriting, serve it up as an area of expertise.

RESOURCES

BOOKS

102 Ways to Make Money Writing 1,500 Words or Less by I.J. Schecter (Writer's Digest Books). This guide has an extensive section on corporate writing.

The Wealthy Writer: How to Earn a Six-Figure Income as a Freelance Writer (No Kidding!) by Michael Meanwell (Writer's Digest Books). Meanwell reveals how to launch a freelance career—and be successful at it long-term. The book includes case studies and sample documents.

The Well-Fed Writer: Financial Self-Sufficiency as a Freelance Writer in Six Months or Less by Peter Bowerman (Fanove). With an engaging style, Bowerman discusses different kinds of corporate freelance jobs (brochures, ad copy, etc.), writers' rates, dealing with difficult clients, finding new clients, and more.

PROFESSIONAL ORGANIZATIONS

Always keep an eye out for local and national organizations that can help you improve your networking opportunities.

> **American Marketing Association.** Has forty thousand members and provides marketing information through research, case studies and journals that stay on top of emerging trends. www.marketingpower.com
>
> **The Association for Women in Communications.** Promotes advancement of women in communication fields by recognizing excellence, advocating leadership, and positioning members at the forefront of communications. www.womcom.org
>
> **Public Relations Society of America.** World's largest organization of PR professionals. Offers continuing education, information exchange forums, and more. www.prsa.org

TECHNICAL WRITING

While the goal of creative writing is to entertain and that of advertising writing is to sell, the primary goal of technical writing is the accurate transmission of information. Technical writing, then, can be described as putting complicated information into plain language in a format that is easy to understand. The tone is objective and favors content over style. (This does not mean, however, that you should present the subject in a formal, stunted style.) Above all, technical writing should be concise, complete, clear, and consistent. The best way to achieve all these is to make sure your writing is well organized.

By far the biggest area for technical writers is in the computer industry, though there are a wide variety of possible assignments, including preparation of customer letters, utility bills, owner manuals, insurance benefit packages, and even contracts (some states have "plain language" laws requiring contracts and insurance policies to be written in simple English). In any technical field, writers who can bridge the gap between engineers who design things and the customers who use them are in high demand.

Technical writers do not necessarily need formal training in the areas they cover. To the contrary, one of the greatest talents a technical writer brings to a project is the ability to take a step back from the technical details and see the subject from a different perspective than the engineers, scientists, and experts. Thus, a technical writer becomes familiar with a subject by interviewing experts, reading journals and reports, reviewing drawings, studying specifications, and examining product samples.

Technical writers themselves often shy away from the term *freelance writer*, preferring to be known instead as *independent contractors* or consultants. This probably has a lot to do with the fact that technical writers work mostly with corporations, where the term *independent contractor* sounds more professional. It's very important to establish and maintain a high degree of credibility when working with firms.

The number of ways to enter the technical writing field are as varied as the people entering it. If you're cold-calling large companies, you'll want to contact the manager of technical communications or manager of documentation. Local employment agencies may also be of service. The easiest way, of course, is to have been at a company full-time in the past and have all of those connections and freelance possibilities in hand when you leave to start your own business.

For this initial contact you will want to send a cover letter, resume, and some samples of your work. Be very clear about the kind of work you're seeking; although it seems counterintuitive, writers who present themselves as having particular areas of experience and expertise come across as more professional than those who claim to be generalists who can do any brand of corporate writing. Target each cover letter to the specific company in question, emphasizing its products or services, and highlighting those brochures and writing samples that are most relevant to the work you're seeking. If you're contacting the regional ballet about writing their fundraising material, include the donor letters you penned for the cash-strapped symphony last year. If you're contacting a hospital about writing patient brochures about how to manage diabetes, send in any other clips you've written on consumer health.

What if you don't have such clips and writing samples? If you lack the experience, build a portfolio by volunteering to write material for a nonprofit organization, or offer to help your colleagues prepare reports and presentations. If you are interested in pursuing this type of work, it is probably a good idea to join the Society for Technical Communication (www.stc.org), where you can network to gain contacts in the industry. Many businesses hire writers from the STC talent pool.

RESOURCES

PROFESSIONAL ORGANIZATIONS

American Medical Writers Association. Provides educational sources for biomedical writers and offers networking opportunities. www.amwa.org

Council of Science Editors. Offers networking opportunities and cutting-edge information for those who work in science writing, editing or publishing. www.councilscienceeditors.org

Society for Technical Communication. The STC supports the arts and sciences of technical writing with networking and learning opportunities. It has over fourteen thousand members and is available to anyone whose work makes technical information available. www.stc.org

BOOKS

Handbook of Technical Writing, **ninth edition by Gerald J. Alred, Charles T. Brusaw, and Walter E. Oliu** (St. Martin's Press). This alphabetically organized manual is an industry standard, now updated with new information on integrating visuals, handling copyright law, and addressing ethical issues.

Kaplan Technical Writing: A Resource for Technical Writers at All Levels **by Diane Martinez, Tanya Peterson, Carrie Wells, Carrie Hannigan, and Carolyn Stevenson** (Kaplan). This book teaches technical writing for user manuals, intranet teaching, and even e-mail. It's also available for download on the Amazon Kindle.

Opportunities in Technical Writing **by Jay Gould** (McGraw-Hill). Looking to get started as a technical writer? This book teaches you how to market yourself, deepen your technical expertise, and find jobs, while also discussing career details like starting salaries and possibilities for specialization.

CATALOG COPY

Ever pick up the J. Crew catalog and wonder who writes their descriptions of stylish khakis and heather-gray sweaters? Have you ever read through the Trader Joe's catalog and wondered how they came up with such tantalizing and adventurous portrayals of avocados? Remember: *Someone* has to write the copy you read as you're paging through the catalogs in your mailbox. Why can't it be you?

It's not terribly difficult to break into writing catalog copy, even if you don't have any experience in advertising. You will need to start small with niche businesses and work your way up. It helps if you begin with products you know. This could mean creating a flyer for a local farmer's market or a catalog of a regional stationer—anything to get your foot in the door. Once you have some of those under your belt, you will be ready to start pitching larger accounts.

Begin with the creative director of the company you're interested in; if there is no such person, try the marketing director. Your pitch letter will need to demonstrate that (1) you have experience, (2) you already know and like their product line, and (3) you write well. Study their existing catalog or website copy to become familiar with the style in use. Every company has its own history and way of communicating its product to customers, and you want to show that you can be creative while also respecting the existing style. Note that most very large companies utilize an advertising agency for their accounts, so you may be referred to a middleman.

Catalog copywriters are kind of the original Twitterers: They have learned to make every character count. Catalog copy must be snappy and short. Most products are introduced by a quick but memorable headline that creates a feeling for the product but doesn't merely spit out the product's name (e.g., "Weekend comfort. Workweek style" for a women's oxford cloth shirt from Lands' End). This is followed by an ultra-short description of the product and its specs. More companies have gone to bullet points in recent years with the idea that people don't really read anymore—especially when they shop online.

Many catalog copywriters do "B2B" catalogs: business-to-business catalogs, rather than consumer or trade catalogs. In other words, they are helping one company sell their goods or services to another company, not directly to Joe or Jane Shopper. One of the hazards of typical B2B copy is that it can be overly technical and boring. If you can write sharp copy and be both entertaining and informative, you will get jobs.

RESOURCES

BOOKS

88 Money-Making Writing Jobs by Robert Bly (Sourcebooks). Robert Bly claims to make $600,000 a year as a writer. Some will find this claim difficult to swallow, but the book contains great tips on starting a writing business, including suggestions for catalog copywriting.

The Complete Guide to Writing Web-Based Advertising Copy to Get the Sale: What You Need to Know Explained Simply by Vickie Taylor (Atlantic). Writing web-based copy is not the same skill set as writing print catalogs. Taylor discusses pitfalls to avoid and also dissects trends in Web advertising.

> **_Start & Run a Copywriting Business_ by Steve Slaunwhite** (Self-Counsel Press). This book has tips for creating your business from the ground up, including how to get clients, how and how much to bill them, and how to tackle different kinds of projects.

COPYEDITING AND PROOFREADING

The real heroes of the writing profession are the copyeditors and proofreaders who labor to make the rest of us look good. If you've ever known someone who excels at copyediting and proofreading, you know that both take real talent. For those who possess the unique ability, copyediting and proofreading can be a good source of additional income.

To get work you will almost certainly have to pass a test. To do this, study the stylebook for your chosen field or publication (most likely _The Associated Press Stylebook_, _The Chicago Manual of Style_, or the _MLA Style Manual and Guide to Scholarly Publishing_). Also memorize a list of most commonly misspelled words. You'll most likely out-test most of the competition.

Once you have the credentials, you're ready to start selling yourself. The traditional route, of course, is to e-mail your resume to magazines, publishing companies, newspapers—any place that routinely hires copyeditors. Sometimes a more assertive approach works as well. We know one enterprising proofreader who got frustrated with a regional magazine that didn't pay nearly enough attention to apostrophes, dangling modifiers, and Oxford commas as she would wish. Photographs were mislabeled and interviewees' names were inconsistently spelled. Rather than merely getting annoyed, she sent a corrected, marked-up copy of the magazine to the editor-in-chief, offering her services as an experienced and eagle-eyed proofreader. She got freelance work from that magazine right away.

What's the Difference Between a Copyeditor and a Proofreader?

Although some people use the terms interchangeably, "copyeditor" and "proofreader" are not the same. Here's the difference.

- **Copyediting:** The writer's direct supervisor or editor usually edits stories for content and organization. The role of the copyeditor, then, is to look for additional spelling errors and typos. He may raise questions about conflicting statements and may be charged with smoothing awkward text transitions and ensuring uniform style. In some cases, a copyeditor may even rewrite portions of copy to improve the flow of text or to maintain a uniform tone. A copyeditor may also be expected to keep an eye out for libel. At newspapers and magazines, it is often the copyeditor's job to write headlines and photo captions. Copyeditors are sometimes also called upon to design pages. This may involve deciding which stories, photos, and graphics will run and which will be featured most prominently. (Before beginning any job, freelance editors should determine the level of work expected and base their fees accordingly. See Appendix A for market rates.)

- **Proofreading:** Proofreaders are charged with looking for typographical and mechanical errors after all other editing is complete. A proofreader may check typeset copy word for word against a manuscript and identify any deviations. They look for misspellings, missing copy, typos, misnumbering, mislabeling, and incorrect cross-references. Proofreaders may also check copy for conformity to type specifications and ensure attractive typography by checking letter or word spacing, margins, and repetitive word breaks.

The extent to which a copyeditor or proofreader must verify facts varies widely. In the past, this has traditionally been the job of a separate fact checker. A fact checker does not make editorial changes but simply verifies accuracy. One client may request that the fact checker verify all statements, while another client may request the verification of addresses and trademarks only. However, cutbacks at many companies have meant that some no longer hire a separate fact checker, so you will do yourself a favor if you can include fact checking in your standard services.

Copyeditors and proofreaders are in high demand, so if you look hard enough and are willing to start small enough you are likely to find work. Smaller newspapers frequently need help. The pay may not be great, but jobs like that can build a resume and provide an extra source of income. Keep in mind that there is plenty of copyediting and proofreading work at places other than publications. So don't overlook nonprofit organizations and big companies—any place that publishes anything.

RESOURCES

CORRESPONDENCE AND ONLINE COURSES

If you want to improve your copyediting and/or proofreading skills, there are plenty of correspondence and online courses available:

> **The American Copy Editors Society (www.copydesk.org).** Has links to various training opportunities for people who wish to become accredited copyeditors.
>
> **Editcetera (www.editcetera.com).** Offers courses in developmental editing, copyediting, proofreading, and more either in the San Francisco Bay area or via mail correspondence.
>
> **The New School Online University (www.newschool.edu/online).** Offers coursework, information, class discussions, and research links all online.
>
> **University of California Berkeley Extension Online (http://learn.berkeley.edu).** Has a variety of interactive courses online for professionals, including a four-course editorial track.

INDEXING

The indexes in the back of most nonfiction books are another source of income for freelance wordsmiths. While the index is sometimes the responsibility of the book's author, few actually do it themselves because frankly, it can be a royal pain. Freelance indexers hired by the author or publisher usually do the work.

There are two basic kinds of indexing:

> **1. Conventional indexing.** To do this job, an indexer will typically receive a set of actual hardcopy page proofs, which are exact images of how pages will appear in the book, complete with page numbers. The indexer reads these proofs and compiles a list of subject headings, subheads, and the

location of each key reference. Upon completing a rough draft of the index, the indexer then edits, organizes, and proofreads it.

2. Embedded indexing. Increasingly, powerful computer programs have made the old slog of hardcopy indexing obsolete. In Microsoft Word and other programs, the indexer can tag certain terms and phrases as items they want in the final index. The code for this is not visible in the printed version, but the document will automatically generate a final index with the information arranged alphabetically. The advantages of this system are that it updates the index's page numbers automatically if the author makes last-minute changes to the page proofs, or if there is ever a new and expanded edition of the book.

Since indexing is one of the last steps in completing a book, indexers frequently work under intense pressure and time constraints. Indexing cannot be started until final page proofs are available. By that time the printer wants to get the job on the press and the publisher is clamoring for a finished product. As a result, skilled indexers must possess more than good language skills, attention to detail, patience, and an analytical mind—they must also be able to work well under pressure.

Probably the best way to break into the business is to send resumes with cover letters to publishers. You can find their addresses in *Literary Market Place, Writer's Market,* and *Books in Print.* It is hard to get established in the indexing business, but once you do get work—and do it well—it is easier to get jobs through word of mouth and a little networking.

RESOURCES

PROFESSIONAL GROUPS

Joining a professional indexing organization may help improve your indexing skills and provide you with excellent networking opportunities:

The American Society for Indexing. The only professional organization in the United States devoted to the advancement of indexing. www.asindexing.org

National Federation of Abstracting and Information Services. Serves groups that aggregate, organize, and facilitate access to information. They address common interests through education and advocacy. www.nfais.org

BOOKS

Indexing Books, **second edition by Nancy C. Mulvany** (University of Chicago Press). Written by a professional indexer, this book covers the indexing process from start to finish. The second edition has new information about software programs and technological developments.

The Indexing Companion **by Glenda Browne and Jon Jermey** (Cambridge University Press). This award-winning guide covers different types of indexes, how to index from PDF files, and various software programs.

GHOSTWRITING

When a book is ghostwritten, the person whose name appears on the book as primary author has done little or none of the actual writing. He is merely a source of information—providing content, background information, and, hopefully, credibility. Typically this person is a celebrity or someone well respected in his field of expertise. While he has the experience and the name recognition that can make for a best-selling book, he lacks professional writing credentials. As a result, the so-called author relies on a more experienced writer—a ghostwriter—to put his ideas into book form.

The ghostwriter gathers information for the book by interviewing the author and will often conduct her own research and interview several other sources as well for background material. While each collaboration is different, the author usually will review the manuscript and possibly even edit it for content. For their part, ghostwriters may be credited as co-authors or get no visible credit at all. (Their motivation is often a five- or six-figure check and the opportunity to get even more lucrative work either as authors or as ghostwriters.)

The arrangement that a ghostwriter walks into is inherently more complex than the typical relationship between a writer and publisher (which is complex enough). It's easy for misunderstandings to arise between the so-called author and publisher, with the ghostwriter being caught in the middle. In one sense, the ghostwriter is a translator, taking what the author has to offer and trying to deliver what the publisher expects. The best way to diffuse some of this conflict is to clearly map out in writing what each party expects from the arrangement. When all is said and done there may still be misunderstandings, but at least the ghostwriter can justify what he has done.

There are a number of ways to break into ghostwriting. One is to seek out a rising star in sports, entertainment, business, or politics. Publishers are often in search of new talent and new celebrities. Armed with a collaboration agreement and the right amount of talent, you can sell your services to a publisher.

As you gain experience and become specialized in a certain subject area, you will find it easier to sell your talents to publishers who are looking for ghostwriters in that field of expertise. Along the way you can build your resume by collaborating on magazine articles with celebrities or experts in your chosen field of specialization. Magazines do not knowingly accept ghostwritten articles, but they would accept, for instance, an article on the modern history of baseball, "as told to" John Doe.

Very often, successful executives or entrepreneurs are looking for writers who can help them self-publish a book of their own. The finished books are then distributed through their businesses to clients, co-workers, and relatives. This is a great way to get work and hone your talents, and possibly even make a name for yourself.

RESOURCES

BOOKS

Ghostwriting: For Fun & Profit by Eva Shaw (Writeriffic Publishing Group). Shaw, who has been a professional ghostwriter for thirty years, discusses breaking into the business, how to capture clients' stories, how much to charge, and how to negotiate a contract.

11
WHAT ABOUT
SELF-PUBLISHING AND
PRINT ON DEMAND?

IN 2007, THIRTYSOMETHING novelist Lisa Genova couldn't get a literary agent. The Harvard-trained neuroscientist queried more than a hundred agents, but was rejected or ignored by all of them. She went to writers conferences, e-mailed editors, and tried to generate interest in her novel *Still Alice*, about an academic who discovers in the height of her career that she is suffering from early onset Alzheimer's disease. Nobody nibbled, so Genova plunked down $450 of her own cash to iUniverse, a company that specializes in one-stop self-publishing. Although an industry professional told her that self-publishing her first novel would be the death of her fledgling career, precisely the opposite happened. Word-of-mouth recommendations from independent booksellers led to bigger endorsements, and eventually a top-drawer agent. Genova then snagged a contract with Simon & Schuster's Pocket Books division for "a mid-six-figure advance" (translation: around half a million dollars). When the book debuted as a Pocket title in early 2009, it did so with a splash, hitting the New York Times best-seller list at number five. Genova called the rags-to-riches transformation a journey from "extreme to extreme," noting that, "this time last year, I was selling the book out of the trunk of my car."

Not every self-publishing success story is quite as dramatic as Genova's, but many other tales can give courage to disheartened writers. Even in small numbers, self-publishing can work financially, and authors often wind up keeping more money than they would in a more traditional setup. For example, Peter Bowerman, author of a series of books on writing and publishing (www.wellfedwriter.com), had $11,000 of sales in the first two months for his second book *The Well-Fed Writer: Back for Seconds*, of which roughly 80 percent was profit. In a third book, *The Well-Fed Self-Publisher*, he tells his story of self-publishing, claiming that his first book alone provided him with a full-time living for the better part of five years.

Sound too good to be true? Not necessarily. It has never been easier, cheaper, or more efficient to self-publish. In the last decade, self-publishing has gone from being a highly stigmatized Method of Last Resort to a respectable backup plan or even a first choice. Although few people set out to self-publish (as Bowerman says he intended to do from the beginning), many begin to consider it seriously after years of attending writers conferences, submitting to agents and publishers, and having no success. Striking out repeatedly using the traditional route has pushed many authors toward self-publishing, and some will never come back.

THE BAD OLD DAYS

Up until very recently—i.e., the dawn of the twenty-first century—people in the know could simply look at a book and tell you whether it was self-published. The covers were often ugly, for starters, with the cheapest kind of stock art and the least attractive typeface. And that's not even counting the number of typographical errors in the jacket copy or even on the front cover. Flipping through the book—which was often too long and obviously showed the lack of much-needed editorial intervention—book professionals could find poor writing, inconsistent fonts, and other unprofessional qualities. The books *looked* self-published. Joe Writer simply couldn't compete with what a professional publishing company could do, especially in terms of design, layout, marketing, and distribution.

Technology has leveled the playing field in an astonishing way, and Joe now has a fighting chance. (Jane, too.) According to *The New York Times*, "Gone are the days when self-publishing meant paying a printer to produce hundreds of copies that then languished in a garage … for as little as three dollars, an author can upload a manuscript or collection of photos to a website, and order a printed book within an hour." Not surprisingly, more authors are turning to self-publishing because of its low cost and ease of use. In 2008, the self-publishing company Author Solutions published thirteen thousand titles, up 12 percent from the previous year; in 2009 it purchased rival company Xlibris and is poised to expand even further. Near the end of 2009, the world's first-ever Self-Publishing Book Expo was held in New York City. Overall, self-published and print-on-demand titles accounted for 285,394 of the 560,626 books published in 2008—with self-publishing overtaking traditional publishing for the first time ever in terms of title output. Clearly, a revolution is underway.

CAN SELF-PUBLISHING WORK FOR FICTION AS WELL AS NONFICTION?

Self-publishing is an especially attractive option for writers of nonfiction how-to guides. In nonfiction, if a customer needs a book on how to breed Labrador retrievers, they're going to enter "breed Labrador retrievers" into Amazon.com's search field and seriously consider whatever pops up, no matter who wrote or published it. They might not even realize they're ordering a self-published book.

In fiction, though, sales are primarily author-driven rather than content-driven. Customers don't suddenly decide they want to read a novel about two Labrador retrievers who fall hopelessly in love. (Would *anyone* want to read that?) That's not to say it's impossible for fiction authors to sell their self-published works, but it's more difficult, because the topic can't drive sales in the way a nonfiction book can. In other words, there will be no "easy" sales for self-published fiction in the same way that there might be at least a few easy sales for some nonfiction topics. It will require even more of the trait that every self-published author needs in spades: to be a self-starter.

Such was the case with William P. Young, whose novel *The Shack* was rejected by every major or minor traditional publishing house he tried. So he and some friends created their own micro-publishing company, Windblown Media, in 2007. They aggressively sold the book to churches, schools, and individuals, with customers often buying ten or twenty copies at a time to give to friends. By 2008, multiple publishers were bidding on the book, including some who had rejected it the first time around, and Young signed with Hachette Book Group. By the middle of 2009, the novel had six million copies in print and had spent double-digit weeks on the national best-seller lists.

There are other success stories too: Christopher Paolini, teenage author of the fantasy franchise *Eragon*, got his start by publishing his book himself, as did techno-thriller novelist Daniel Suarez (*Daemon*). Success can happen if you are persistent—and self-publishing fortune favors the brave.

ARE YOU A SELF-STARTER?

Self-publishing is not for everyone. This method favors the creative, the self-promotional, and the persistent. If you have any wallflower tendencies, or you shudder at the thought of surrendering a boatload of time to the nonwriting aspects of your publishing career, this is not the route for you. Self-publishing can take an obscene amount of effort, so if you won't enjoy the process, stick with a traditional publisher.

However, if you are in possession of an entrepreneurial spirit and feel passionate about matching your product (a book) with an audience's need, keep reading. Here's a side-by-side comparison of the pros and cons of both self-publishing and traditional publishing.

SELF-PUBLISHING	TRADITIONAL PUBLISHING
You get to keep most of your profits	You will get a small royalty, usually including some money up front and some over time as the book sells
You can usually publish your book within a few months of completion	Your book will usually release six months to two years after you turn it in to your publisher
You have to do your own editing or hire an editor privately	You benefit from the editorial expertise of at least one editor at your publishing house

You have complete control of the book's cover design and title	You may have input into the cover design and title, but you will not have the final say
You will be responsible for getting your book into bookstores—a difficult task—and driving sales online and at your events	Your publisher (and its distributor or distributors) will handle the legwork of getting your book into stores and tracking sales
You retain all the legal rights to your work, permitting you to spin off other brands and licensing agreements without a third party or intermediary	Your publisher controls the rights to your book and must approve any spin-off products or licensing agreements
You will be the primary publicist for your book, calling media, mailing out review copies, writing press releases, etc.	You will benefit from having a professional publicist, though she sometimes handles dozens of books each season and then needs to move on to the next season's frontlist books
If you do your job right, you will probably be exhausted	If you do your job right, you will probably be exhausted

We're going to see in chapters twelve and thirteen that some of the most time-consuming aspects of self-publishing are actually things all writers should be doing anyway: promoting, blogging, making media contacts, visiting bookstores, and the like. The amount of promotional effort differs in degree but not in kind. Still, there are other elements of the self-publishing process you'll want to consider.

QUIZ: IS SELF-PUBLISHING RIGHT FOR YOU?

Self-publishing is not for everyone. In the spirit of *Cosmopolitan* magazine and inane quizzes everywhere, please take the following short quiz to determine if self-publishing might be the best path for you.

1. When I think of being a published author, I:
   a) see it as one facet of a career in speaking and traveling.
   b) see it as the culmination of my creative work.

2. Where money is concerned, I tend to:
   a) get irritated when I think of how little of the retail price of the book actually comes to me. There must be a better way.
   b) am above caring about pecuniary matters. I don't write for money.

3. I consider myself:
   a) an extrovert.
   b) an introvert.

4. In the first year after the publication of my book, I plan to devote _____ hours a day to its promotion and marketing:
   a) one
   b) four

5. It matters _____ to me to have my book put out by a press that can enhance my reputation and prestige:

a) a great deal

b) very little

6. On a scale of one to ten, the number that represents my comfort level with the early adoption of brand-new technology is:

a) two—I am the writerly equivalent of a Luddite. What's a blog again?

b) an eight—I get excited about all the possibilities of new media.

7. I think of myself as:

a) basically creative, but not a salesperson.

b) someone who could sell the devil a heater.

Okay, it's reckoning time. Give yourself ten points for each of the following answers: 1 = A; 2 = A; 3 = A; 4 = B; 5 = B; 6 = B; 7 = B. If you scored 40 or below, self-publishing may not be the best route for you. (Though you can, with determination, overcome some of your gut-level responses: Introverts can *choose* to promote their books unceasingly, and artsy people can educate themselves about the business end of things.) If you scored 50 or higher (or you scored a ten but you're determined to prove the quiz wrong), consider self-publishing.

OH, THE MANY HATS YOU'LL WEAR

When you're a self-publisher, you have to get used to many different roles. Here are ten of the different parts you'll play:

1. Writer. You're familiar with this one; it's what got you here in the first place. But if you're a self-publisher, this is just the first and most publicly recognizable of many hats you'll wear.

2. Marketer. Take a look at chapter twelve on what a book marketer does. As a self-publisher, you'll need to do a lot of homework about branding your name and positioning yourself in the marketplace. How can you drive word-of-mouth sales? How does "viral marketing" work, anyway? Successful marketing involves knowing how to connect with your target audience(s) consistently, repeatedly, and with a message they actually like. (Or at least one that doesn't annoy them.)

3. Book Designer. You'll be amazed at how important cover art is to book sales. For starters, good cover design is the key to getting your book carried in bookstores. (Did you think the buyers at chain stores actually *read* the books before they decided whether to stock them? Not typically.) Your book's cover absolutely must look professional, which is why many self-publishers decide to splurge in at least this one area and hire a professional designer. This is not the place to cut corners. Even if you are hiring someone, study examples of cover design and evaluate what works and what doesn't. Start with the bestsellers in your genre or field.

4. Editor. Most writers flatter themselves that they don't need editing, but almost everyone does. Even the most experienced writers have tics and problems they may not even be aware of (like that phrase just now that ended with a preposition, and the next sentence that will begin with a conjunction). But don't worry. There are numerous freelance editing services available; post your job at www.gofreelance. com and watch as freelancers approach you to hawk their services. Be clear about what you want: Fees range widely, with some editors working only to improve the manuscript and others acting as product managers who also oversee such things as design, layout, and distribution.

5. Product Manager. There are a surprising number of stages involved in publishing a book, including obtaining an ISBN-13 and a bar code (www.bowker.com), getting a copyright (www.copyright.gov), and other details. You need to be a highly organized individual to undertake this multistep process. It isn't rocket science, but it does require you to stay on top of things.

6. Warehouser. In bygone days, this role was played by Your Basement or Garage, with boxes of books stacked high to the ceiling and being commandeered for kindling in literary hard times. Today, however, self-published authors can choose to outsource warehousing to a third party, so they don't have to actually store the boxes themselves. And with the small print runs now made possible by improved print-on-demand technology, warehousing may become a thing of the past altogether.

7. Distributor. If a warehouser is someone who stores your books until they're needed, a distributor is someone whose job it is to actually get them into bookstores. (Sometimes the same company will perform both functions.) Distribution is often the Waterloo of self-published authors, as traditional bookstores (especially chains like Borders and Barnes & Noble) don't take kindly to self-published books and often refuse to stock them. Check out chapter fifteen of *The Complete Guide to Self-Publishing* by Tom and Marilyn Ross for ideas on how to get bookstores to carry your books by using an intermediary.

8. Publicist. When you are your own publicist, you are responsible for setting up media interviews, sending out review copies, following up with contacts, arranging book signings, and a thousand other things. This can be frustrating work, especially as you will have to overcome the traditional stigma that has been associated with self-publishing. Reviewers might toss a self-published book into the recycling bin, and newspaper book editors (the few who remain) will barely glance at them. It's your job to make them care. For ideas, see chapter fourteen.

9. Website Guru. It is absolutely necessary for any self-published author to have a first-rate website, preferably one where readers can interact regularly with you, get information about interviews and author events, and buy books directly (which is to your advantage, as far more of the profit will come to you when they buy from your site instead of from Amazon.com). If you are not an experienced technical person, by all means hire someone to build and maintain your website, and don't skimp. Your website is your face to the world.

10. Speaker. A crucial part of being an author, self-published or not, is to go out into the world and create demand for your message. That means a lot of public speaking.

As a self-published author, you will be doing even more of this than if you worked with a traditional publisher. Book yourself at libraries, coffeehouses, bookstores, community centers, historical societies, nature centers, cruise ships—whatever is relevant to your book and your audience. If you do well, you'll get more invitations—and can earn a nice side income as a speaker while you sell books at your events.

WHAT IS PRINT ON DEMAND?

Although "self-publishing" and "print on demand" (POD) are often used interchangeably, they are not the same thing. Self-publishing, as we've already seen, is where an author publishes a book herself—sometimes hiring a company to help with printing and distribution, etc., but retaining the creative rights to the work. POD books *can* be self-published, but don't have to be. Traditional publishers use POD when they have a book for which they predict a very small audience and need only a few copies, or when a book has gone out of print and there isn't any reason to do another full print run. When demand is low, POD is a great option for traditional publishers, who can print only as many copies of a book as they think they can sell, and avoid the expense and hassle of warehousing unsold books. POD enables publishers to maintain a large catalog of backlist titles, and it also allows them to meet demand in the weeks or months between traditional print runs—which used to be a nail-biting time for publishers, who were frustrated knowing that they'd lose customers if a desired book was not immediately available.

In either case—whether POD is employed by a self-published author or by a traditional publisher—POD books are not printed until there is demand for them. POD is a digital technology, which means that it is less difficult and expensive to reprint than it is for traditional offset printing. Small, even tiny, print runs are now economically feasible.

What does this mean for the self-published author? Well, if you have a very small print run (say, one hundred copies) you are definitely going to want to utilize a POD company rather than a traditional offset self-publishing company, which usually has rates that are cheaper the larger the print run. (Some of the self-publishing companies like Xlibris now offer POD rates, too, so be sure you're comparing apples to apples.) With traditional printing, you will get a far lower rate per book if you order a thousand copies than if you order a hundred. POD, on the other hand, is a great equalizer. The per-book cost is going to be significantly more than with offset printing, but if you have a small number of copies you'll usually wind up ahead financially and save some trees in the process.

One thing to be aware of with POD is that it may be harder to get your book on Amazon.com unless you use their POD arm, called Book-Surge. In 2008, Amazon.com came under fire with allegations that it was refusing to allow other POD companies like Lightning Source to sell their authors' books through Amazon.com. A lawsuit is pending.

FIVE GUIDELINES FOR PICKING
A REPUTABLE SELF-PUBLISHER

Unfortunately, there are always people who are out to make a buck at someone else's expense, and the exploding growth of the self-publishing industry has not escaped the attention of scam artists. As more and more authors decide to go it alone with very little publishing experience, some become easy prey for unscrupulous people and companies. Here are some general suggestions. (For more information, a great source is the website Writer Beware, which is specifically geared to science fiction and fantasy authors, but whose advice is almost universally applicable: www.sfwa.org/beware).

1. **Demand to see sample products of any company you decide to use for self-publishing.** Anyone can build a fancy website, but it's hard to tell from a website what a company's finished book might look like. Some companies that have catered to self-publishers have cut corners by using inexpensive paper, which doesn't sound like a big problem until you're trying to read a book that's been printed on it—the typeface can bleed into the reverse side of the page, and the paper doesn't bind well, sometimes resulting in a book that literally falls apart in your hands.

2. **Be careful about using fly-by-night companies and startups.** In self-publishing, the biggest and most established names are iUniverse, Lulu, AuthorHouse, and Xlibris, and there are many other reputable firms as well. (For a detailed comparison of the largest and most well-known self-publishing outfits, check out *The Fine Print of Self Publishing* by Mark Levine.)

3. Be wary of firms that want to charge you editorial fees, or direct you to a particular freelance editor, unless you specifically ask for that. Some past scams, including one from EditInk in the 1990s, had so-called literary agents referring writers to EditInk's services, with the agent receiving a portion of the bogus and inflated editorial fee.

4. Steer clear of firms that promise to get your book into Walmart, Costco, or Barnes & Noble. The odds of this happening are really unlikely, at least before you've proven through your own aggressive sales that the book has "legs." While it may sound appealing to think that your self-publishing company will be able to get your book this kind of distribution, don't kid yourself. Move on.

5. Consider hiring an attorney by the hour to vet any self-publishing contract. Some of these boilerplate contracts are definitely not in the author's favor.

WHEN PUBLISHERS COME CALLING ... FINALLY

As some of the success stories in this chapter have shown, traditional publishers are basically interested in one thing: profit. If you have self-published successfully, you may find yourself in the unexpected position of fielding offers from the very publishers who once turned you down. (If this does happen, please promise to savor the feeling, and blog about it for other struggling writers.)

One thing you should immediately do, before signing a contract with a publisher, is consider finding an agent. The ball is definitely in your court now: You have a demonstrated history of strong sales with this title; you have shown you are the kind of self-promoter that agents and publishers love; and you already have an editor or two wanting to buy your book. Almost any agent would love to represent you at this point because it's a guaranteed sale.

Go through the advice in chapter five about choosing an agent. You are in a position to interview several and choose the very best. You might consider one with legal and contractual experience, because there are going to be some particular issues you want your agent to pay attention to as you morph from self-published author to traditionally published author. For example, say you still have several thousand copies of your book in your garage. You want to retain the ability to sell those yourself at your author events. Your publisher may decide to lower the price of their edition of your book—you had originally set it as a $19.95 paperback, but the publisher wants to sell it at $16.95, which is in line with the industry standard. Which is the price at which you can sell your extra copies? For these and other questions, you'll need an experienced agent going over the fine print of your publishing contract.

One more word on self-publishing vs. traditional publishing. There's no law that says that just because someone wants to marry you, you can't stay single. In other words, just because a publishing house is now interested in your book doesn't mean you are obliged to sign with anyone. You might instead choose to continue self-publishing, especially if you find you are making more money that way and distribution is not a problem. Study the options, get good advice, and then go with your gut.

RESOURCES

If you're serious about self-publishing, be sure to join both the Independent Book Publishers Association (www.pma-online.org) and the Small Publishers Association of North America (www.spannet.org). Here you'll get loads of marketing information, tips, connections, and links to resources.

BOOKS

The Complete Guide to Self-Publishing **by Tom and Marilyn Ross** (Writer's Digest Books). Now in its fifth edition, this has over five hundred pages of information about every stage in the process. This manual is essential if you plan on tackling many of the business aspects of self-publishing, like contracts, order fulfillment, taxes, and printing.

Dan Poynter's Self-Publishing Manual, Volume 2: How to Write, Print and Sell Your Own Book **by Dan Poynter** (Para Publishing). Poynter's popular guide has been updated for the twenty-first century with new information on new technologies, audio options, international rights and more.

The Fine Print of Self-Publishing: The Contracts & Services of 45 Self-Publishing Companies Analyzed, Ranked & Exposed **by Mark Levine** (Bascom Hill). If you are bewildered by all of the choices available among self-publishing, this book compares their services side-by-side, with actual sample contracts from each one.

The Well-Fed Self-Publisher: How to Turn One Book Into a Full-Time Living by Peter Bowerman (Fanove). The subtitle may be a little over the top (you will probably not make a full-time living from one self-published book), but the advice here is creative and first-rate. Almost two-thirds of the book is devoted to marketing and publicity. www.wellfedsp.com and www.wellfedwriter.com

PART THREE

BUILDING YOUR READERSHIP

WE'VE ALL SEEN successful authors on television, describing their books and their seemingly inevitable journey to bestsellerdom. Many of us have felt pangs of writerly jealousy at such moments, imagining ourselves in their chair as they chat with Katie Couric or Diane Sawyer. This is what it will be like when we have arrived. This is what is in store once we get published.

What we don't see is the tremendous work those authors and their publishers put in behind the scenes, often for many years, to get to that place. Far too many new writers simply expect that of course their first book will be featured on *Oprah* and *Good Morning America*. Their book is fascinating and is going to change the world, right? They're just as smart as those "experts" on *Oprah*. So they sit around and wait for the phone to ring. When it doesn't, they blame the person whose job it is "supposed" to be to get an author on national television: the publicist. Why, it's her fault that the book is not a *New York Times* bestseller!

Believe us when they say that these newbie authors simply don't have a clue. For starters, at most publishing companies, publicists are responsible for an unbelievable number of books. We've heard of some publicists who are supposed to promote ninety titles in a year. That's not even including the backlist titles (older books) for which they still sometimes get media inquiries. This kind of expectation is impossible and insane—so the last thing publicists need is a whiny author on the phone berating them for not being star-makers.

So before we start this all-new section of our book—which will contain dozens of realistic, proven publicity ideas and also teach the difference between publicity and marketing—we need every would-be author reading this book to recite The Creed. Go ahead and say it out loud. Commit it to memory.

1. "More than half a million books will be published this year.
2. Only a couple of them will be on *Oprah*.
3. I am in charge of my own publicity."

There now, don't you feel empowered? Your expectations are more realistic, you're in the driver's seat, and you're ready to learn. You may not get your book on national television (though it does happen), but there are tons of things you can do to get the word out. Read on.

12 A CRASH COURSE IN MARKETING AND PUBLICITY

IT'S GREAT TO write a book, and if you've published one, either with a traditional publisher or on your own steam, you deserve congratulations. However, just because you've written it doesn't mean your work is done. In fact, it's probably not even half done in terms of the hours you should be putting in. Even if you are lucky enough to have a professional publicist assigned to your case, you are going to have to work very hard to promote it. This book can't emphasize enough how much book promotion is your responsibility—so this section has been created to show you how to get started.

After a short foray into book marketing, the bulk of this chapter deals with book publicity—as do the two chapters after that. Don't wait until your book is already published to read these chapters; by then, some of the best kinds of publicity are already next to impossible.

WHAT IS MARKETING?

We're going to get book marketing out of the way first because less of it is up to you than publicity is. Although people sometimes assume that publicity and marketing are the same—and they are certainly complementary—they serve different functions.

In the words of Jacqueline Deval, author of *Publicize Your Book!*, marketing is, "quite simply, how to sell books as fast as possible to as many people as possible." Book marketers determine who the readers of a particular book might be—which is often the easy part—and how to reach them success-fully—which is the hard part. Is your Southern novel going to appeal to middle-aged women who enjoy middlebrow contemporary Southern fiction, like fans of Anne Rivers Siddons, or are you aiming toward more of a comic chick-lit Southern audience, such as readers who enjoy Joshilyn Jackson? Are your readers liberal or conservative? Gen-Xers or baby boomers? Dog lovers, nature lovers, bikers? All of these questions are relevant. As an author, you won't be privy to most of the marketing meetings that happen on behalf of your book, but you can help your cause tremendously by having some de-tailed information about the potential audience in your book proposal from Day One.

Here are some issues that a marketing director at a publishing house might deal with:

- **Format and binding.** The marketing team helps to decide whether your book will be hardcover or a "paperback original" (meaning one that debuts in trade paper without a hardcover edition first). Size is also important. They might feel that a Christmas novella needs to be bound as a smaller gift book, perhaps with a ribbon marker. Size, binding, and format all help to set the tone for what type of book yours will be—and what audience will desire it.

- **Book titles.** The right title is paramount in reaching the market for your book. Although some authors resist an audience-specific, niche-oriented title, these often sell better than generic titles. For example, the book *Eat Well, Lose Weight While Breastfeeding* is not terribly catchy, but it successfully identifies its target market right off the bat: new mothers who are nursing and want to lose some of their pregnancy weight. Some titles can be funny and memorable (e.g., *Don't Just Do Something, Sit There*, a book about

Zen meditation), while others are serious (e.g., Fareed Zakaria's *The Post-American World*), and still others are gently evocative, which is the case for most fiction titles (e.g., *Seducing an Angel*). At a publishing house, people on a titling committee actually hold meetings to find just the right title for your book's market. The title you suggested in your book proposal may or may not be the one that winds up on the book's cover. And unless you are already famous and title approval is part of your negotiated contract, you probably won't have much say in the matter. Even if you are famous, you may still be overruled: F. Scott Fitzgerald wanted to call his third novel Trimalchio and was shepherded instead to the title *The Great Gatsby*. Sometimes, publishers really do know what they're doing.

- **Book covers.** The right cover is enormously important for your book. It's not just that consumers make purchasing decisions based on whether they find a cover enticing, it's that store buyers do it as well. One sales representative explains that when he gets his coveted biannual meeting with the fiction buyer at a major chain, he has about thirty minutes to present the entire season's list—which may include fifteen or twenty novels. Store buyers place their orders after a cursory description of each novel and its author, along with a good look at the cover art. Needless to say, a bad cover can defeat a book before it even gets out of the gate, so publishers usually invest a good deal of time and money in getting the right design.

- **Catalog placement.** The marketing team is responsible for preparing a publishing house's seasonal and topical catalogs. Where a book goes in the catalog is often a significant indicator of its prominence on that season's list. The most important books tend to appear at the front of the catalog (or at the beginning of that month's releases, if the catalog is in chronological order), and the oldest books—the backlist—appear in the back. (Get it?)

- **Advertising.** Whether, where, and when to advertise is a nagging question for folks in the marketing department. National book ads are very expensive—thousands of dollars for a small black-and-white placement in *The New York Times* or *The New Yorker*, and many thousands more for a fifteen-second recurring spot on NPR, for example. As it happens, many studies have shown that ads are one of the least consistent or effective ways of selling books. Many ads don't give enough of a sense of the book for its target audience to get excited. Some of the more useful (and cheaper) advertising is actually done in niche publications, like small magazines that target a particular demographic. An ad for a new book about Google's founding is more likely to appeal to the specialized readers of *Wired* than it is to all of the readers of the *San Francisco Chronicle*.

- **In-store placement.** Ever walked into a Borders or a Barnes & Noble and gotten immediately sidetracked by the new or recommended books on the front table? Ever thought, "Hey! This book must be outstanding if it was recommended by the smart people who work at this store"? Well, the truth is that those books actually got "table placement" because their publishers paid for them to be there for a limited period of time, not because a chain store buyer actually read them and thought they were brilliant. That also goes for whether a book is placed on an endcap (an end-of-row display) or a specialized table further back in the store (e.g., "holiday reads" or "book club favorites"). One of the discussions that goes on in the marketing department up to a year in advance is whether to pony up the considerable cash (at least four figures, and often five) that is required for advantageous store placement. They also discuss whether to get a book into some kinds of stores, like airport stores, in the first place. Every book on the shelves of an airport store has paid for the privilege of being there.

Your Marketing Plan

Although you will not be in control of most marketing decisions, especially the ones regarding store placement, catalog placement, and advertising plans, you can and should take the lead in establishing the audience for your book. Do this as early as the book proposal, where you will lay out exactly what the target audience can be and where to find them. Throughout the process, keep the marketing team alert for niche opportunities they might not normally hear about. For example, one author of a book about *Buffy the Vampire Slayer* got hooked into *Slayage*, the online international journal of Whedon Studies, and learned that there would be the first-ever "Buffy Studies" conference right around the time her book was launching. Once she notified her publishing house, the marketing and publicity people got together to actually launch the book at that conference, where the author was a featured speaker. Due to the uniqueness of a "Buffy Studies" conference (yes, there really is such a thing), some major media, including CNN, covered the gathering and interviewed the author. It was a super launch to the book and couldn't have happened if the author had not alerted the publishing house to this unusual opportunity.

You know your book better than anyone, and you should be able to come up with a list of niche publications, conferences, and organizations that could help sell your book. Stay in touch with the marketing director throughout the prepublication months and be sure to let her know about any sales leads you have.

RESOURCES

BOOKS

1001 Ways to Market Your Books, sixth edition by John Kremer (Open Horizons). This reference book is chock full of useful ideas and hints for authors who want to learn about market share and how to expand sales.

The Complete Guide to Book Marketing by David Cole (Allworth Press). Cole offers advice on how to build a brand and market to niche audiences.

Guerilla Marketing for Writers: 100 Weapons for Selling Your Work by Jay Conrad Levinson, Rick Frishman, and Michael Larsen (Writer's Digest Books). This entrepreneurial guide doesn't deal with the Internet, but it does address classic ways to sell your work more traditionally.

WHAT IS PUBLICITY?

Remember when we quoted from Jacqueline Deval's statement that marketing is trying to sell as many books as fast as possible to as many people as possible? Well, the role of publicity is to help people know about those books and their authors. Whereas much of marketing is paid for by the publisher—advertising, the right placement in the store, the perfect cover—publicity is aimed at getting free media coverage. Well, it's *sort of* free. Authors can't simply pay journalists to interview them, but getting their attention can take a lot of expert time and follow-up, so in that sense good publicity can be costly indeed. Here are some helpful things to remember about publicity:

- **Advertising is not publicity**. As we learned in the marketing section, when you see a commercial on television, or a book ad in the incredible shrinking book pages of America's newspapers, those are paid for by someone—usually the company that is pushing the product. In the case of books, that's usually the publisher, though sometimes the author digs deep into his pockets and buys ad time. Although it's a great stroke to authors' egos to see their books advertised in prominent places so their family and friends can see them (as well as any high school bullies who once taunted them), advertising is actually a weak way to generate interest in books. Book consumers are smart people—even smarter than the beer customers who buy a Budweiser just because some frog in a commercial told them to. (We have no actual research to back that last part up, but it *feels* true.) People who buy books know where advertising comes from, who pays for it, and why it exists. They've seen ads for plenty of books that turned out to be a waste of trees, so they're not usually going to buy a book just because of an ad. The best that an ad can do is create what's called an *impression*, and it actually can take several of these before something might actually register on a consumer's radar.

- **The best publicity campaigns succeed in generating word of mouth.** After a book's cover design, the second most effective means of driving sales is "word of mouth" recommendations. Basically, this means that the book needs to be fodder for general conversations:

TED: "Did you hear Thomas Friedman on *The Daily Show* last night? That's the book I was recommending to you about climate change."

CINDY: "I sure did, and after work I'm going out to buy his book!"

Most people trust the opinions of their friends, moms, spouses, and colleagues about what is good to read. And as we just learned, sometimes it takes multiple "impressions" of a product before consumers are ready to actually buy: In the above example, Ted had already told Cindy that *Hot, Flat, and Crowded* was a book she would enjoy, so she was predisposed to listen to the author when she was channel surfing one night and found him chatting with Jon Stewart. Ted's mentioning it to her the next day was a third "impression," and for Cindy, the third time was the charm. Publicity (in the form of an author interview on national television) worked hand-in-hand with grassroots word of mouth to close the deal. The goal of a publicist is to garner enough media coverage to get people talking about a book and recommending it.

- **Publicity capitalizes heavily on what is in the news.** One of the genius aspects of publicity is its timeliness. In the Thomas Friedman example above, we know that *Hot, Flat, and Crowded* became a *New York Times* bestseller, but timing played a role in that success. The book released in September of 2008, just after the highest-ever spike in gasoline prices to around $4.50 a gallon and just before the election of President Barack Obama. Everyone was talking about energy, oil, the Middle East, and politics; the situation was perfect for Friedman's book. Good publicity works in tandem with the news and helps connect potential readers with books that can help them understand timely issues. Of course, this works most seamlessly for nonfiction, but savvy fiction authors do it, too, connecting their novels to items in the headlines. (Sometimes novelists also succeed when people long to get *away* from the news: In late 2008, during the worst economic recession in half a century, sales at Harlequin, the nation's largest romance publisher, were up by 9 percent.)

PUBLICIZING YOUR BOOK

As you can see, it's your job to create the kind of "word of mouth" discussions that can drive sales of your book. Success as a writer often depends on speeches, book signings, newsletters, blog posts, TV appearances, radio interviews, websites, visits to groups, campus talks, and more. Who else knows your book better? Who else is as dedicated to its success? Who else can talk about it as ardently?

In fact, even though you may have a wonderfully written nonfiction book, oftentimes, good writing isn't all that is needed to make it a success. How much you are willing to talk about your book is essential because many publishers are not able to give each book the promotional attention it needs to make it a success. That is up to you, the writer. If you have a book with a wide national audience, the promotion plan is equally, if not more important, than the actual contents of the book. Even well-known authors go on the road, give talks, and do interviews to promote their works. Self-promotion is even recognized by writers as a technique as much a part of writing success as knowing the difference between active and passive voice.

Speak Up

While public speaking is frightening to some writers, it is important to take advantage of any opportunity that allows you to speak about your work to an audience. Not only should you be willing to speak when asked, but also seek out speaking opportunities. Speaking gives you the chance to create excitement about your work in a personal way. You are forming a memorable relationship with the audience if you are prepared and enthusiastic. Getting to hear about an author and his work firsthand will prompt many people in an audience to be interested in your book. They will also be likely to tell someone else about it. If you can walk away with even just a handful of people interested in your book, you have created more potential sales than would have otherwise occurred.

Be imaginative about what groups to address. You'll know some of the best venues in your own area, but there are general resources around to help you. *The Encyclopedia of Associations*, available at libraries, is a compendium of organizations around the world. It can help you find audiences. If you write about nursing, for example, you can find dozens of nursing associations, each of which may have newsletters for members and meetings where you may be permitted to give a presentation. Look up local businesses, churches, and groups that may agree to let you promote your work to their members.

When you speak, it helps to use visual aids. Whitney Otto created a slide show to promote *The Passion Dream Book*, a novel that explores the relationship between art and the lives of artists. The slides also helped her add originality to her tour and broaden it to include libraries and art schools. Visuals are a great way to make your presentation more interesting and engaging, and even more importantly, more memorable.

Go Visit

Remember, part of your job as a writer is also to be a publicist. One way to publicize and promote is to make a point of visiting local bookstores to meet the staff and talk about your book. If bookstore staff know you, they're more likely to put your book in the window (if they get to decide which books belong there). They also may be more likely to recommend your book to customers interested in your topic because your book will stand out in their minds above the others.

Jeanne M. Dams used the *Deadly Directory*, which she calls an indispensable reference for mystery writers, to find mystery bookstores. (Unfortunately, that publication is now, well, dead, having been murdered in 2008 by the brutal economy.) Dams visited every store within driving distance to supplement the book tour arranged by her publisher. "Even when I drew very few people, I established a personal relationship with the bookseller," she says. "That really matters because mystery bookstores hand-sell their books."

If your publisher doesn't spring for book tours (and few will), don't be afraid to plan your own. Some writers have combined book tours with family vacations, hauling the kids and sometimes even the dog along as they traverse the country. Libraries and bookstores often welcome visiting authors who wish to speak or give readings; call or e-mail several months in advance of your planned visit to set things up. E-mail a jpeg or pdf of a flyer about your visit and ask the library or bookstore to please post it widely in the community two to three weeks beforehand.

Once you plan your tour, send a news release to media outlets in every city you'll visit, then follow up with a phone call before you arrive. This will help ensure that you get some media coverage and publicity. Remember that *you* are primarily responsible for getting people to attend signings and readings. Such events succeed or fail based on the author's ability to mobilize her own network.

News Releases

If your publisher doesn't do it for you, write a news release and send it to your media and to any other publication or electronic news organization you want to visit. If you've written a speech, it should be easy to adapt into a brief news release, focusing on whatever major aspect of your work is most useful to a general audience. For tips on how to do this, see Jodee Blanco's *The Complete Guide to Book Publicity*.

Send your release to the editor of the appropriate department at a newspaper, and also to the book editor if the newspaper employs one. For example, releases about books on management go to the business editor; those on relationships go to the features editor. Send your release to the producer of any TV shows you are pitching.

Radio and Television

In some ways, radio is a medium made for authors. You get the chance to talk about your book, and even read aloud from it, which is one of the strongest ways to hook a reader. You also may get the opportunity to interact with readers and potential readers who call in to a radio show to ask questions of the author. And you don't even have to worry about how you look! Seek out radio opportunities whenever you can; if you feel nervous, begin with a few podcasting forays as described in chapter fourteen.

Directories such as *Bradley's Guide to the Top National TV Talk & Interview Shows, Talk Shows and Hosts on Radio,* or *Talk Show Selects* also are helpful in finding hosts on radio and television. Television demands different skills than radio or print interviews, because your appearance is critical. If you're going to be on a TV show and can't afford a media coach, try role-playing an interview and then watching a tape of it. Are any of your mannerisms distracting? Are your answers clear? Can you speak in sound bites of thirty seconds or so? Is your voice expressive? Are you entertaining? And, despite all those questions, do you seem relaxed?

Television can be an intimidating medium, so it's best to start small with your local cable station. Your chances of scheduling a TV interview will be better with a local station, and it won't be as overwhelming. These stations aren't as hectic and will be able to make you feel more comfortable about your experience. They may be more encouraging because they know you are a beginner. Knowing that the audience for these stations is smaller should also help to calm some of your public speaking fears.

If you're still intimidated and can afford it, consider hiring a media coach, who can help you learn how to do interviews. Don't feel like this is necessary, though, because as long as you are passionate about your topic, even if you aren't perfect, you will still be successful.

Write

Another way to promote your work involves writing about it. You are already a writer, so this avenue should appeal to you.

- Newsletters can be highly effective ways of finding and keeping readers, especially as you build a career over many years. You could do your own newsletter, or team up with other writers you know who are looking to promote their work as well. Jeanne Dams and three other mystery writers, Barbara D'Amato, Hugh Holton, and Mark Zubro, started a newsletter to promote their books. They started their mailing list by asking their publishers to slip a postcard for a subscription into their books. They mail their newsletter to anyone who responds to the postcard and also to anyone else they think might be interested. Into it goes an article by each author, mystery quizzes, even recipes for foods mentioned in their books. Most importantly, the newsletter always includes a list of the authors' appearances and their books in print. It can be a time-consuming and expensive promotional tool, but if you team up with other authors, you can split the costs and still reap the rewards.

- Instead of mailing print newsletters, consider doing an e-mail newsletter. The cost for this could be significantly less. If you have a website or blog (which you should; see the following chapter), you can add a link asking people to subscribe to your free e-mail newsletter. Include information about your books, appearances, and anything else that might interest people who enjoy your work or the topics you write about.

- Op-ed pieces are another great way for writers to build enthusiasm for a book, especially with more serious nonfiction, where an author's expertise is a critical component of selling the book.

Network

Everyone was a beginner once, and many successful authors remember how difficult it was to become established. These authors are often a tremendous resource to beginners. The book you're reading now wouldn't exist without the generosity of writers, agents, and editors who took time to share their expertise.

Joining a writers' association and attending writers' conferences can help you learn how to write and sell your work, but more importantly, these networks help you meet people who may be able to help you—and whom you may be able to help. You must be sincerely willing to help others and unafraid to ask for help yourself. You never know what someone else is willing to do for you until you ask.

Writers' groups also can help their members promote their work. C.J. Songer, author of the Meg Gillis crime novel series, used a list published by Sisters in Crime, a group for mystery writers, to reach independent bookstores. Through the group, she also bought a discounted ad in *Publishers Weekly*. "Although it was a fair amount of money, *Bait* was my first-ever book and it was a treat to myself," Songer says. Because she had taken that ad, she also earned a discount on a promotional page for her book on the *Publishers Weekly* website. "It was very gratifying to be able to go online and see my own book, plus it was accessible for family and friends (and acquaintances) all across the country," she says.

Networking is infinitely easier now in the age of social media, which we'll cover in the next chapter. Online affinity groups and public forums like Facebook have made it easier than ever to reach thousands of like-minded readers with a single click.

RESOURCES

The Complete Guide to Book Publicity by Jodee Blanco (Allworth Press). This book is actually geared for professional publicists, teaching them how to pitch to the media, find multiple story angles for the same book, and handle PR disasters. But authors should read it too, to learn how publicists think and glean ideas for successful book promotion.

Get Known Before the Book Deal: Use Your Personal Strengths to Grow an Author Platform by Christina Katz (Writer's Digest Books). This excellent book focuses on the platform-building and networking that happen before you even submit a book proposal to an editor or agent. Much of the advice is also applicable to the crucial months just before and after your book is published.

Publicize Your Book!: An Insider's Guide to Getting Your Book the Attention it Deserves by Jacqueline Deval (Perigee). Now updated, this how-to guide puts authors in the driver's seat and empowers them to create pitches, develop a press kit, prepare for interviews, and more. The author also has a helpful website at www.publicizeyourbook.com.

13 WEBSITES, BLOGS, PODCASTS, AND SOCIAL NETWORKING

LET'S TAKE A little walk through literary history, shall we? It used to be that authors' main connection with readers, if it existed at all, was through touring and correspondence. In the nineteenth century, famous novelists like Charles Dickens and Mark Twain went on tour, often for months at a time, filling great lecture halls and taking questions from readers. In the twentieth century, with the advent of radio and then television, authors could communicate with thousands or even millions of readers at a time through interviews and readings on the air. This was an enormous leap forward for book publicists, who worked tremendously hard to maximize exposure for authors and get them booked on the most popular programs.

Now, however, it is the twenty-first century, and the rules are changing once again. According to Penny Sansevieri, author of *Red Hot Internet Publicity*, the advent of blogs and podcasts has meant that "the TV programs we would have traded a kidney for in the past are not even skimming the surface of the media that really drives readers to books, and consequently, to sales." Nowadays the Internet has brought us an unprecedented democratization in how books are publicized.

What makes the difference is peer groups: Whereas traditional print, TV, and radio publicity hit a broad audience in a shallow way, these new online media target a narrower audience in a deeper way. Blogs, podcasts, and social networks tap into word-of-mouth book recommendations, which have always been a powerful means of driving sales. Potential customers who might just breeze by an ad or even a well-placed radio interview will give serious thought to buying a book that's recommended by a blogger they trust or given five stars on www.goodreads.com by their sister.

What's marvelous about the Internet is that it has the potential to link you directly to like-minded readers who might be interested in your book. You have the chance to get direct access to your target audience. And best of all, it's basically free.

YOUR WEBSITE

Five years ago, it was enough for an author just to have a nicely designed, professional-quality website. It was the end-all destination, with an author biography, a page for each book the author had to her credit, and maybe a few links to media articles.

Nowadays, you need to change the way you think about your author website. It is no longer a destination or end goal, but a *portal*. As Internet publicity has exploded, a website has become a starting point in driving sales, but it is not the last word. Here are some things your website might have:

- **A place to buy.** The fanciest author sites allow customers to buy the book right from the site, but this can be difficult and expensive to do. Others link directly to Amazon.com through the Amazon Associates program so customers can click through to buy the book, and the author gets a small kickback from the sale.

- **A very obvious connection to your blog.** Some writers have made the move to have the front page of their website be their blog; others prefer to have the "official" site be more formal but have a clear place where visitors can click to get to the regularly updated blog. We'll explore blogging in a moment, but for now just know that if you decide to have a blog, you need to integrate it seamlessly with your author website.

- **A clear connection to your podcast,** if you have one.

- **A place to sign up for your e-mail newsletter.** As we saw in the last chapter, an electronic newsletter (preferably HTML and not just text) can be a great way to communicate with your readers. Make sure your website is designed to capture the names and e-mail addresses of readers who want to keep abreast of your writing and speaking engagements.

- **Links to related sites.** Add links to other websites that will be relevant to anyone interested in your work. If you write about science, for example, include links to scientific websites.

Building Your Website

If you don't already have a website, you need to reserve your domain name immediately. Preferably, this is your own name as it will appear on all your books (e.g., www.AmyMarieAuthor.com). If that domain name has been taken, either by another person with your same name or an entrepreneurial computer program that is looking to make a buck, you need to decide what to do. If you haven't published your first book yet, change your author name. Seriously. Use a pen name or another version of your real name (James instead of Jim, Kathy and not Katherine) if your name's site has already been taken, or try your first and middle initials with your last name. If that's not an option, you can try to buy the real domain name from the current user.

Once you have registered a domain name, it's time to build your site. Most authors tend to hire a professional for this; a clunky, unprofessional, or ugly site is actually worse than having no site at all. If you can't afford to hire an experienced web designer, try a student, whose rates will be much cheaper. If you can't afford to hire a student, you can go it alone with template software and then upgrade the site after your career is better established. Remember that the website is a portal, not a destination, so your links are crucial. So whether you hire a designer or try the DIY method, make sure your site is accessible and interactive.

SEO: Search Engine Optimization

It's great to set up a beautiful website, but what if you build it and they don't come? What if it's like that old *Brady Bunch* episode where Peter throws himself a hero party and none of his friends show up?

That's why you have to let technology work for you—to invite others to your party. You can do this through SEO (search engine optimization). Try a little experiment right now and Google yourself. (Yes, it seems immodest, but it's really okay.) Ideally, what you want to find on the first page of the Google search results, in roughly this order, are:

1. Your book's website or author website.
2. The Amazon.com page for your book so these prospects can easily "convert" into becoming paying customers.
3. Various media interviews or blog reviews of your book.

If your book isn't out yet, or you don't even have a publisher yet, you're not going to see those last two items, but you at least want your author site to be one of the top things that comes up whenever someone Googles your name. If you are already published, you will probably also see some library results too, plus any op-eds you've written about your topic (you *have* been working on those, right?).

You'll probably notice that your author site will slowly climb the Google rankings in the weeks surrounding your book's release, especially if your site has an active blog. You can actually use your blog to generate a higher Google ranking by linking, linking, linking. For more tips on optimizing your Google ranking, go to www.smartzville.com/google-homepage.htm. One key element of success, especially for nonfiction, is getting your name so associated with your topic so your name comes up very high on the list when someone Googles your topic. There are many ways to do this: by writing and blogging so often about the topic that other people link to your page, which will help your Google ranking; by getting multiple media interviews about your topic; and by focusing on popular keywords and metatags on your site.

BLOGGING

If you are serious about your writing—and especially if you plan a career in this rather than just one book—you need to create a blog. A blog, short for "weblog," can be anything from a public diary about your life to a running commentary about a specific topic: figure skating, science fiction movies, celebrity gossip, whatever interests you. There's even a wildly popular blog devoted to cakes gone wrong, where every day the owner posts photos of a different cake disaster.

As an author, your blog needs to be devoted to things that are relevant to your book. Now, listen up for a very important distinction (which will also come into play in this chapter's section on podcasting): *The sole purpose of your blog cannot be to advertise yourself or your books.* People lose interest very quickly when they feel they're being subjected to an endless round of "Look at me!" promotions.

What people want instead is good information. If they've looked you up and have thought about buying your book, it's because they're interested in the topic you write about (for nonfiction) or the genre you write in (for fiction). As an example, let's take the hypothetical case of a popular romance novelist we'll call Amara Love. Amara updates her blog about five times a week with fresh content, sometimes discussing trends in the romance writing business, sometimes revealing where she is with a forthcoming book, sometimes making movie recommendations for the latest romantic comedy to hit theaters. She has book giveaways every once in a while to drive traffic to her site (both her own novels and other favorite writers), and she takes reader questions all the time by publicly answering some of the e-mails she receives via the "contact me" button on the blog.

Some novelists have taken blogging a step further by actually blogging as their characters. Meg Cabot, author of the YA *Princess Diaries* series, blogs in the voice of Princess Mia at www.miathermopolis.com. Teen readers love the free extra content they're getting via the blog, and the blog helps document Mia's life in "real time" as teens are experiencing it themselves: spring break, summer break, holidays, etc. You don't have to go to the extreme of blogging as a character, but you do need to create a community and give useful information.

Getting Started

From a tech standpoint, blogging is quite easy. While we suggest hiring a real web designer for your author portal site, even a neophyte can create a blog in about half an hour using the templates on Blogger, TypePad, or WordPress. You'll often pay a monthly fee for administration, though others are free and offer free templates online. Some authors have a blog professionally designed, and if you can afford this, knock yourself out. But know that you don't have to unless you expect the audience for your book to be exceptionally tech-savvy.

The things your blog must have are links, contact information, and a tagline up top that succinctly describes what your blog is about. A tagline could be "There's an App for That" for an iPhone-news related blog, or "Cats Say the Darndest Things" if you wrote a book about how felines communicate and want your blog to be a meeting place for fellow cat lovers.

TEN HOT TIPS FOR YOUR NEW BLOG

1. **Be sure to enable "trackbacks,"** which will help to drive traffic to your site. Also, set it up so your posts are stamped with the date so readers will be able to recognize fresh content.

2. **When you post, learn how to link to almost anything you can**—other blogs in your field, the pages of books and movies you write about in your posts, articles you find interesting, etc. Every time you do this, you help Google to "spider" your blog. On the Internet, a spider is actually a good thing: It's a web of incoming and outgoing links, all of which help to drive up your Google ranking and generate traffic.

3. **Let friends, family, and acquaintances know about your new blog.** If they are bloggers, politely ask if they would mind linking to your blog from theirs. These incoming links are even more valuable for your blog's Google ranking than your outgoing ones.

4. **Allow reader comments.** Sometimes authors worry about editorial control issues with blog comments, but as the site's

owner you can choose to remove any individual comments if they should ever be offensive. Ninety-nine percent of comments should be welcome, though, so open the doors!

5. **Don't be afraid to be opinionated.** Some of the liveliest blog discussions happen when you take issue with something or persuasively express a strong opinion. Always be respectful, however.

6. **Periodically search Google for your blog's topic, and follow those links to other people's blogs.** If they are discussing something you have just posted about, leave a comment about their discussion and also a link to your own blog. This is a great way to find blog readers who are already interested in your topic.

7. **Try to blog five to seven times a week.** You can do this by keeping your posts short (say, 200 to 500 words) and by having some of your posts be links to articles and questions under discussion. You can also invite "guest bloggers" or post interviews with other people in your field. If doing multiple posts a week is unrealistic, commit to blogging twice a week on the same days—say, Monday and Thursday. You will build more of a following when readers know when to expect your posts.

8. **Make sure to enable "pinging" with each blog post.** This is what alerts blog directories that you have published a new post.

9. **Allow your blog to utilize RSS (really simple syndication),** which is a subscriber feed that people can sign up for when they're interested in your blog. This alerts readers automatically whenever you've updated your content.

10. **Have a contest or giveaway every few months.** You can hold trivia contests, haiku competitions, whatever you like. Readers who normally "lurk" (read but don't comment) will come out of the woodwork when there's free merchandise on the table.

The Secret, Most Important Reason Why You Should Blog

Still not convinced you need to start a blog? Here's the real reason why you must, especially if you are a nonfiction author trying to establish yourself as an expert on some topic: A blog is now the expected vehicle through which members of the media will find sources. Not only will they cyberstalk you on your own author website and blog, they will also monitor how often your book and blog are mentioned on *other* people's blogs using services like Technorati (www.technorati.com). How often other people cite you as an expert or favorably review your book increases your stature in the eyes of the media.

Journalists also trawl blogs to get a feel for how "hot" a topic is, which is one of the reasons why you want to encourage comments on your blog. They often want to see how so-called ordinary people might be experiencing a particular topic. For example, if you've just written a book about a double-digit fall in housing prices, a journalist will be interested to see that forty people have commented on your most recent post about new housing legislation, some of them sharing personal tales of foreclosure.

Be sure to have a "contact me" button on your blog. Your e-mail address won't be on it for readers, so it's one-way communication and you don't have to worry about mad fans showing up at your house. (As if.)

Remember that for members of the media, time is of the essence. They might only have a couple of hours before they need to turn in their copy or book a radio interview for the end-of-day rush hour, and they're going to want to hear back from you right away. If you're lucky enough to have generated media interest, don't blow it by not checking your messages. Arrange to have the "contact me" messages from your blog sent to an e-mail account you check several times a day.

MANAGING THE FLOW—MAKE THAT AVALANCHE—OF INFORMATION

Many writers complain that they just don't have the time to blog or follow other people's blogs, and it's true that the blogosphere can be an enormous time sink. To help you manage the flow of information, sign up for Google Reader, a tool that customizes your blog reading and keeps you up-to-date with new posts from other people. (www.google.com/reader)

With Google Reader, and other services like it, you can subscribe to any blog you like or want to keep up with, and it will customize a sort of home page for you and chart which posts you have and have not read. You don't have to click on each post to go to it; the posts

PODCASTING

It's safe to say that many successful authors are now blogging, and that blogging is all but required if you want to have a strong career and regular interaction with readers. Admittedly, that's not yet the case with podcasting, which hasn't yet hit the mainstream author community as strongly (yet), but is still a powerful tool for you as an author. So think of it as an optional, but potentially influential, path for you. If you are already a talented oral communicator and feel comfortable in chatty conversation, a podcast may be just the ticket.

What Is a Podcast?

A podcast is a new-fashioned kind of radio show. It's all on the Internet, and listeners can either hear the show online or download it to their MP3 players or iPods. One advantage of podcasting is that the start-up costs are quite low and you don't have to worry about attracting advertisers. (Though you can certainly sell ads if you want to.) You do have to worry about attracting listeners, though. A podcast isn't like a traditional radio show where some listeners just stumble onto the content because it happens to be on the air. With podcasting, listeners have to know to look for your show.

Luckily, that is getting easier all the time as podcasting becomes more mainstream. You can syndicate your podcast through a site like Google Feed-Burner (http://feedburner.google.com), which works like a blog's RSS feed in alerting your listeners whenever there's a new episode of your show.

Unlike blogging, which is easy to set up, podcasting requires a little more technical expertise. You're going to need either an external microphone for your computer or a site like AudioAcrobat (www.audioacrobat.com), which permits you to record your show by phone or via Skype from anywhere in the world. (Skype is an online service that allows users to make phone calls and conduct video conferences, often for free, over the Internet. See www.skype.com.)

What Kind of Podcast?

You may be wondering what a good podcast might sound like. Really, the Skype's the limit (pun intended); think of your podcast like an audio blog. There are as many different kinds of podcasts as there are authors, but here are three basic types.

> **1. The interview podcast.** This is the one that most closely resembles a traditional radio show. Say you've written a book about minor league baseball. Your weekly podcast might involve interviews with present and former minor league players, umpires, fans, and the like. You'd be surprised how easy it is to get guests on your podcast, especially if you give them a good idea of what to expect and keep the interview under fifteen minutes. (By the way, always encourage your guests to link to the podcast on their own sites and blogs to help drive traffic to your podcast.)

> **2. The commentary podcast.** This is a talking-heads type show, where you are the expert giving commentary on your topic. For example, in the minor league baseball example above, you would offer opinions on new draft picks, spring training observations, bad umpire calls, and the

like. Be sure to keep it short and have the length of your podcasts be fairly consistent. Ten to twenty minutes of commentary is plenty.

3. The call-in podcast. From a technical standpoint this is the hardest type of show to produce, because you have to worry about the audio quality not only for yourself and your guest but also for the callers, but it's potentially the most riveting in terms of interactions with interested callers.

As you've probably noticed, there's no law that says your podcast can't combine these elements. Some of the most compelling shows are the ones that mix your opinion and your guests' expertise with your callers' questions, *Talk of the Nation* style.

Be creative but consistent with your content; you are building a brand, and listeners should know what to expect. Link to your podcast from your website and/or blog. Ask listeners and blog readers which guests they would like to hear you interview, or which issues they'd like to have you cover. Remember: It's all about community.

SOCIAL NETWORKING

If blogging and podcasting are steps toward building a community, social networking is like an enormous potluck: You never quite know who is bringing what or how many people will be there, but you're pretty much guaranteed to get a good meal. (Even if you feel a little bloated afterward.)

Social networking is still recent enough that many people are just learning the ropes, and no one is quite sure of the best methods for using it to sell books. This means that authors have a great opportunity ahead as they try different things to see what works with their particular audience. In this section we'll explore three of the most popular kinds of social media, but be aware that there are many more already and will undoubtedly be dozens of niche sites in the future, including some focused on books.

MySpace

MySpace, which according to *The Wall Street Journal* has consistently had between 100 million and 120 million users, has been eclipsed recently by Facebook, which had that number in early 2008 but had grown to 300 million users by the middle of 2009. Still, MySpace is one of the most important social media sites. Billed as "a place for friends," MySpace emphasizes interpersonal relationships and the accumulation of contacts. Most authors are not on MySpace, and this is fine unless you fall into either one of these two categories:

- YA. If you are a YA novelist or even if you write nonfiction books for teens, you absolutely need a MySpace page. That's because the site remains the most important social networking medium for teens and young adults. Everyone who is anyone is going be there—which means you should be, too.

- You write about music. MySpace has become the It Site for bands and those who love them. All types of music are represented on MySpace, from classical and pop to rap and hip-hop. Artists can post streaming video of performances, upload digital audio files, and enlist fans and friends. If you write about popular culture and the music scene, you need to create a presence on MySpace.

It's easy to set up a MySpace account, post pictures, and find friends. When you set up your account, use a couple of author photos and also your book cover(s) among your "top eight" photographs. You want potential friends—who are also potential customers—to be exposed to your book visually as well as in any blog posts or updates you do on MySpace.

Facebook

Facebook, now the top social networking site in the world, grew 127 percent in 2008 and as of press time had surpassed 300 million users. It vaulted past MySpace so suddenly in part because Facebook's ads were less obnoxious and obtrusive; many adult MySpace customers began switching loyalties when they discovered that Facebook might be less aggressive about constant sales pitches.

This should tell us something. No one joins Facebook to become fodder for sales pitches. They join because they want to connect with old or distant friends they never get to see. If authors (or companies) exploit Facebook as a sales tool in too obvious a way, people will simply tell Facebook to "block" that person.

TEN HOT TIPS FOR USING FACEBOOK

1. **"Friend" promiscuously.** Yes, you'll be hearing from some people you never imagined you would see again (and weren't terribly sorry to lose in the first place), but you'll be amazed at how much most of us have grown up since high school. Old friends and acquaintances can turn out to be among the strongest supporters of your writing. Once you get a name established as a writer, you'll also start getting friend requests from readers you've never met. Some writers friend everyone who asks but set parameters on Facebook for which ones will appear in their news feed; others create separate accounts for their work and personal lives.

2. **Comment widely on other people's links and status updates.** Facebook is all about community, so don't just stand

---

on a platform and shout about your work with a megaphone. Get involved in conversations about other people's status updates, links, and photographs. It's fun in its own right, and it makes people more likely to pay attention to your posts.

3. **Don't just promote yourself.** All work and no play make Facebook a very dull place indeed. While you don't want to overwhelm Facebook friends with details about the fight you just had with your teen or the bills you're struggling to pay, it's great to post status updates and photographs about your life and family outside of work. What movies are you seeing? Who do you think should win on *American Idol*? Writers are people, too, and readers like to see that they are interested in sports, volunteer opportunities, and the like.

4. **Alert friends to new releases, book signings, and works in progress.** When there's something concrete and specific going on with your book, don't be afraid to shout about it. Friends who stay with you through all the steps between "An agent finally wrote back and said she wants to represent me!" to "I got a good review in *Library Journal*!" want to know these things. Let them know about upcoming author appearances and speaking engagements. Link to reviews or discussions about your latest book.

5. **Push your blog posts and tweets to Facebook.** One way to cut down on the tendency many people have to feel overwhelmed by social media is to arrange your various accounts to talk to each other. For example, most blog programs have

a tools section to help you automatically update the blog with any new tweets. The reverse is true if you also use Twitterfeed, which pushes any new blog entries to all of your Twitter followers.

6. **Become a fan of your publishing house.** Most publishing houses now have a presence on Facebook, and you'll want to show your support for your press (and also receive any important general updates about products and breaking news) by becoming a fan.

7. **Create a fan page for yourself or your book.** It's easy to create a fan page, but some people feel awkward or conspicuous doing this. It can be a bit much for friends to receive a news update that says, "Amy Marie Author became a fan of Amy Marie Author," inviting them to also become a fan. If you don't feel comfortable creating your own book or author fan pages, ask a friend to do it for you. You can send this friend any updates or announcements to post.

8. **Create a Facebook "event" for the month of your book's launch.** Ask friends to RSVP if they will buy the book during that window of time, and make them eligible for special giveaways if they also blog about it then, review it on Amazon.com, link to the book or its trailer in their status update, etc. (You can choose to hide the guests who are not attending, and only show the ones who are definitely or maybe attending.)

9. **Follow other authors on Red Room (www.redroom.com).** Launched in 2008, Red Room, another social media site,

claims it has an "author centric" mission to connect authors with readers. It works with publishers to sell authors' works on the site, and with Facebook to upload member-writers' Red Room blog posts to their social media profiles. Red Room is selective about the authors it represents, but it costs nothing to become a follower, and you can learn a lot about promotion this way.

10. **Remember the three Ps: Public + Permanent = Privacy Settings.** The default mode on Facebook is always open sharing. Unless you tell Facebook otherwise, almost anyone—and not just designated friends—can have access to your friend list, profile, and even your photographs. And unless you tell Facebook otherwise, absolutely anyone in your "default network" (which would be your hometown, high school or college, or city of residence) can see your status updates. All this openness can lead, and has led, to some very embarrassing situations for people who didn't realize that information or photos they thought were private were in fact in the public eye. Remember Miss New Jersey 2007, who was publicly disgraced when her humiliating Facebook photos made the national news? Learn from those mistakes and adjust your privacy settings to allow your photos, videos, and status updates to be seen by the friends you approve. Even after doing this, just work under the assumption that everything you post will be both public and permanent, and exercise appropriate caution.

Twitter

(Note: If we were being true to form, then this section would only be 140 characters. We're already more than halfway there!)

Think of Twitter as "microblogging." It's only been around since 2006, and really just took off at the end of 2008, so it's still untried—and has yet to make a profit for its creators. And yet Twitter is exploding in users. We won't venture any statistics, because by the time you read this book those numbers will be hopelessly out of date. Millions of people are now following other people on Twitter, some of whom they have met, and many they have not. Followers read these people's 140-character "tweets," often "retweeting" them to others—i.e., forwarding them on. Once people have signed up to read your tweets, they can follow you on their smart phone, on Facebook, on your blog, or online at www.twitter.com.

Some adventurous authors have begun to use Twitter to keep in touch with readers—even before their books are published. According to *Publishers Weekly*, author Rebecca Skloot began tweeting about her 2010 science book *The Immortal Life of Henrietta Lacks* in early 2009. She assembled an audience for the book by building her tweets around similar content that science readers would care about. "I treat my Twitter feed like a mini-publication, a place where I tell readers about things I think they'd be interested in, as in, 'if-you-like-my-stuff-you-should-definitely-read-this,'" Skloot told *PW*. "I interact a lot with readers there, but I very rarely post personal stuff, except for occasional posts about the progress of my book, which let people know that it's coming."

Other authors tweet about their signings, appearances, and media interviews, as well as what they're thinking about national issues and things in the news. Since Twitter is so new, publishers and authors are just now learning strategies that work successfully. In 2009 Chelsea Green Publishing made news by having a contest for readers to "Tweet This Book" for one of their new releases. During the four-minute contest time, they had twenty-seven contestants and forty-five total entries of people who tweeted about the book to their own followers. Now, that doesn't sound like much, but according to tech blogger Chris Webb (www.ckwebb.com), that doesn't account for how many people actually saw the forty-five tweets from these twenty-seven people: 14,216 Twitter users. As a bonus, The Huffington Post picked up one of the funniest entries, which further expanded the network of people who had been exposed to that book title. So here's the breakdown:

> Potential customers reached: Fourteen thousand plus
> Time spent: Less than five minutes
> Cost to publisher: One book given away to the winner

That sounds like a pretty decent promotion to us. As you can see, the possibilities of using Twitter to generate word of mouth are endless.

GETTING STARTED ON TWITTER

If you're thinking of beginning to Twitter, spend a week or two as a follower first. Sign up for some of the wonderful tweets about writing that Writer's Digest Books puts out every Friday. Like Facebook, Twitter is free to users, so you've got nothing to lose except time. Go to www.twitter.com to learn more.

You'll need to decide what kind of Twitterer you're going to be. Your followers don't want to be pitched your book constantly. They want to get an author's take on a subject they're passionate about—or in the case of fiction, characters they love. In fact, some novelists actually use Twitter as if they were microblogging as their characters.

You'll want to decide how much information is too much information (TMI). Most of the people who follow you on Twitter want to know about your work, not what you're grilling out on the deck tonight. (There are exceptions, of course, but most followers get annoyed if your tweets are often frivolous. Some authors have two Twitter accounts: one for friends and family, and one for readers. This may be more trouble than it's worth, so try to keep your Twittering professional. Ask yourself what information will be truly useful to your followers. A restaurant that tweets out its daily pie and soup specials each morning is useful to patrons; a restaurant that tweets about the &*!@*$$ coffeemaker being on the fritz again is just irritating.

RESOURCES

The Facebook Era: Tapping Online Social Networks to Build Better Products, Reach New Audiences, and Sell More Stuff **by Clara Shih** (Prentice Hall). Although this is not specifically about book marketing, it does have excellent information about how to use Facebook to your advantage, with examples from established retail companies.

Plug Your Book! Online Book Marketing for Authors by **Steve Weber** (Weber Books). This guide deals with search engine optimization, Google rankings, tags, and click ads as well as social networking sites, especially MySpace.

Podcasting for Dummies by **Tee Morris, Chuck Tomasi, and Evo Terra** (Wiley). How to envision, create, and promote your podcast.

Red Hot Internet Publicity by **Penny Sansevieri** (Morgan James). This book focuses on how to use the Internet to create word-of-mouth success, with chapters on blogging, podcasting, virtual book events, and Amazon.com.

Twitter Power: How to Dominate Your Market One Tweet at a Time by **Joel Comm** (Wiley). Though this focuses on how businesses can use Twitter to build brands and provide better customer service, there are lots of tips that would also apply to authors.

14 FIFTY IDEAS TO GET THE WORD OUT ABOUT YOUR BOOK

IN *1001 WAYS to Market Your Books*, John Kremer discusses—you guessed it—just over a thousand things you can do to promote your writing and build your audience. However, he cautions that most people should choose half a dozen to a dozen of those things and try to do those few things exceptionally well. Not all writers will be successful at everything: Not everyone is an electrifying speaker, for example, and not everyone would feel comfortable cold-calling radio talk show hosts to ferret out an invitation to speak on the air. Play to your strengths.

In this chapter, we've offered just fifty ways for you to get the word out about your writing. Make a commitment to implement ten to start out with (no cheating—they can't just be things you planned to do anyway). Some are marked "fast," indicating that they are ones you should be able to implement in ten minutes or less.

BEFORE YOUR BOOK IS PUBLISHED

1. Write a fantastic press release. Good publicists know that a "media kit"—all of the elements that are mailed to potential reviewers and journalists—doesn't try to give away the contents of the entire book. The press release, which is the linchpin of a strong media kit, will usually be just a page long and will focus only on the most salient aspects of the book. Work with your publicist to craft a good one. You know your book cold (and will be very fortunate if the publicist has had time to read it); the publicist knows what issues the media actually care about. For tips on getting started, consult Writer's Helper (www.writershelper.com) and eHow (www.ehow.com).

2. Write an author Q&A. Many great press kits include a short Q&A with the author. Don't wait for someone to ask you probing questions about your work; ask and answer them yourself. If you have a publicist, give her the Q&A several months before the book's release so the interview can be sent alongside any advance galleys and press releases. Here are some tips:

- Keep your answers short. You don't want to give away the store; you just want to give a taste. A good Q&A whets the appetite but does not give away so much of the plot or information that the reader no longer needs to buy the book.

- Aim for a total of 500–750 words, including questions.

- Try to make it lively and engaging, unless that detracts from the spirit or gravitas of your book. (If you are writing a how-to guide to a respectful funeral, for example, you may want to skip the humor.)

- Don't make the interview merely an expanded outline of your book. Rather, use the interview to discuss how and why you came to the topic or story, how writing the book has changed you personally, and what you hope it will offer to readers.

- Make it personal without oversharing; this is the story behind the story.

- "Repurpose" the interview for your book's website and link to it on your author site. Also, don't be surprised if members of the media quote from it in articles or ask you the same questions in radio interviews. They are busy people who love it when you do their grunt work for them.

3. Understand that your publicity campaign needs to begin months before the book is published. By the time your book is released, it's already too late for some of the major national media attention you'll want to try for, including author interviews or spreads in magazines or reviews in *Publishers Weekly* and *Library Journal*. Six months ahead of time is not too early to send galleys to those publications, and three months ahead of time is usually too late. Also, realize that many of the most important conversations about your book happen before it is even published, when chain stores like Barnes & Noble decide how many copies they're going to order. Try to learn the timeline of these events from your publisher so you can help your successes to feed off one another: A strong, early buy-in from the chains can help to fuel prepublication buzz, which generates early reviews, which lead to foreign rights sales and publicity opportunities, which drive stronger consumer sales. So start early! Once the book is published, many of the most important promotional avenues will be closed to you.

4. [FAST] Make sure the media kit has the publicist's full contact information—and yours, if the publicist is willing for the press to contact you directly. It's amazing how many press releases and media kits bury the publicist's contact information, or fail to provide an e-mail address (the default initial method of communication for most busy reviewers and journalists).

5. Don't blow off your author questionnaire. Your AQ is designed to help the publishing house help you, which is why it's perfectly amazing how many authors complete it hastily or never turn it in at all. The AQ normally includes the author's background information, media contacts, speaking engagements, and a list of potential reviewers and endorsers to whom the publisher should send the book. Use the AQ to describe specific conferences, selling opportunities, and connections.

6. Understand that bound galleys are expensive. It might cost your publisher three times as much money to print up a bound advance reader copy (ARC) as it does to print a copy of the finished book. Have realistic expectations about how many bound ARCs your publishing house is going to be able to print and mail for you, and help your publicist target the list of recipients so those precious ARCs don't just wind up in someone's recycling bin. (And don't send them to your friends and family.) Some publications, like *Library Journal* and *Publishers Weekly*, will not usually take an electronic galley or pdf, but many smaller ones will   which is both cheaper and easier for your publisher. And some journalists who are interviewing you don't even need to see the whole book, but will be fine with the press kit and an e-mailed version of the first few chapters.

7. Prepare a press list to give your publicist four to six months prior to publication. Give your publicist a list of targeted niche publications, explaining why these publications should get a review copy. Publicists are usually happy to send out review copies (up to a limit) if they honestly believe it will help. If you've been doing your research about the most effective blogs, e-zines, and journals in your area of expertise, prepare a list of those to supplement the standard list your publicist probably uses for almost every book. Also identify any major anniversaries or conferences related to your topic (e.g., the bicentennial of Lincoln's birthday for a historical biography). Your publicist shouldn't be expected to be an expert on your topic's unique sales opportunities.

8. Ask if you can speak briefly at the publisher's launch meeting. A "launch meeting" is a multiday conference where almost everyone at your publishing house gets together to hear presentations about books that are coming on the next season's list. It's a great chance for personal interaction and for the sales force to hear you describe your book with humor and passion. If you do it well, this will ignite *their* passion for your book.

LEARNING ABOUT THE INDUSTRY AND GETTING KNOWN

9. Subscribe to *PW Daily, Publishers Lunch, Mediabistro*'s daily e-mail newsletter, and other free industry alerts.

Reading these regularly will give you a better sense of the business end of publishing and bookselling, and help you intuit what kinds of story angles might interest the media. Writer's Digest also runs several blogs you can subscribe to for up-to-date information on publishing, agents, writing techniques, and more.

10. If you know *any* members of the media, bloggers, or other "big names" who can help, add them to the press list you give to your publicist. Explain how you know them and provide full contact information.

11. If you're a novelist, work on a nonfiction hook. It's much harder to publicize fiction than nonfiction, so work hard on ways to tie your novel in with the news. Does it deal with medical ethics, like Jodi Picoult's novel *Handle With Care?* Is it about commercial developers encroaching on a beloved landscape? A child who doesn't fit in? All of these fiction topics are potential fodder for nonfiction buzz and conversation.

12. Contribute op-ed pieces. Op-ed essays, or "opinion editorials," are a wonderful way to elevate your status as an expert on your topic. It's hard to break into the national newspapers like *The New York Times* or *USA Today*, but some of the regional dailies are part of syndicated news services (e.g., Knight Ridder, Reuters) through which your piece might be picked up by other papers. Mention the name of your book in the byline.

13. Create an e-zine. This one takes some effort, but can pay off handsomely. In the past, many successful authors rewarded their readers with quarterly newsletters that described new projects, book tours, and appearances, etc. Unfortunately, these newsletters were expensive to print and to mail, so the authors often wondered whether it was all worth it. Today, authors have no excuse! An e-zine has no printing costs, no shipping costs, and fewer headaches than a print publication. It does take some time and effort to generate content, but it's worth it if it helps you communicate with your audience. You can capture potential readers' e-mail addresses from your blog, your book signings, and your personal networks.

USING YOUR WEBSITE, BLOG, AND E-MAIL

14. [FAST] Turbocharge your e-mail signature. This one should take five minutes, tops. Go into your e-mail program and choose "settings" or whatever menu allows you to change your signature (the contact information that belongs at the bottom of every e-mail you write). Without being overly gimmicky or cutesy, use the e-mail signature to get the word out about your book. At the very least, "author of *Your Title Here*") should appear alongside your name, phone number, and address. Some authors will hyperlink the title so that when recipients click on it they are automatically directed to the book's website or Amazon. com page. Some authors may also include tiny snippets of reviews (keep these super-short) or even a thumbnail-sized jpeg of the cover of the book.

15. [FAST] Make sure your website address is listed on the back cover of your book—and that the site is alive and kicking by launch time.

16. Set aside an hour or two every week to browse other people's blogs, make comments, and drive traffic to your blog. You want to get known as an expert in your field.

17. Write to relevant bloggers individually. Bloggers are a little different than journalists. Whereas journalists are accustomed to receiving a generic press release and an un-solicited copy of your book, bloggers need to be e-mailed individually. Tell them how you found their blog and why it is directly relevant to your book, and ask if they would be interested in reviewing it. Remember to politely follow up with them a few weeks after sending. Bloggers usually do their blogs in their spare time for the love of a particular topic, and they are almost always unpaid. Be patient if they seem a little slow to respond.

18. Blog early and often. Read chapter thirteen for some ideas on blogging—remember that you are helping to build a community around your book, not just sell a product. Your blog cannot be all-advertorial-all-the-time. One way that some authors get started is to begin as a guest blogger on a site created by a friend or colleague, or their publisher. This way, they can get a feel for blogging before diving in feet first.

One tip: Many authors tend to think in thousand-word increments. (Hey, we're writers. We write.) But online, shorter is actually better. If you have a lot to say, divide it up over the course of several posts, and remember to interact with readers' comments by addressing them in your remarks.

HACKING THROUGH THE AMAZON JUNGLE

19. Register as an author on Amazon.com, and create an Author Profile. You want to establish yourself on Amazon.com so when readers click on your name, they will have the option of going to your Amazon.com author page. Here you can blog (with either the same or different content than your regular author blog), post news of signings and release dates, and link to your own website and/or blog. Amazon.com's Author Profile becomes especially useful as you establish many books to your name. Readers can easily call up (and hopefully purchase) every book you have to your credit.

20. Become an Amazon.com reviewer. You can spread word of mouth about your own book (gently) while also directing like-minded readers toward worthy books in your field. Don't just trash the competition; balance praise of the good works with criticism of the second-rate ones.

21. Send your book to Amazon.com's top reviewers. Amazon.com's book reviews are increasingly important to the sales of books (and lawnmowers, and ice cream scoops, and everything else that's sold on Amazon.com). One way to get some attention is to send copies of your book to Amazon.com's top reviewers, who are classified in the top ten, top fifty, top hundred, top thousand, etc. These are the people whose reviews consistently receive "helpful" ratings from other customers. They can usually be contacted via their reviewer profile pages on Amazon.com, which you can access by clicking on their names. Be aware that these people are rock stars in Amazonland, and are thus very busy. You will want to research their other book reviews to see if they enjoy books in your genre, and also e-mail them first to see whether they might be interested in looking at yours.

22. Sell autographed copies of your book through Amazon.com's Sell Yours Here program. Some collectors love having a copy signed by the author. It's free publicity for you, and it helps to get your name associated with something rare and coveted.

23. [FAST] Ask friends and family to review your book on Amazon.com. But be sure to tell them not to refer to you by your first name! There's nothing quite like the dead giveaway that comes with, "John did such a wonderful job with this book. When we were in kindergarten learning our letters, I never dreamed that John would have it in him to write a novel." Your friends need to make their reviews impersonal and informative—and be sure they know your friendships will survive even if they don't give you five stars. Also, self-published authors should know that having a strong showing of Amazon.com reviews may actually help to obtain better product placement through the AmazonEncore program, launched in 2009.

24. Create a Listmania! list. Remember that you want to be involved in the *community around your topic*; you're not just plugging your own book. With that in mind, create a list on Amazon.com of some of your favorite books and authors. If you write a novel that's set in Alaska, for instance, you'd want a list that includes your favorite travel guides to the region, books about Eskimos, and even the best parkas. (Yes, they do sell parkas on Amazon.com.) Do include your own book in the list.

RADIO AND PODCASTING

25. Practice mock interviews. If you have friends who are media-savvy, or even if you don't, practice a mock interview or two before your first real podcast or radio interview. Your friends can help you crystallize your message in sound bytes, which are between thirty seconds and two minutes maximum, with emphasis on at least one pithy takeaway phrase. Friends can also alert you to any vocal tics you may have, such as too many long pauses, unfinished sentences, and *ums*. Practice answering the most common questions: why you wrote the book, what's in it for the listener, what it's about, etc. Also think about the questions you are most fearing, and have your mock interviewers pose them to you. You probably won't ever be asked those questions, but just knowing you would be able to handle them will help you to exude confidence.

26. Broadcast yourself. Create a few short (two to three minutes long) videos of yourself discussing your book and upload them to YouTube. Try to avoid the boring "talking heads" approach by having video of yourself talking interspersed with images of the book's cover, footage of you interacting with readers, etc. You may need to hire a professional to help you with this, but you can also learn the basics yourself with a program like iMovie for the Mac. Post these little vidlets on YouTube. Be sure to tell friends and family about them, link to them on your Facebook and/or MySpace pages, and link to them from your book website or author blog.

27. Do a short podcast of your own about your book. We talked about podcasts in chapter thirteen, so do a quick refresher course there if you need more information about the basics. If your publisher doesn't have its own podcasting program (which more and more are starting to do), you'll need to do a Google search of podcasts that deal with your subject matter. Contacting podcasters is similar to contacting bloggers: Be sure you listen to several of their episodes so you can show them you have a sense of what they do and feel you would be a good guest. Once the podcast goes live on the Internet, link to it on your own site and make it your status update on Facebook.

28. Invite yourself to someone's podcast. Most podcasts, even the ones with broad circulation, are just mom-and-pop-outfits, with hosts who have other full-time jobs. Research the most listened-to podcasts in your area of expertise, then e-mail the producers of each show and offer yourself up as a guest. Make it clear why your book is directly relevant to their podcast and why their listeners would be interested; also offer to send the producers a copy of the book. If you have a link to your own podcast or YouTube video, send that so the producers can see you're for real.

29. Do radio interviews. One of the great things about doing a podcast or two is that you have an audio sampler you can now use when you're pitching local radio stations. Radio deejays don't want to put just anyone on the air. The guest needs to be both informative and entertaining, feel at ease, and target remarks to what listeners really want to know. Not everyone can do this—some people are too garrulous, others too timid. If you have a podcast you can link to when you e-mail radio stations, this gives you a leg up on the competition. If stations are serious about having you on the air, they'll regard this as a sort of audition tape. Be sure to follow up by phone so the producer can hear what you sound like without being edited.

30. Have a one-night stand. No, not *that* kind of one-night stand—we mean the kind that Penny Sansevieri recommends in her book *Red Hot Internet Publicity*. This is a prearranged evening event where you host a sort of online book party, a virtual seminar about your topic. Keep it educational—what does the audience want to know?

WHEN THE BOOK IS PUBLISHED

31. Keep a log of interviews, review copies, media contacts, book events, and other information. Organization is key to successful book promotion. Work with your publicist to share information about where the book is being sent and which media members have been pitched. You don't want to pitch someone who has already accepted or rejected a pitch from your publicist.

32. Go with the "one in ten" rule. Rejection is part of being a successful author, and you simply have to get used to it. Assume that nine out of ten of your pitches for reviews, endorsements, interviews, and events will be rejected. If you pine over the opportunities that *don't* come your way, you'll be blind to all the ones that *do*. If you make ten strong pitches a day, that means that at least one person a day, on average, is going to say yes to your book.

33. Follow the news. Publicity is news driven (for more on this, refer back to chapter twelve). What this means for you is you will have a much better chance at getting media interest if you can tie your book topic to a big item in the news, as Jon Krakauer did with *Under the Banner of Heaven* and the Elizabeth Smart kidnapping. However, be tasteful and sensitive about tragedies in the news. For example, one magazine editor was distressed that within two hours of the Amish school shootings, she received a press release about a romance novelist who was touted as an "expert" on the Amish community. The editor felt it was disrespectful and exploitative—a real turnoff.

34. Always keep your books with you to sell. When Jan Karon, author of the *Mitford* novels, was starting out, she always kept a box of books in her car trunk and would stop at bookstores all through the South to introduce herself. Keep books on hand for unexpected sales opportunities, and also create your own opportunities.

35. Crash a trade show or two. Trade shows are the great confabs of the publishing world, where thousands of people gather to see and be seen. The largest of these is BookExpo America, usually held in the late spring. It's unlikely your publisher will pay to bring you, but if you can pay your own way, the publisher can probably spring for a badge to get you onto the show floor. It's worthwhile just to ogle all of the new and forthcoming products, to talk to publishers and agents, and attend panels and workshops. Remember also that there are dozens of smaller trade shows for niche areas of publishing, as well as regional writing festivals, conferences, and workshops.

SIGNINGS AND APPEARANCES

36. Go on the road. Children's fantasy novelist Obert Skye (a pen name) has taken to the road regularly to promote his middle-reader series *Leven Thumps*, with great success. He speaks at elementary and middle schools all across the country, often hitting several different schools' assemblies in a day. It's exhausting but effective: After his visits, local booksellers can hardly keep his stories in stock. You can do this yourself, if on a smaller scale. Publishers rarely send new or midlist authors on the road anymore, but they're thrilled to have you create your own opportunities. Think about your own niche audience—children, expectant parents, dog breeders—and how you can travel to speak to them.

37. [FAST] Give yourself face-out presentation. Okay, this one is just a wee bit underhanded. If you have been lucky enough to get your book into large bookstores, you can help your book put its best face forward. Research shows that covers sell books—but what if your book is shelved spine out, so book buyers don't get a chance to see its cover? Don't move your book on the shelf—it is probably in alphabetical order by last name—but do turn it so it gets "face-out presentation" on the shelf.

38. Get to know your local booksellers. Booksellers are some of the greatest people in the world—they love books, right? So get to know them. Ask them about what is selling in your category, and what authors can do to promote their books.

39. Do a hometown book signing or launch party. Twenty-city author tours are a thing of the past for all but the national best-selling authors—they are expensive to mount and often don't succeed in selling very many books. One kind of book signing that *does* work, however, is the hometown launch party, held at a traditional bookstore or even a restaurant. One debut author guaranteed her local bookstore that if they let her have the signing there for free, she could sell at least fifty copies of her first book—and if her friends didn't show, she would buy them herself at full retail price. This was a financial gamble, but her friends (and proud mom) came through. The bookstore made money, not just on the sales of her book but on the other books, cards, and magazines the customers bought that night. It was a win-win.

40. Don't be a whiner. One bookseller who used to work at Barnes & Noble reports that a local author persisted so relentlessly about having a store signing that the harassed staff finally scheduled one for him. When he arrived, he looked around and griped, "Where are my meats and cheeses?" He had expected to be treated as a celebrity, with a red carpet and a full buffet. He also wondered aloud why the store hadn't done more publicity and almost no one showed up. He became something of a legend among the staff, and not in a good way. The lesson here? Don't be whiny and demanding, like Mr. Meats and Cheeses. If you are lucky enough to get a local book signing, know that it is *your* responsibility to get people to come to your events—and there will not be free hors d'oeuvres.

BOOK CLUBS

41. Write a free reading group guide that is downloadable from your blog. If your book is even remotely bookclubbish, you will want to make it as easy as possible for book clubs to discuss it. Check out the examples at ReadingGroupGuides (www.readinggroupguides.com). Book clubs are important not only because you might sell ten to fifteen copies of the book at a time, but also because they tend to attract "real" readers: the ones who discuss and even blog about the things they like, who buy them as gifts for other people at holidays, and who wear pajamas made out of recycled paperbacks. Okay, maybe not that last part, but the point is that book clubbers are your people. Do what you can to court them.

42. Learn how to Skype. More and more authors, especially novelists, are using free Skype technology to make short appearances at book club gatherings, answering questions in real time. One author we know advertises on her website that she will appear for free for half an hour at any book club with a group of twenty or more people by using Skype. Skype (www.skype.com) is free and easy to use for anyone with a high-speed connection. Readers love having a personal connection with this author, and she never needs to leave her house.

SOME NICHE OPTIONS

43. Hire an outside publicist. This can be a very costly option, with great publicity firms charging ten to twenty thousand dollars and up for a no-holds-barred six-month campaign. One novelist, Lisa Tucker, bit the bullet and spent almost all of her twenty-thousand-dollar advance from her first book, *The Song Reader*, on an outside publicity firm. It was a gamble, but the decision paid off handsomely, with major media (including CBS's *The Early Show*) spurring sales of the book. If you can afford it, by all means try this route. Your publisher can usually recommend good outside publicity firms. (And incidentally, twenty thousand dollars is an extremely high advance for a first-time author. It's not unheard of, but it's certainly not common.)

44. Think outside the box store. Some of the most successful book signings don't happen in bookstores at all, but at niche venues where likely readers may be found. Bill Nye the Science Guy books events at aquariums; an organic cookbook author might do a signing-and-cooking tour at local farmers' markets; an African American genealogist does signings and informational events at libraries and museums of American history. Be creative, and be persistent.

45. If you're a professor, assign your book for your classes. Given the stereotype of the egotistical academic, it's surprising how many professors are overly modest about their published works. Academic publicists complain all the time that their wallflower authors won't spread the word about their own research and writing. Get your book on the syllabus, talk it up with colleagues who may wish to assign it to their classes, and be sure to speak about it at academic conferences.

NICE AUTHORS FINISH FIRST: WORKING WELL WITH PEOPLE

46. Don't undermine your publicist. Publicists are very hardworking and often underappreciated. Think about what life is like on their end: They call media all day long, and nine times out of ten the answer is no—if someone picks up the phone at all. Then they get blamed by their authors for not getting books reviewed in *The New York Times*. Don't be whiny, demanding, or visibly insecure. Do be proactive, helping your publicist all along the way and coordinating communication. Emphasize your willingness to help with all aspects of the campaign.

47. Do favors for others. Karma matters in publishing. Write that book review you've been asked to do, even though you don't have time. Offer that letter of recommendation. Doing favors for others feels good for its own sake, but it also has a way of coming back to reward you down the road. For example, when you help a member of the media when she's doing research related to your topic and stumbles upon your very helpful blog, she may well remember you two years later when you send her a galley of your book to ask for an endorsement.

48. Send personal e-mail requests, not e-mail blasts. Journalists and reviewers get dozens of e-mailed press releases every day, and most are deleted unread. Help yours stand out by writing a personal (and correctly addressed) opening paragraph that explains why you are contacting this person, why you think (based on your research) she may be interested in your book, etc. The answer may still be no, but at least your e-mail won't be immediately trashed.

49. Write thank-you notes. On real paper. It seems a bit out of date in our high-tech world, but an old-fashioned thank-you note never goes amiss. Send one (or several) to your publicist. Send one to each journalist who interviews you, each reviewer or blogger who takes the time to read your work (even if the review was not one your mother would have written), and each bookseller or librarian who sticks his neck out for you by agreeing to host an event. Heck, while you're at it, write one to your eighth-grade English teacher and thank her for helping you on the road to being a published author. She'll be thrilled.

50. Above all, be known as an honest, good, hardworking person. Believe it or not, old-fashioned character is still the best route to success—in publishing as in life. When people love and trust you (which is also its own reward), they are more likely to go out of their way to help you by introducing you to opinion-makers, showing up at book signings, linking to your blog, subscribing to your e-zine, and a hundred other things. In the end, being a successful author is about having strong and caring relationships. So be a mensch.

PART FOUR

YOUR WRITING BUSINESS

AS WE'VE SEEN, writing isn't just about the creative work you do in obscurity while you leave the business end of things to the professionals. A successful career in writing is as much about your ability to be an "authorpreneur" as it is about your skills in actually putting words on paper. We learned in Part Three that you're the one who is primarily responsible for getting the word out about your book. In Part Four, we'll see that you also bear the main responsibility for running a good business: negotiating favorable contracts, staying on top of legal issues, filing your taxes, and making sure you don't get sued for libel.

We'll also learn, though, that you don't have to do all these things alone. You can hire specialized professionals to handle some of these issues for you (e.g., an agent or attorney for contract negotiations and a CPA for your taxes), but even writing itself can be done more collaboratively. In this section we'll look at all kinds of writerly communities where you can share creative ideas and learn what has worked (or not worked) for others.

Hemingway famously said that writing is, "at its best, a lonely life," and to some degree that is true. Yet it doesn't have to be. This section is about getting connected and reaching out to others: people you can help, and people who may be able to help you.

15 CONTRACTS, AGENTS, AND THE FINE PRINT

MANY WRITERS LIVE in large part by trusting editors and publishers they've never met without anything prudent souls would consider security. Clearly the best security you can have as a writer is a written contract. For books, contracts are the norm. But understanding the contract's implications can be difficult. For articles, contracts are more common than they used to be. Of course, a contract is only as good as your ability to enforce it. If the language is vague, or the cost of a lawsuit far outweighs the benefits, the contract becomes fairly useless. And if drafted the wrong way, a contract can become more like a chain than a bond.

As a writer, you probably can't afford to level the playing field by having a lawyer on retainer. But you can learn the important legal issues. This chapter describes contracts and laws that apply to writers to help you avoid some of the common and more costly mistakes.

YOUR RIGHTS

Understanding what rights you're selling to a publisher is important. The term *selling* may not even be a good word. In most cases, it is more like you are leasing your work to a publisher. Here, then, is an overview of the options you have when offering your work to a publisher.

- **First Serial Rights.** Rights that the writer offers a newspaper or magazine to publish the manuscript for the first time in any periodical. All other rights remain with the writer. Sometimes the qualifier "North American" is added to these rights to specify a geographical limitation to the license. (Note: When content is excerpted from a book that's scheduled to be published, and it appears in a magazine or newspaper prior to book publication, this is also called first serial rights.)

- **One-Time Rights.** Nonexclusive rights (rights that can be licensed to more than one market) purchased by a periodical to publish the work once (also known as simultaneous rights). That is, there is nothing to stop the author from selling the work to other publications at the same time.

- **Second Serial (Reprint) Rights.** Nonexclusive rights given to a newspaper or magazine to publish a manuscript after it has already appeared in another newspaper or magazine.

- **All Rights.** This is exactly what it sounds like, and for book contracts it's usually something you want to avoid. "All rights" means that authors are selling every right they have to a work. If you license all rights to your work, you forfeit the right to ever use the work again. If you think you may want to use the work again, avoid submitting to such markets.

- **Electronic Rights.** Rights that cover a broad range of electronic media, from online magazines and databases to CD-ROM magazine anthologies and interactive games. The contract should specify if—and when—electronic rights are included. The presumption is that unspecified rights remain with the writer. As you can imagine, this area of rights negotiation is the most disputed right now, since it's the one that's constantly changing. In the last couple of years, some publishers have also inserted "Kindle rights" and "Google rights" into their boilerplate contracts (see sidebar on page 283).

- **Subsidiary Rights.** These may include various serial rights; movie, TV, audiotape, and other electronic rights; translation rights, etc. The contract should specify who controls the rights (author or publisher) and what percentage of sales from licensing of these rights goes to the author.

- **Dramatic, TV, and Motion Picture Rights.** Rights for use of material on the stage, in television, or in the movies. Often a one-year option to buy such rights is offered (generally for 10 percent of the total price). The party interested in the rights then tries to sell the idea to other people—actors, directors, studios, or TV networks. Some properties are optioned numerous times, but most fail to become full productions. In those cases, the writer can sell the rights again and again.

Rights are nearly always negotiable. If you feel uncomfortable with a publisher's proposal, ask if he would consider other terms. If you do sign away all rights to a piece of work, you are normally only selling the rights to a particular group of words set in a particular order. In some cases you can take the same information, rewrite it from a different angle, and resell it, but read your contract carefully first to make sure there is no clause about competitive works.

In the absence of any written agreement, in most cases the copyright law assumes that an author is only giving a publisher one-time rights. The key exception is a work-for-hire arrangement. In these cases, the work becomes the property of the publisher. Generally, something is considered a work-for-hire if it is produced by an employee, such as a staff writer. In some cases freelancers are also given work-for-hire arrangements. But in most instances, freelancers and independent contractors own the rights to their creative work unless stipulated otherwise in writing.

ELECTRONIC AND DIGITAL RIGHTS

With the proliferation of books and magazines on the Internet, electronic rights have become a controversial issue between writers and publishers. In one high-profile case (*Tasini v. The New York Times*), the federal courts initially sided with publishers, allowing them to reproduce articles in electronic form without owing the authors additional compensation. The court ruled that putting articles into electronic databases and onto CDs fell under the "collective works" provision of the Copyright Act. The Supreme Court reversed that ruling in 2001, deciding that newspaper and magazine publishers had infringed on freelancers' copyrights by republishing their work in online databases.

Given the rapidly evolving state of technology, such issues are bound to come up again and again. For example, some publications are developing pages on the Internet that hold the potential of becoming quite profitable. Tracking user "hits" on particular articles is relatively easy, and some writers want a share of those profits.

And what about Google? In its oh-so-modest quest to make all information available to anyone at any time, Google has become a catalyst for controversy. In 2005, The Authors Guild sued the search engine because of Google's project of scanning millions of books from university library collections. Although many of these books were older and in the public domain (i.e., no longer subject to copyright), some were still copyright-protected. The Authors Guild felt that Google's mass digitization would reduce the need for consumers to actually purchase the books, thus making it more difficult than ever for authors to earn a living. "Google countered that its digitization of these books represented a 'fair use' of the material," wrote Authors Guild President Roy Blount, Jr. "Our position was: The hell you say." The $125 million settlement the two parties struck late in 2008 mandates the creation of a Book Rights Registry to track authors' royalties, and grants authors the right to opt out of digitization if they so choose. It also severely limits the number of book pages a Google user can examine for free.

Nearly all print publications these days seek some control over electronic rights. When all is said and done, your primary goal is to retain as much control of your material as possible so you can profit from its use in the future. Following, then, are some additional terms relating to electronic rights you will likely see in contracts, and some words of advice for dealing with these issues.

- **First Electronic Rights.** These rights give the publication the first shot at using your material while allowing you afterward to sell reprints in any medium.

- **One-Time Electronic Rights.** This grants publishers the nonexclusive right to use material once in an electronic publication. You can grant this right to more than one publication at a time.

- **Nonexclusive Electronic Rights.** Publications are likely to ask for such rights in perpetuity, or indefinitely. Because the language is nonexclusive, you can still resell or reuse your material electronically at any time. The downside is that the original publication can also resell your work without compensating you.

- **Exclusive Electronic Rights.** If a publisher asks for any type of exclusive rights, it should only be for a reasonable period of time (usually three to six months). Afterward, you are then free to resell or reuse your own material.

- **Archival Rights.** Many print and electronic mediums expect to archive material online indefinitely. Make sure this request is non-exclusive so you are free to resell or reuse your own material.

- **First Worldwide Electronic Rights.** Since the Internet does not stop at any border, "First North American Serial Rights" has little meaning in the online world. Many publications are therefore using the first worldwide clause as a result. As always, try to avoid signing away exclusive rights indefinitely.

WHAT'S THE CONTROVERSY ABOUT THE KINDLE?

In 2009, The Authors Guild alerted its members that behemoth bookseller Amazon.com was unveiling an updated version of the Kindle, its electronic reading device. Although most people who use the Kindle download the printed text and read it on a screen, the Kindle 2 also has a text-to-speech capability for most books it services, meaning the device can read the book out loud to you while you are doing something else. This new frontier is great news for the visually impaired and people with learning disabilities, but it may not be such a terrific deal for writers. The Authors Guild is concerned that Amazon.com is not planning to pay authors any additional fees for audio rights, which have traditionally been a separate (and lucrative) line item for authors and publishers.

While The Authors Guild investigates this issue, it encourages writers to resist granting Amazon.com unspecified rights: "We recommend that if you haven't yet granted your e-book rights to backlist or other titles, this isn't the time to start. If you have a new book contract and are negotiating your e-book rights, make sure Amazon's use of those rights is part of the dialog."

MAGAZINE CONTRACTS

Contracts and negotiations for periodicals are relatively simple. In some cases there will be no contract at all, just an editor giving you the go-ahead to write an article. Yet whenever possible, try to get some kind of written agreement, even if it's just an informal, e-mailed assignment letter from the editor. If you get nothing in writing, try sending your own letter confirming the assignment. It may clear up costly, frustrating, and time-consuming misunderstandings.

If you are presented with a contract or letter of agreement, it should cover the key issues listed below. In cases where there is no written agreement, at least talk through these key issues so you are clear on what the publication expects of you.

- What rights are you granting to the publication? First rights (as defined earlier in this chapter) are a good starting point.

- How and when will you be paid? The best option is to be paid on acceptance, since publication will often occur months later.

- What kill fee will the publisher pay if the finished article is rejected? And under what circumstances is a kill fee normally paid?

- What expenses will the publisher cover?

- Is the publisher responsible for defending you against a libel suit?

- Will you have the right to approve the final version of your work? Most publications "retain the right to edit for space and style." This can mean almost anything. But generally if you write professionally and follow the style of the publication, you won't experience much revision.

- Are you expected to provide additional materials such as sidebars, photographs, or illustrations? If so, the agreement should spell out whether you will be paid separately for them.

- Will you receive complimentary copies of the publication in which your work appears? You should be given at least a couple copies of the publication.

- What is the deadline for the completion of the work? This should be spelled out clearly in the agreement.

When you are presented with a contract, remember that many points can be negotiated. If you're new to the game you may have less of a chance to negotiate. But as you gain more publishing credits, along with a solid reputation, you will also gain more leverage.

BOOK CONTRACTS

Regardless of your excitement about getting a book deal, take a long, hard look at how you're treated under the terms of the contract. Better yet, consider getting a lawyer or agent who can. After all, you will have to live with the terms of the contract for years to come.

Book contracts fall within a fairly standard format, but you have every right to negotiate the individual terms. There are no "right" ways to handle the various issues in a book contract. Simply hold out for the best overall deal you can. Some points are more important to the publisher than others, just as some points are more important to you. Try to hold firm on the issues of most importance to you, while giving in on other points that are more important to the publisher.

The following are some contract issues that may come up:

- How much of an advance will be paid? The amount is often negotiable, even for first-time authors. Publishers of course want to pay as little money as possible, as late as possible in the process, to reduce their financial risk. But first-time writers can usually expect a few thousand dollars if not more, depending on the author's platform, the size of the press (larger companies often pay more), and how many copies the publisher thinks it might sell in the first year. (This is not true for academic and university presses, where advances are often under a thousand dollars or nonexistent. At university presses, the expectation is that the publisher is doing *you* a favor in helping you obtain tenure, so financial compensation is negligible.)

- When is the advance to be paid? If payable in two or three stages (as is the norm), what are these stages? If some stages are delayed for reasons beyond your control, is there a time limit to prevent foot-dragging by the publisher? An ideal contract would pay you half upon signature of the contract and half upon receipt of an acceptable manuscript. Be wary of contracts that pay you more than half of the advance after the publication of the book (when the money, by definition, is no longer an "advance").

- Are royalties based on a percentage of the list price or the publisher's "net," which is what the publisher actually receives after giving a 45 to 55 percent discount to the retailer? In the latter case, getting a fair accounting becomes harder. Most writers' organizations recommend royalties be based on list prices, but this is becoming unusual. Remember that a royalty of 7.5 percent off the list price of a book is equal to 15 percent or even 17 percent of the net price, so if you are weighing contracts between different publishing houses, be sure you are comparing apples to apples. Also, is there a provision for an audit of the publisher's records in accounting for royalties due you?

- Does the contract provide a time frame in which the manuscript is considered to be accepted even if the publisher does not expressly indicate it?

- Do you have the right to review the edited manuscript? If so, how long is the review period? Does the contract specify a time frame in which you must complete any revisions? If so, is it enough time?

- If an accepted manuscript is never published, does the contract become void, allowing you to sell it elsewhere? If so, do you retain the money paid in advance?

- Is there an arbitration clause that allows for peaceful resolution of disputes? If arbitration of contract disputes is called for, the arbitration should be in accordance with the American Arbitration Association's (www.adr.org) rules. Also, does the contract state the place for the arbitration? It should be a locale equally convenient to both parties.

- If the book is to be indexed, who is responsible for hiring and paying the indexer? Who is responsible for the cost of providing photographs and illustrations? Who will secure and pay for permissions to use long quotations from other works? If you are responsible for such costs, are they to be withheld from the advance or royalties, or do you need to pay for them separately in cash? (For tax reasons it can actually be better to have the publisher deduct these fees from your advance so you never receive that money as income.)

- Do you have veto power over the title of the book and the cover design? Rookie authors almost never do, but you can ask.

- Does the contract provide for free copies to be furnished to you? The default number for most publishing houses seems to be ten, but there's no reason you can't ask for more. This is one of the easiest concessions a publisher can make.

- Are you allowed to purchase additional copies at a discount? Many contracts stipulate that authors can buy "author copies" at a 40 percent discount. Don't be afraid to ask for 50 percent, which is roughly the discount that most publishers provide to large retailers.

- Does the contract specify a dollar amount for the publisher's promotional expenses? Does it obligate you to make promotional appearances without being paid for your time and expense?

- Does the contract give the publisher any options on your future work? Also called the "right of first refusal," this clause means that you are contractually obligated to show your next book to the publisher of your first book before you shop the second book around to anyone else. If your first publisher wants to buy the book, you have to sell it to that house, even if you know you could get a better deal elsewhere. Unless the publisher wants to pay you for this option, try to reject it.

- Does the contract have a "noncompete" clause prohibiting you from writing, editing, or publishing another competing book without written permission of the publisher? Some clauses are so vaguely worded that they seemingly would give the publisher control over virtually anything else you produce. If you must have such a clause, make sure it's narrowly worded and that there's a deadline involved, meaning that after a certain amount of time (three years is fair), you will be free to write a competitive work.

- Do publication rights revert to you when the book goes out of print? (See sidebar on page 290.) Do you have the right of consent to any sales of subsidiary rights, such as motion picture, book club, or anthology rights?

- Is there a provision for full subsidiary rights to revert to you should the publisher fail to exercise such rights in a specified time? Many writers mistakenly hand over potentially lucrative rights to publishers who have no interest or expertise in exercising such deals.

- Does the publisher promise to pay for legal expenses arising from any libel action in connection with the book? If so, do you have the right to choose your own lawyer? If you are partly responsible for any of the legal costs, does the publisher agree not to settle any claim without your consent? Finally, can the publisher freeze royalty payments after a suit is filed? If so, what are the provisions for the resumption of payments following a settlement?

WHAT DOES IT MEAN TO GO OUT OF PRINT?

In old-school publishing, it used to be relatively easy for publishers to decide when a book was considered out of print. It was when the publisher ran out of copies and didn't think there was enough of a market to go back to press for another full print run. Authors would usually get a letter from the publishing house, announcing that the book was going out of print and offering them the right to purchase the last remaining copies at a substantial discount. Then the rights would "revert" back to the author, who could choose to do nothing, self-publish a new edition, or sell the work to another press.

Nowadays, though, print-on-demand technology (discussed in more detail in chapter eleven) has meant that publishers can go back to press cheaply for much smaller print runs than they could do in the past. It's now fairly trivial for publishers to print up fifty extra copies for the Christmas season or for a specialized conference where they know a particular book is going to sell. But this means that publishers now hold the rights to books much longer than they used to, and this may not always be the best thing for authors. If you can, make sure your contract spells out precisely what your publisher means by "out of print." Do the rights revert back to you after a certain number of quarters in which sales have been under a particular threshold? Is the book considered "out of print" once it has sold fewer than five hundred copies in one year? Whatever the standard, make sure it is clearly stated and specific.

AGENTS AND ATTORNEYS

Whenever you are faced with a lucrative contract or complex negotiations, consider the services of a literary agent or attorney. This is the norm. Four of five books sold to major publishers are sold through agents. Many book publishers and film producers will not even deal directly with writers when it comes to contract issues and negotiations.

Of course, the money in question must be substantial for the services of an agent or attorney to be worthwhile. Most agents want a 15 percent share of your proceeds. Attorneys can charge two hundred dollars or more an hour, and most negotiations will consume at least several hours of expensive legal service. Accordingly, it is not in your best interest (nor theirs) for an agent or attorney to get involved unless several thousand dollars are at stake.

We talked at length in chapter five about who needs an agent and how to go about finding one. Here, let's just explore the financial angle. In some cases, agents and attorneys are well worth the cost and can increase your net income. Here's how:

> **1. Good agents and attorneys know more about contracts and negotiations than most writers can ever learn.** And by keeping you out of the direct negotiations, they enable you to preserve your working relationship with publishers and editors.
>
> **2. Professional representation by an agent or attorney shows a publisher that someone with credibility thinks your work is worthwhile.** It means more when someone else does your boasting for you—especially when it's an agent or attorney who understands the publishing world.

3. Most important of all, agents and attorneys relieve much of the work and stress involved in building a successful career. This allows you to be more productive as a writer.

While both can be equally beneficial, there are major differences in what agents and attorneys can do for you. Agents are often necessary early in the process to help you find a publisher. An agent's role can be that of salesman and business consultant. Some will even work with you to develop your talent. And if an agent is making 15 percent of everything you make, the agent should be interested in strategizing your whole career, not just placing a single book.

Attorneys, on the other hand, only come into play once you have a contract to negotiate. Try to find an attorney who regularly negotiates author contracts and is experienced in publishing law. You can usually find one through writers' organizations. Note that some literary agents are also trained attorneys, and some of them will negotiate contracts on a work-for-hire basis for authors who are not regular clients. It pays to do a little research.

WHAT THE AUTHORS GUILD CAN DO FOR YOU

Every profession needs a guild, right? Writers are no exception. As you've already seen in this book, The Authors Guild (www.authors guild.org) is at the forefront of the fight for authors' rights, whether it's taking on media giants like Amazon.com and Google or offering telephone seminars to help writers negotiate everything from book promotion to finding an agent or filing self-employment taxes.

But one of the most wonderful, and underreported, services The Authors Guild provides to its members is a free contract review by an experienced attorney. Not only does the Guild go over every clause of the contract to make sure you are getting a fair shake, but it can also compare your proposed contract with prior ones from that same publishing house, which gives you leverage in negotiation. If you know, for example, that your publisher has done a graduated royalty before for a similar midlist novel, or that your publisher agreed to axe the option clause in other contracts, you are in a better bargaining position.

It costs new authors ninety dollars a year to join the Guild, but it is money well spent. To become a member, you either need to have a book published by an established American house or have published three articles or essays. If you have a book under contract, you can join as an associate member with full benefits.

LEGAL ISSUES

Copyright

The basic rules of copyright are easy to understand. All works created after 1977 are protected for the length of the author's life and another seventy years thereafter. After that, the work falls into the public domain and anyone can use it without permission.

Obtaining a copyright for your work is truly effortless. The way the law is structured today, copyright is assumed the moment your words hit the paper or the computer screen. You need not even place a copyright notice on your work. There are, however, additional benefits to registering your work with the U.S. Copyright Office:

- Adding a copyright notice allows you to defeat claims of "innocent infringement."

- You must register your work with the Copyright Office before you can file suit against someone who steals your work. If you wait to register your work until after the theft takes place, you may not recover attorney fees or some damages from the defendant.

If your book is being published by a traditional publishing house, the publisher will undertake the copyright procurement for you. If you're self-publishing, or just want to have the secure knowledge that you own the copyright before you start submitting your work to publishers or agents, you'll want to obtain the copyright yourself. To register a copyright, request the proper form at www.copyright.gov. In 2009, the fee was thirty-five dollars.

Fair Use

Aside from protecting their work, the copyright issue of most concern to writers is the doctrine of fair use. It is this principle that allows you to quote briefly from someone else's work. It's important to note, however, that the rules of fair use have never been clearly defined by the courts, nor have they been spelled out in law. Fair use can only be judged in the context in which it occurs, but one general guideline for quoting from someone else's book is that you can usually use 250 to 300 words without permission. Some publishers will even go to 500 words. But be aware that if you're quoting other kinds of works, like short stories, and especially poems and song lyrics, the rules are far more strict. That's because part of what determines "fair use" is the percentage of the total work you are using. Quoting 300 words from the definitive biography of Robert Frost would be far less than 1 percent of the total work in question, and should therefore be free, but quoting just two lines from one of Frost's poems constitutes a goodly percentage of the total work—so it's going to cost you. If you are unsure if what you want to use is within the limits, obtain permission before quoting from any copyrighted material. When in doubt, choose to err on the side of caution.

To get permission to quote from copyrighted material, you must submit a request to the copyright owner, which usually means contacting the publisher. Larger publishing houses have a "rights" or "permissions" button on their websites, often with an application form you can fill out online. For smaller houses, the standard method is to contact the rights specialist by e-mail. In a brief message, explain exactly what you want to quote, and note when and where it was first published. Be sure to include information about how you will use the material and the name of the publication in which it will appear. In most cases, you will be granted permission on the condition that you credit the original source. In some cases, you may have to pay a fee, which can range from a few dollars to a few thousand dollars. You must decide whether the material is worth the cost involved.

Libel

You are guilty of libel if you publish a false statement that is damaging to another living person's reputation. The false statement can be unintentional and still be ruled libelous in court, which is why the law requires writers to take every reasonable step to check for accuracy. While it is up to the plaintiff to prove falsehood, it is up to you to prove that you made every reasonable effort to be accurate.

Few writers would knowingly publish falsehoods, yet the pitfalls for writers are numerous. You can accurately print what you have been told and still commit libel—if the person giving you the information was wrong in his facts. Many writers get in trouble simply by failing to check minor facts, which is why you must double-check and triple-check information—even when you believe it is correct.

Misspell someone's name while writing about a crime and you can implicate an innocent person in wrongdoing. That's libel. You can be held just as libelous if you falsely state someone has died. The "lucky living" have won such cases on claims of undue hardship and emotional distress. Errors in something as innocent as a high school sports story have even resulted in libel suits. While such instances are rare, the important point is that nearly any form of writing can put you at risk of libel.

The only way to be safe is to always be 100 percent certain of your facts. *The Associated Press Stylebook and Briefing on Media Law* is an excellent source of information on libel and how to protect yourself.

RESOURCES

ORGANIZATIONS FOR LEGAL ADVICE

The writers' groups below offer legal advice and contract help for writers. Contact them or check their websites to find out what specific legal services they offer.

The Authors Guild. Offers legal advice regarding contracts and also can step in and help resolve legal issues and disputes, or help writers find an attorney. www.authorsguild.org

National Writers Union. Offers contract advice and guidance on dealing with grievances and what to do if they occur. The organization also advocates for rights of freelancers and writers. www.nwu.org

ORGANIZATIONS FOR LOCATING LITERARY AGENTS AND ATTORNEYS

The organizations below offer listings and reports on various literary agents and attorneys. Some are free of charge, but some require a fee.

Agent Research & Evaluation. Offers services to help you locate the right agent. www.agentresearch.com

Association of Authors' Representatives. Agents in this organization must meet professional standards, such as no reading fees. www.aar-online.org

Writers Guild of America, East. Offers information and tools for writers and represents writers in motion picture, broadcast, cable, and new technologies industries. www.wgaeast.org

BOOKS

Guide to Literary Agents by Chuck Sambuchino (Writer's Digest Books). This book details where and how to find the right agents to represent your work. (Note: The author also runs a helpful blog at www.guidetoliteraryagents.com/blog)

How to Be Your Own Literary Agent by Richard Curtis (Mariner Books). Billed as "an insider's guide to getting your book published," this teaches you to think like an agent and do many of the things an agent would—including successful contract negotiations.

Kirsch's Guide to the Book Contract by Jonathan Kirsch (Acrobat Books). The definitive guide for writers, agents, and attorneys who are seeking to negotiate a book contract.

The Writer's Legal Companion: The Complete Handbook For The Working Writer, **third edition by Brad Bunnin and Peter Beren** (Basic Books). This thorough reference guide covers contracts, copyright, libel, and defamation.

16

FINANCES
FOR WRITERS

EACH YEAR, THOUSANDS of writers fail in their dream of becoming freelancers. Sadly, many fail not because they couldn't write well enough, but because they never mastered the business side of the profession.

While just as important to success, the business side of freelancing is often a lot less appealing. So it's easy to shove business matters into the bottom drawer, where they slowly kindle into a blaze of uncollected bills and overdue taxes. If you take the right approach, however, the details of business need not consume much of your hard work and talent. A few hours a week keeping your business matters well organized and up-to-date is all it really takes.

This chapter focuses on what you need to know to keep the business side of freelancing from overwhelming you—so your success as a writer is unfettered by the mundane details of business and taxes.

SETTING UP YOUR BUSINESS

Creating a simple budget is not only essential for business, it can make your life easier as well. For our purposes we'll assume you are a full-time freelancer, or are about to become one. If this is not the case, you can still benefit from having a more complete understanding of the business side of the trade. Keeping your budget, however large or small, in order will help your life run smoother month to month and will spare you panic-stricken moments come tax time.

As with any budget, what you're trying to create is only a rough representation of what's likely to happen. As you go through the steps, keep in mind that it will get easier each year. Once you are established as a freelancer you'll have the previous year's income and expenses as a basis for planning. You'll also have a regular base of clients to make your income more predictable.

The best way to start the budgeting process is to estimate your costs. Monthly overhead (what you must pay whether you work or not) should be the first category. This includes any payments on your computer or other equipment, office rent, publications, Internet service, and an estimate of auto expenses. Whenever possible, you'll need to keep track of business expenses separately from home expenses. Some budget items are used for both work and home (e.g., your car), so the IRS expects you to keep track of things like work-related mileage separately. Later in this chapter, we'll discuss how to use that information to your advantage at tax time.

After figuring overhead, take a look at your household budget and calculate the minimum amount you'll need for living expenses. Include your rent, mortgage, car payment, other consumer debt, groceries, utilities, and the like. Then, subtract from this amount any take-home pay from your spouse or other sources of steady income.

Financial planners recommend freelancers have three to six months of overhead and living expenses available when they start their business. Even if you start with as much work as you can handle, still count on two to three months for the checks to appear in your mailbox. One survey by the Editorial Freelancers Association found that freelancers waited anywhere from a week to a year to get paid, with one or two months being typical.

Ideally, your capital reserve will be your savings account. Realistically, the start-up costs for a freelance writing business are small enough that most can get by without borrowing. If you need to borrow money, it makes sense to apply for a separate credit card for business use. (It can still be in your name.) It's a lot easier to maintain your books with a separate business account. If your card has a grace period and you pay your balance every month, your card works like a rolling line of credit with no interest cost whatsoever—but be careful not to carry debt from month to month.

Planning Your Earnings

The overhead calculation you did earlier is important in figuring how much you should charge for your services. Different freelancers' websites post information about typical fees, so launch a Google search about what free-lancers are charging so you at least know the ballpark rates.

To calculate an hourly rate, figure the amount you hope to earn. That may be what you used to make at your old job or what you dream of making at your new one. Then, add in your annual overhead expenses. Divide that figure by the number of billable hours you expect to work in a year. (Count on spending a quarter of your time marketing your services, maintaining your records, and reading professional publications. These are not billable hours, but they are necessary ones if you want to run a successful long-term business.)

Most magazines and clients won't pay by the hour but by the word, inch, or article. You can, however, estimate how long an assignment will take and multiply that by your hourly rate. Factor in writing time, of course, but also the time you'll spend researching and revising your piece. Remember to consider expenses, too. Try to estimate your costs for phone charges, mileage, research, and other expenses. Add these to the fee you negotiate.

Always keep in mind what the market will bear when making your calculations. Check with other freelance writers in your area to find out what they charge. Don't charge more than you can get, but don't under-estimate yourself, either. Lowball pricing may get you a few jobs. But it will hurt your image with clients and editors, and often, your self-esteem. It won't do your bank account any good, either. (For more information on setting your prices, see Appendix A.)

RECORDS AND ACCOUNTS

Nobody becomes a freelance writer to do bookkeeping, but freelancers quickly find it becomes an important part of their jobs. Again, it need not be cumbersome. Ideally, record keeping should take no more than two hours each week.

Your record keeping system can be as simple as a daily log of income and expenses. If you're more comfortable keeping records on your personal computer, your local computer store should have a wide array of software that can do the job. Quicken Home & Business, for example, is a program that enables you to create estimates and invoices, generate business reports, record mileage, track accounts payable, and watch your cash flow. Financial planners recommend that you set up a separate checking account for your business. This will keep you from tapping your business funds for personal needs, and it will provide clearer documentation of your income and business expenses.

Some tips on record keeping:

- Save and file your receipts from every business expense—travel, books purchased, blog fees, office supplies, postage, etc.

- The IRS strongly recommends you keep expense records for as long as the period of limitations for audits. In most cases, that's three years from the date the return was filed or two years from when the tax was paid, whichever is later.

- Keep income records for six years after each tax return is filed. That's the IRS period for going after unreported income.

- You'll need records for the cost of your home or improvements for as long as you own the home if you take the home-office deduction.

- Also, you must keep records of items for which you claim depreciation, such as cars, for as long as you depreciate them, plus the three years after you file your return.

Though costly and time-consuming, audits are relatively rare. The IRS audits less than 1 percent of tax returns each year. Among businesses and the self-employed the chances are about 4 percent. Even if you're audited you won't necessarily owe money. About a fifth of those audited don't owe any additional taxes, and some even get refunds.

YOUR INCOME

Expenses are only half of what you'll be tracking. You'll also need to record income as you receive it and keep pay stubs that document your earnings. Each source that pays you more than six hundred dollars a year must report your earnings to the IRS and send you a 1099 form showing the amount. Income records are important for comparing to the amounts reported on each 1099.

If you've been bartering with other businesses (receiving goods or services rather than cash), the law requires you to report the fair market dollar value.

Cash Flow

That first big check you receive for your writing will be a thrill, but don't rush out and spend it. There's going to be a lean period. With the right strategy you can minimize the ups and downs.

The best way to avoid cash-flow problems is to continually work on developing new clients. That means sending out queries or contacting potential clients even when you're busy. Try to set aside a couple days each month for such marketing.

Additionally, never rely too much on any one source of income. Developing a few key accounts, preferably large and reliable enough to cover your overhead and basic living expenses, is important. But don't become complacent. Nothing lasts forever, so don't let any single account become more than a third of your business.

Meticulously track what your clients owe you. Record who owes you money, how much, and when it's due. As best as possible, arrange payment on your terms. Remember, book authors are not the only ones who get paid some money in advance. You may be able to get money up front for copywriting or even expense money from magazines.

For article writers, publications that pay on acceptance are obviously more desirable than those that pay on publication. If you're getting paid on publication, you could wait months for your article to be published, and at least a month after that to get paid. If paid on acceptance, you should get paid within a month of your final rewrite. Some tips:

- Fast action is the key to good cash flow. To maximize your income, incorporate billing into your weekly schedule.

- Tabulate your phone or other expenses as soon as the bill comes due.

- Bill clients as soon as payment is due.

Don't let a new, unproven account run up huge tabs before you get paid. In most cases, you won't know how good a publisher's or client's payment practices are until they owe you money.

Getting Paid

Waiting for checks is one of the most nerve-racking parts of being a writer. Let's face it: As writers we rely heavily on the creative side of our brain. Business and finances are not something most of us enjoy dealing with. So we like to think that our creative efforts will always be rewarded fairly. Yet even when our rights are carefully spelled out in a contract, there's no guarantee that payment will arrive when it's due.

For sure, one skill that writers acquire is patience. But we needn't be *too* patient. No matter how bad the publisher's cash flow, it's usually better than ours. So when the wait gets too long (i.e., thirty days past due), call or e-mail immediately. You need not be confrontational. Simply send a late notice, or call to check on the status of payment or to make sure your invoice wasn't lost. If you call, be sure to get a commitment from the editor or accounting office on when the payment will be sent. If that doesn't work, your next step is to deal with the accounting department directly and find out when the check was cut or mailed. If that still doesn't work, you can consider legal action such as arbitration or small claims court.

TAX ISSUES FOR WRITERS

Becoming a freelancer means saying goodbye to those carefree days when you spent thirty minutes filling out your annual taxes. As soon as you make any money freelancing, you'll have to fill out the long form 1040 and Schedule C for business profit or loss. If you plan to deduct car or equipment expenses, you'll have another even more complex form to fill out.

Estimated Taxes

Freelancers don't have any tax withheld from their income. Doesn't that sound great?

Unfortunately, it isn't. Any self-employed person must pay estimated taxes on earnings, not just annually but quarterly. You can use IRS form 1040-ES to calculate and make your estimated payments, which are due on the 15th of January, April, June, and September. For more information, go to www.irs.gov and type in "estimated tax" in the search field.

Writers do well to plan ahead. If you can't estimate this year's income accurately, you will usually be safe from penalties if you base your quarterly taxes on what you owed the prior year. Your state and city may also require you to withhold taxes. To be safe, put aside at least 33 percent of your net earnings to cover your federal, state, and local taxes. It is better to be prepared than to be surprised.

Self-Employment Tax

If you thought the news about quarterly taxes was bad, you're going to want to sit down before reading this section. Writers and other self-employed people get to pay *more* tax than most other people. Don't you feel special? That's because in addition to ordinary income tax, freelancers must pay a self-employment tax to cover Social Security and Medicare. Employees pay Social Security tax, too, but the self-employed pay roughly twice as much (about 15 percent), because they're expected to cover both the "employee" half and the "employer" portion. When you look at your tax bill, you'll find that's one of the strongest motivations for taking every deduction you're allowed, which we'll cover in the next few sections.

Auto Expenses

If you work from home, you can deduct mileage from home and back to any interview, trips to the library for research, or travel for any business function. This is true even if you don't qualify for the home office deduction. If you work from an office outside the home, however, you can't deduct mileage for commuting to the office.

You can calculate auto expenses using the standard mileage rate or the actual-cost method. To use the standard mileage rate, multiply the mileage driven by the current mileage rate (fifty-five cents in 2009). The rate frequently changes but is stated each year in the instructions that come with Schedule C, the IRS form for reporting business income and expenses. Using the standard mileage rate is the easiest method in terms of record keeping.

As the name implies, the actual-cost method measures what it really costs you to operate your car. For this method you'll have to keep receipts for all automobile expenses, including gas, maintenance and repairs, insurance, taxes, loan interest, and depreciation of the car's cost.

If you use the car for both business and personal reasons, calculate the percentage of business miles each year and deduct that percentage of your costs. There are limits to how much of your car's value you may write off each year. For details, you'll need a current copy of IRS publication 917.

Home-Office Expenses

Qualifying for the home-office deduction means jumping through regulatory hoops (learning what the rules are) and increasing your risk of an audit. But the tax savings can be worth it. You may be able to deduct a percentage of your mortgage interest or rent, utilities, and upkeep for your home each year.

To qualify for the deduction you must use an area of your home regularly and exclusively for business. Occasional or incidental use of your home office won't cut it, even if you don't use the space for anything else. The most accurate way to calculate the business portion of your home is to divide the square feet of the work area by the total square feet of your home. Expenses you can deduct include the business percentage of:

- Mortgage interest.

- Utilities and services, such as electricity, heat, trash removal, and cleaning services.

- Depreciation of the value of your house.

- Home security systems.

- Repairs, maintenance, and permanent improvement costs for your house.

- All costs of repairs, painting, or modifications of your home office. (You can write off repairs the first year. Permanent improvements are considered capital expenditures and subject to depreciation over several years.).

One other word of caution—you can't use home-office expenses to put you in the red. They can't be used to help create a tax loss.

Before you take any home-office deductions, figure out what the tax savings will be. If the savings are minor, you may not want to bother. What you lose in taxes, you may gain in peace of mind because you'll be saving yourself extra work. You can get more information from IRS Publication 587.

Other Expenses

The IRS applies the "ordinary" and "necessary" rules in judging the validity of a business expense. This means the expenses should be ordinary for your profession and necessary for carrying out your business.

Office equipment is a necessary—and often major—expense for freelance writers. Computers, desks, chairs, shelves, filing cabinets, and other office furnishings are deductible expenses if you use them in your business. These can be deducted even if you don't opt for the home-office deduction. IRS publication 534 provides more details on how to depreciate business property.

Among the largest costs for freelancers are phone and Internet expenses. The IRS prohibits deductions for your personal phone line, even if you use it for business. But you can still deduct the cost of long-distance business calls, even if they're from a personal line.

If you entertain sources or clients you can deduct 50 percent of that expense. You must keep a log of the date, location, person entertained, and business purpose of the entertainment for every item you deduct. If you travel in connection with your writing, you can deduct the cost of transportation, lodging, and meals.

Other deductible expenses include the cost of:

- Dues to professional organizations.

- Newspapers, magazines, and journals used for your business.

- Research, copying services, and online databases.

- Books used for research or comparison.

- Office supplies.

- Postage for business use.

- Cleaning supplies for your office.

- Legal, accounting, and other professional services.

- Business licenses.

If publishers or clients reimburse you for some of your expenses, remember to keep records of those payments and either report them as income or subtract them from the expenses you report.

Schedule C Pointers

Schedule C is a catchall form for all businesses, so much of it can be meaningless and mysterious for a freelancer. Here are a few things to remember if you fill out the form yourself:

- You'll probably be checking the "cash" box for accounting method. That just means you record income when you get the check and expenses when you pay them. Few freelancers will use the more complicated methods.

- Check the "does not apply" box for method used to value closing inventory. You don't have any. Unpublished manuscripts don't count.

- The office expense category is a catchall that includes office supplies, postage, etc.

- You only fill out the pension and profit-sharing portion if you have employees participating in a plan. Your own plan contribution, if any, is reported on form 1040.

- The tax and license expenses that you can deduct include real estate and personal property taxes on business assets, and employer Social Security and federal unemployment taxes.

- A big total in the "other expenses" column can make the IRS very suspicious. Break these items down as much as you can in the space provided.

- Your principal business or professional activity code will most likely be 711510 (the category for independent artists, writers, and performers) unless you work in advertising or related services (541800), the publishing industry (511000), or Internet publishing (516110).

Professional Help

As you've figured out by now, business tax forms are a lot more complicated than ordinary tax forms. So you may want professional help. If so, your options include tax preparation services and accountants.

If you're incorporated or face particularly complex business issues, you may need help from a CPA. Small or medium-size CPA firms are most likely to be familiar with issues that concern you. Franchise tax services provide a consistent, mass-produced product. They're the cheapest option, but they may be less familiar with some of the unusual situations of freelancers.

Don't overlook the possibility of the DIY method through tax accounting software, which is easy to use, very accurate, and updated annually to reflect changes in the tax code. For example, TurboTax Deluxe is an excellent program for freelancers who need to file a Schedule C, and it can be much cheaper than hiring an accountant. Moreover, if you track your business's finances with Quicken or QuickBooks, which are designed by the same company that created TurboTax, you can have the program automatically input all of your business expenses and income into TurboTax.

SAVING FOR THE FUTURE

While you may be able to write in your retirement years, you still will need some other savings if you hope to maintain your standard of living. For many people, this means investing in some kind of Individual Retirement Account (IRA).

The SEP-IRA

An IRA is a personal savings plan that provides income tax advantages to individuals saving money for retirement. Most people who invest in a traditional IRA can claim an income tax deduction for the year in which the funds are contributed into the account. These contributions, as well as any gains, accumulate tax-free until you withdraw the money. You can therefore accumulate greater earnings each year the funds remain in the account. Withdrawals are subject to income tax, generally in the year in which you receive them. Since the goal of a traditional IRA is to provide retirement income, the government assesses a tax penalty of 10 percent if you withdraw money from an IRA prior to age 59½, unless certain exceptions apply.

For freelance writers, the best traditional IRA choice is the SEP-IRA, which is specifically designed for self-employed individuals. The contribution limits are much higher ($49,000 in 2009) than are allowed with a traditional IRA ($5,000 for people under age fifty and $6,000 for people over age fifty), because the government expects that self-employed workers don't have employers pitching in matching funds, pension plans, and other goodies.

The Roth IRA

A Roth IRA is a different type of sheltered retirement account, and it is the best choice for most people if their income at retirement age is expected to be higher than their income is now. (This is true for most of us.) The Roth has a tax structure different from any other IRA in that contributions are posttax, so you don't get an immediate tax deduction. However, this strategy pays off in the long run: Since you have already paid taxes on any money you place into a Roth IRA, your earnings at retirement are tax-free. Moreover, the Roth is the only type of IRA you can pass on to your heirs tax-free.

As with traditional IRAs, you can open a Roth account through a stockbroker or other provider of investment accounts. As with all IRAs, there are restrictions on your eligibility. You can stay up-to-date on the rules with IRS Publication 590 or at www.irs.gov.

INSURANCE

It's not enough just to save for a rainy day—you also have to prepare for disaster. This means having enough insurance.

Health Insurance

Health insurance will be one of the biggest expenses you'll face as a free-lancer. If you're leaving a job with health benefits, federal law requires employers to continue your coverage for up to eighteen months (at your expense) through the pricey COBRA program. Beyond that you can choose from other group plans or individual coverage. Whatever route you choose, expect it to cost no less than several thousand dollars a year—and often much more if you have a pre-existing condition.

Many business or writers' organizations offer group health insurance, including The Authors Guild. Some even offer choices, including major medical plans with a range of deductibles and health maintenance organizations (HMOs). But membership in one of these organizations may not guarantee you'll be accepted for coverage.

Check with the organization or its insurance carrier for details of the plan. Most are perfectly acceptable. But some organizations provide only a fixed amount of coverage based on the number of days in the hospital and cover no expenses for physician treatment outside a hospital.

Depending on your state, an individual plan may leave you vulnerable to cancellation or steep rate increases should you develop a lengthy illness. Also, most independent coverage will have a waiting period of several months.

A less costly approach is to opt for an individual plan with relatively high deductibles and co-payments. It will still do what insurance is supposed to do, which is to keep you from getting wiped out by a huge medical bill. No matter what type of plan you have, most hospitals and doctors will let you pay off what you owe over time if you ask.

One of the best cheap insurance options, if you can find it, is an HMO that will offer you a high deductible in exchange for low premiums. This way your deductible may still be cheaper than the rates charged to those people who have traditional coverage.

Other Insurance

Going in business for yourself should not mean neglecting disability insurance. To the contrary, seek out a plan that covers the highest possible percentage of income for as long as possible. No insurance company will underwrite a policy that pays 100 percent of your income, because that would provide no incentive for you to go back to work. But policies may go as high as 80 percent and last as long as ten years or to age sixty-five.

Many writers' organizations offer group disability coverage. The groups may also offer relatively inexpensive group life insurance that can cover such items as your mortgage. But it's important to look at disability plans closely. Some plans cover only a fixed period, so you'd be out of luck and money in the event of long-term disability.

If you work from home, also check with your home or renter's insurance carrier to make sure your business equipment is covered. Professional liability is another coverage to consider. Your largest liability exposure is for libel. If your work seems likely to involve you in libel litigation somewhere down the road, you may want to take out a separate policy through a group like the National Writers Union.

17 FINDING A WRITING COMMUNITY

WRITING IS A solitary pursuit, but that doesn't mean you have to go it alone. Writers' organizations offer a range of support for writers from writing advice to insurance options. There are also critique groups where writers can get together to solicit comments on their work and give feedback to others. A colony is just another way writers can break out of their creative and physical confines to find a new sense of community among other writers. Writers conferences and gatherings are other options. If your goal is to pick up skills from top professionals or expand your contacts in the business, conferences are probably the best investment of your time. And don't overlook the free money that could be yours through grants, fellowships, and contests. It's not easy to win those competitions, but it can be a great boon to your career, in that success will open other doors with agents and editors.

ORGANIZATIONS FOR WRITERS

Some writers need a group for support or for critiquing their work. Others want advice on selling their writing, finding a job, or applying for a grant. Thankfully, thousands of writers' organizations exist to offer help in these areas and in a variety of others. Some are small groups of writers who meet weekly over coffee to read each other's work. There are also nationwide organizations that offer a broad range of services, including health insurance, for their several thousand members.

Some groups, especially national organizations, have stringent guidelines for membership. Local and regional groups usually are more open to new members and are less expensive to join. They generally emphasize feedback and interaction between members. Other organizations, such as The Authors Guild, work on the business side of writing. Still others, such as the American Medical Writers Association, serve a special niche of writers.

Your involvement with a professional organization depends a great deal on your specific needs. Whatever route you choose, you won't have to spend a lot of money to join. You'll typically pay one hundred to two hundred dollars for a yearly membership to a large group, while many local groups are free.

Joining a Writers' Organization

Before you join a writers' organization, compare your needs and goals to those of the group. Consider the following factors:

1. What are the benefits? If you are a full-time freelance writer and need medical benefits, you'll want to look for an organization large enough to offer them. Visit a meeting before you join to determine whether you'll benefit from the group's programs, or talk to a few writers in the organization to determine what they like best.

2. Are your goals compatible? Some groups are organized solely to exchange business and marketing information. Others focus more on critiquing. You must look at the group as an extension of your interests to justify the time away from the keyboard.

3. What size is the group? For some people, the most beneficial group is one that's small and allows them to participate in each session. Others value the resources of a large group. Some feel the best of both worlds is available through a local chapter of a large organization.

4. What's the experience level? If you're experienced and the majority of members are not, you eventually may feel as though you are wasting time. If, on the other hand, the members are very experienced, they may be unwilling to help you develop in a specific area. Many organizations have membership surveys that state the average experience level.

5. What's the cost? If you're paying for a high-service organization but are not using the services, you might want to consider a less expensive, local group.

CRITIQUE GROUPS

Critique groups are a great way for writers who are ready to share their work with others and receive feedback. Critique groups also can help motivate you to create deadlines for yourself so you have something to show at your next meeting. No two critique groups are alike. Each varies depending on the personalities and experience of its members. If you are interested in joining a critique group, there are a few ways to go about doing it and a few things you need to remember.

Starting a Critique Group

One option is to create your own group. If you know other writers who might be interested in joining a group, this might be a good way to get con-structure criticism about your work. When forming your group, remember to do the following things if you want your group to be successful:

1. Determine your goals. If everyone's not on the same page, this isn't going to be a useful experience. Is the common goal working on query letters? Trying to improve the members' novel-writing craft? Serving as a cheerleading or support network? Your group will be all these things and more at one time or another. But the members must agree on the key purpose.

2. Limit the size. It's best if you keep the group to somewhere between six and a dozen members. Much smaller and you run the risk of quickly losing freshness; much bigger, and there won't be an opportunity for healthy interaction.

3. Set a meeting place and time upon which everyone agrees. You can rotate among each others' homes, meet at someone's workplace, or get together at the local coffeehouse. The starting and ending times should work for everyone—it's aggravating to wait for someone who's consistently fifteen minutes late, or to lose feedback from someone who always has to leave early. Set a regular meeting schedule (preferably twice a month; certainly no less frequently than once a month).

4. Set ground rules and follow them. This doesn't have to be a dictatorship, but an effective critique group has to have some order. What will the standard agenda be? Will all members share work at each meeting? Who's responsible for e-mailing the manuscripts prior to each meeting? Does the work being shared have to be new? Are outside guests welcomed? (We suggest not.) What happens when a member doesn't show up or has nothing new to read for two or three sessions?

5. Determine the form for critique. We all want to know how to make our writing better, and that's what most of us want from a critique group. Agree that when members don't like something about another's work, they will offer solutions: "The first page seems to run a bit long. How would it read if you eliminated paragraphs one through three and started with the fourth paragraph?" is much more helpful—even if the advice ultimately is not followed—than "I thought it was boring."

Locating a Critique Group

If starting your own group is not something you are interested in, you may be able to join an existing group. Check with local community centers, libraries, bookstores, colleges, or universities to see if there are any critique groups near you. When choosing your group, keep these things in mind:

1. Just as in setting up a group, be sure that members share your goals. Do their ground rules and usual agenda mesh with what you hope to achieve? If not, keep looking at bulletin boards at area bookstores, libraries, or local colleges and universities until you find a group more to your liking—or start putting up your own notices to start a group.

2. Ask about the experience level/publication record of the members. It's fun to be a bunch of newbies together, but you won't necessarily learn very much. If you're looking

for a new social circle, this group may be for you. If you are serious about reaching your writing goals, find a group with at least one member who has achieved your goal (finishing a novel, finding an agent, getting a magazine article published) in the past year. While you don't want to be in a critique group with five National Book Award finalists if you're still on the first chapter of your debut novel, it's better for you if the others in your group are a bit more advanced than you are. That way, you can learn from them.

Online Critique Groups

If there aren't any critique groups close to you, or you don't know enough writers nearby to make starting a group feasible, a final option could be to join an online critique group. Online critique groups give you the opportunity to have your work critiqued by other members of the group without having to accommodate each other's schedules. They also allow for a more diverse group because you are not confined by proximity, which means more diverse opinions. Online groups can offer support and assistance in all aspects of your writing from grammar to overall structure, and they can provide you with links and newsletters about writing. It may seem that online groups would be impersonal, but in fact, you may find that you can become just as close to your online critiquers as you would with people in the same room.

If online groups are something you are interested in, there are many possibilities. At http://writing-critique-group.blogspot.com/, you are eligible for up to six critiques of your writing once you have offered three critiques of other people's work. The site will match your submissions with writing in the same category, so scientists aren't reviewing poetry and vice versa. You can also keep in touch with other writers (and potential critics) through Writer's Digest at www.writersdigest.com/forum.

IS A WRITERS' COLONY RIGHT FOR YOU?

Writers' colonies (sometimes called retreats) offer a wonderful change of pace, providing an opportunity to get the most out of your creative powers in a short span of time. The ways in which colonies are set up to do this can be as varied as a writer's imagination.

Some allow you to work virtually uninterrupted. Others provide space for quiet work but also encourage participants to interact and learn from each other during breaks, or through critiques, readings, and workshops. Some even bring together creative people from different disciplines—painters, writers, musicians—believing you can learn more about your own art by talking with others about theirs. At some retreats, the interaction takes place randomly throughout the day as different people gather together informally.

Most colonies require that you submit an application, including samples of your work and a description of how you will utilize your time. All of this is reviewed by a selection committee, whose goal is to make sure applicants are serious about their work. To get accepted, you must demonstrate how you will use your time to begin or complete a project.

Few, if any, colonies enforce a regimented schedule or keep tabs on your progress. Writers respond to this freedom differently. Some overwork and burn out in a short period of time. More commonly, writers need several days to adjust their newfound freedom before they can develop a routine for their work.

Some colonies select writers with substantial professional credentials. Others cater to emerging talent. Still others try to foster a mix of better-known and lesser-known talent. Some colonies are highly competitive—

receiving dozens of applications for every position they have open. One way to improve your chances is to consider going in the off-season when there are fewer applicants—such as going to Florida in the dog days of August.

A typical stay at a colony lasts from a couple of weeks to several months. The cost of colonies is generally inexpensive, with most charging a small application fee and a weekly cost. This can range from virtually nothing to a few hundred dollars per week, depending on travel, food, and lodging expenses, and the availability of scholarships and grants. The majority of colonies stress that payment is voluntary and no qualified applicant will be turned away simply because she cannot pay. Many require that you bring along whatever equipment you plan to use.

Before you select a writers' colony, consider the following:

- Most colonies schedule visits six months in advance, so make sure you assemble your writing samples and apply at least eight months before you would like to attend.

- Look for a colony that fits your lifestyle. Some writers thrive in a rural atmosphere; others find the peace and quiet uninspiring. Some writers like to cook their own meals at their convenience, while others prefer to have their meals prepared for them. Compare all aspects of the colony before applying.

- Some colonies offer weekend programs, but the majority of them want you to stay two weeks to two months. Since most writers work more quickly at a colony, plan your work ahead of time, even if the colony doesn't require it. If possible, talk to other writers who've been to colonies to find out how they used the experience.

Locating Writers' Colonies

Several sources offer information on writers' colonies:

- As a service to its members, The Authors Guild compiles a list of colonies.

- *Poets & Writers* magazine frequently carries advertisements and notices of colonies.

- The Alliance of Artists' Communities (www.artistcommunities. org) is another good source.

- ShawGuides publishes a free online directory with nearly a thousand entries at http://writing.shawguides.com.

- You may also want to check with your state arts council.

GETTING THE MOST OUT OF WRITERS' CONFERENCES

Whether you are just starting in the business or are already a professional writer, attending writers' conferences can be very beneficial. Beginners can learn a lot about the creative and the business sides of writing, while established writers gain added insights into all aspects of the trade.

Writers—whether beginners or seasoned—have many different goals when they attend a conference. Some want to explore a new writing area or learn from a particular instructor. Others are interested in making contacts with writers, editors, and agents. Still others like the inspiration of spending time with fellow writers.

If you are thinking of attending a writers conference, consider the following points:

- Your chances of individual meetings or instruction are greater at a small conference, but smaller conferences are less likely to attract prominent speakers. Instead of focusing on the total number attending, ask about the number in each session. If the number is thirty or less, you'll have more opportunities to ask questions and discuss your work with the instructor.

- Money is a key consideration for almost any writer, but don't choose a conference solely on the basis of cost. Attending a conference is an investment in your future success. The least expensive option may not be the best for you. A one- or two-day workshop can cost up to two hundred dollars. Conferences that last up to a week can cost eight hundred dollars or more, which usually includes the cost of lodging and some meals. One way to work a conference into your budget is to combine it with a vacation. (Hint: The Hawaii Writers Conference, formerly known as the Maui Writers Conference, held three times a year in Hawaii, is a great place to do this.)

- The caliber of the conference faculty is usually the most important criteria when evaluating a conference. Look for writers who have credentials in the particular area they will be teaching.

- Some conferences offer individual consultations with instructors, editors, or agents for an additional fee. Such personal feedback must be arranged ahead of time. If you are paying for an appointment, you have every right to know what to expect from the meeting. Don't go in expecting to find an editor who will want to publish your work or an agent who will want to represent you. Such overnight success stories are few and far between.

- Most conferences attract writers of a variety of skill levels and are geared accordingly. Check the program for clues as to which sessions are geared toward beginners or professionals. Avoid sessions that seem too far below or above your level of experience.

WRITER'S MARKET GUIDE TO GETTING PUBLISHED

- A conference's format can make a big difference. The best conferences are set up to provide interaction between the attendees and the instructors/speakers, rather than just lectures. Also look for panel discussions where writers, editors, and agents offer their opinions on subjects of interest to you.

MONEY FOR NOTHING: GRANTS, FELLOWSHIPS, AND CONTESTS

Several thousand organizations exist throughout the United States to award money to writers in the form of grants, fellowships, or prizes. Publicly or privately funded, many operate on a national level. Many more exist on the state and local level.

Grants are a way to stay solvent through lengthy projects. Fellowships offer opportunities for career-enhancing education that freelance writers may not otherwise get, since they have no chance at paid leaves of absence. Contests and awards can offer not only recognition for a job well done, but also money to do the next job well, too.

While there are thousands of organizations offering financial support, it takes hard work and skill to be accepted. Much like selling an article or a book, getting a grant, fellowship, or award means having a good idea, doing superior work, and then searching for the appropriate market.

Grants and Fellowships

Many grants have strict eligibility requirements. Some organizations allow you simply to apply. Others require nominations from a member of the organization. Grants from state and local arts councils, for instance, require recipients to live in the state or locality.

The more money in question, the tougher the competition. Some of the biggest have rather high hurdles to face even before you apply, such as having a number of years of professional experience, a book previously published, or a set number of articles published in literary magazines.

Every organization approaches the application process differently. Generally, the process involves these steps:

1. Get the details on any changes concerning the deadline, eligibility, and application process by checking the organization's website or sending an e-mail. Be sure to follow exactly any details as far as manuscript preparation or display of published works. If a printed application is preferred, find out if the deadline is when the application must be postmarked or when it must be at their door. You may need to send your application by overnight delivery to ensure on-time arrival.

2. Send in your application, which usually will include samples of your published work and may include an essay or letter of explanation about your plans for future work.

3. Wait for your application to be screened by a committee that chooses finalists. (In some cases there are multiple screening levels or semifinals.)

4. Finalists will often be interviewed before the final decision, especially for higher-paying awards and fellowships.

Grant application is often framed as a mysterious art best left to experienced practitioners. But in many cases, all the bells and whistles you can muster in a grant application won't make much difference. The quality of your work as viewed by the judges is the primary criterion.

With most grants, selection committees must wade through hundreds or thousands of applications for a handful of awards. Other, more specialized programs may only have a handful of applicants.

Like submitting your work for publication, applying for foundation grants and fellowships means getting your share of rejections. Program administrators advise writers not to be discouraged by an initial rejection. Many writers go on to find acceptance elsewhere or even from the same program in later years.

For a more comprehensive and updated listing, visit www.pen.org, which has a database of more than fifteen hundred grants and fellowships for writers. A one-year subscription to the database costs just twelve dollars.

Contests

There are more contests available to writers than you probably realize. Like grants and fellowships, winning a contest is not necessarily easy. In order to create the best "luck" for yourself, make sure you consider these things before submitting your work. Winning a contest is subjective so there are no guarantees, but there are things you can do to put yourself in a position to compete.

>1. **Understand the categories.** Many competitions group different genres or types of writing together. This is so each entry can be judged by the best person in that category. Find out which categories are offered, then define your entry. Choosing the wrong category is easy to do, but often results in a poor—and ultimately unfair—judgment of your work.

>2. **Stay within the word limit.** Nothing will disqualify your work faster than exceeding a predetermined word limit.

(When entering poems, double-check the number of lines or stanzas allowed.) Many competitions have a maximum word count, and contest judges make sure the winning entries adhere to the guidelines. This is especially the case now that computers have made it so easy to follow this rule. Using the word count function on your computer (in Microsoft Word, you'll find the function under Tools), cut your story until it's within the parameters set by the contest. And remember to leave a little breathing room: If you're ten words over the limit, cut twenty-five just to be safe.

3. Adhere to contest rules. If a contest calls for a double-spaced entry, don't submit it single-spaced. If it asks for your name and address to appear in the top right corner, make sure that's where your information appears. Don't include your own illustrations when the contest guidelines state, "No artwork accepted"—your entry will be discarded. Also, be sure to send the correct fee amount with your application.

4. Stick with the details. Before you hit the print key for the last time, give your manuscript one more read-through. Do all the characters' actions make sense? Is your timing off? Did you use "oversees" when you meant "overseas"? These small details are easy to miss during the editing process but stick out like a sore thumb when a judge is combing through your entry for the first time. Make sure your manuscript is perfect, then send it out.

5. Mail early. First of all, you can bypass all those expensive "express delivery" services by simply mailing or e-mailing your entry early. This will also give you time to add more postage or change the address if your envelope is returned to you. Second, judges often read the first few entries with enthusiasm and excitement. Don't wait until the judge is reading his three hundredth entry only days before his final deadline.

6. Be patient. Remember that running a contest takes time. The contest entries must be received and processed before the judges even get to take a look at your work. Then, after they've made their decision, the final results have to be compiled by the sponsor or organizers of the contest before being announced. Trying to contact the contest via e-mail or phone will only slow down the process, and most likely aggravate whomever you manage to reach.

Even if you take all of this into consideration, know that every judge looks for different things in a manuscript. So don't worry if you can't find your entry on the list of prize winners. All judging is subjective. Next year's judges might be more keen on your word usage and writing style. It's also possible that other entries had tighter writing, clearer character descriptions, and fewer grammatical mistakes than yours. Rework your manuscript to make it even better for the next contest.

A final thing to understand with contests is that many will want to buy one-time rights or first rights for your manuscript. But some ask (and require) "all rights," which means your stellar entry becomes property of the contest sponsor. If that's the case, you can never enter that same piece of work in another contest, publish it, or use part of the material verbatim in any other way. Relinquishing all rights is only worth it when the prize or recognition is higher than average.

Making the Most of Winning

Once reassured that, yes, it is your manuscript in the winner's circle, you might be tempted to believe an award equals a free ticket to publication. This is not necessarily the case. There are so many contests in today's writing world that a winning entry won't automatically lead to publication, nor will it ensure large cash prizes in other contests. You can, however, take steps to keep your entry from fading in the minds of editors. Here's what to remember if you want to go from contest winner to oft-published writer:

- **Embrace feedback.** Many contests offer winning recipients (or sometimes every entrant) feedback from one of the contest judges. These contests are excellent to enter, since advice from someone who's made it in your field is priceless. If comments are made on your entry, study them. Make a mental note to fix any problems in future manuscripts.

- **Market yourself.** You won or placed in a contest because your writing was good. Now let the world know. Bring up the contest on your website; discuss it with others on Facebook and Twitter; mention it to contacts in the publishing business; and be sure to highlight it in future queries to publishers and agents. State the contest name and, if the number is impressive, how many entrants you beat. If the contest is split into various categories, mention which category claims you as the top winner. Bottom line: Winning a contest is hard work. Your friends and family aren't the only ones who will be impressed.

- **Keep in touch.** If you know the names of your judges, keep this information in the back of your mind. Is one a book publisher?

Remember to send him the book proposal that's been sitting on your desk. Does another work for a magazine? Think of an article idea and send it to her attention. Perhaps the contest sponsor is a certain magazine or publishing house—talk yourself up among other editors in that organization. Another bonus to keeping in touch: You may be included in future updates. For example, Writer's Digest often keeps track of the writing kudos received by past winners. This is the perfect opportunity for free press if you're lucky enough to score a writing contract or finish a manuscript down the road.

- **Understand where you stand.** If you didn't win, take a look at the winning entries. (They're often published in a booklet, which you'll be able to purchase from the contest sponsor.) What did they do differently? Take a look at the judges—do they have professional experience in your specific genre? Multiple factors go into choosing a contest winner, so don't beat yourself up if you didn't happen to make it this time. It's the feedback that'll be most helpful to you.

IMPROVING YOUR ODDS

Contests are tough to win, but you can improve your odds considerably by adhering to the following suggestions:

1. **Research the judges of each contest.** They should have professional experience in whatever niche they're judging.

2. **Approximate how many entries are submitted to the contest.** An easy way to do this is to see how many entries were submitted last year. Placing out of fifty entries is easier than placing out of three hundred entries.

3. **Check to see if the contest accepts published and non-published work.** If the contest only accepts one or the other, chances for a level playing field are better. Contests that are open only to members of a specific organization also help narrow the field.

4. **Look for contests that accept manuscripts in particular or prescribed categories.** By entering your fiction manuscript in a strictly fiction category, your entry will do better than when placed in a general contest with entries from multiple fields all vying for one award.

Finding fellowships, grants, and contests that are a good fit for your writing is possible, but don't be discouraged if they are hard to find. Keep checking sources such as *Writer's Market* or www.writersmarket.com for possibilities. Talk to other writers you know and see if they have any suggestions or contacts. The effort you put into locating possible sources of extra money for your work will be well worth it if you put the same amount of effort into the work you submit. Like submitting to an agent or editor, don't give up simply because you've been rejected once. Persevere until you get the award you've been hoping for.

APPENDIX A: PRICING GUIDE

AS A GROUP, writers are underpaid. Surveys by organizations such as The Authors Guild and the National Writers Union show that income growth for most writers lags behind that of most other professions. The question for you, then, is how do you maximize your earning potential either as a full-time or a part-time writer? In actuality, freelance writing is similar to other creative fields like art, photography, and music. You can either earn hobby rates or you can earn a professional wage. The difference is in how seriously you take your work.

Freelancers who command top dollar are experienced professionals who have spent years perfecting their skills either as freelancers or as writers employed in journalism, advertising, public relations, or publishing. Beyond being talented writers, they are reliable professionals who respect deadlines and have mastered the fine details of running an independent business. They are especially good at marketing themselves. A freelancer, like any independent business person, must also set goals and develop a business plan. The plan doesn't have to be as formal as those for bigger businesses, but at the very least you have to decide what writing skills you have to sell, who might buy them, and how you will prove you are the best person for the job.

KNOWING WHAT TO CHARGE

While producers of other products can check out the competition's prices at malls and markets, writers are lonely souls, left to negotiate individually with publishers and clients. Joining a writers' group can broaden your perspective on pay rates, particularly a national group, such as the Editorial Freelancers Association or the National Writers Union, which publish data about how much their members earn for jobs. Reading books like Writer's Market, which annually publishes lists of pay scales for dozens of types of writing, can also help you determine what to charge. Joining a bulletin board discussion at websites like www.everywritersresource.com allows you to simply post your rates and ask plugged-in counterparts, "Am I charging enough?"

Freelancers find most of their work networking with other writers, editors, and potential clients. Other good leads come through e-mail and/or hard-copy queries, or networking through Chambers of Commerce and similar organizations. But the best referrals come from satisfied clients who tell others about your work.

As is the case in most professions, beginning writers also earn less than those who have been in the business longer. In addition, asking for more money is never easy. Some clients may be more willing to negotiate with writers who have already produced materials that meet their needs, but many are not willing to do so when dealing with a new freelancer. To get your feet wet, you may have to settle for less—at first. The trick is to raise your prices as your reputation grows. Remember: The best client is one who is willing to pay you more than once.

HOURLY RATE CALCULATION

It is important to know the hourly rate you need to earn in order to meet your needs. Follow these steps to calculate what your earnings must be in order for you to be a successful freelance writer.

> 1. Covering expenses. To figure out how much you'll have to earn per hour to pay for expenses, first decide how much time you'll have to devote to writing per month. To calculate the break-even hourly rate, divide your monthly expenses (see

chapter sixteen) by the number of hours you plan to work. In the example below, if you can work 160 hours each month on your writing, the hourly rate would be $1,488/160 = $9.50 per hour.

Consider this your bare minimum hourly rate, because it does not include any remuneration for your expertise or any profit. If you use this figure to give an estimate for a job, you'd be valuing your time and talent at zero.

MONTHLY EXPENSE CALCULATION		MONTHLY EXPENSE WORKSHEET	
Computer ($1,600/12 months)	$134	Computer (divided by 12)	$_____
Printer ($200/12 months)	$17	Computer (divided by 12)	$_____
Telephone	$35	Telephone	$_____
Office Supplies	$25	Office Supplies	$_____
Postage	$15	Postage	$_____
Taxes	$1,250 (estimate)	Taxes (50% of gross)	$_____
Other ($144/12 months)	$12	Other (divided by 12)	$_____
TOTAL	$1,488	TOTAL	$_____

2. Setting fees. One way to make sure you are paid market rates is to estimate how much a company would pay an employee to do similar work. Remember that a company may also pay for health insurance, retirement funds, unemployment insurance, vacation time, holidays, etc. These costs can range from 25 to 45 percent of an employee's annual salary,

depending on which perks the employee gets and where she lives. Use a 35 percent estimate to get a rough idea.

- Estimated yearly salary: $40,000 divided by 2,000 (40 hours per week for 50 weeks) equals an hourly pay rate of $20. (This formula assumes you will take two weeks of vacation a year. Adjust the formula as needed.)

- Adding fringe benefit costs of 35 percent ($7) gives you an hourly rate of $27.

- Add to this amount your minimum rate to cover overhead ($9.50) and you have a total hourly rate of $36.50.

- In addition, you might want to add another 20 percent of profit ($7.30) to cover things like self-employment tax, the additional costs of insuring yourself, etc. This makes for a total hourly fee of $43.80, which you would round up to $45 or $50.

A rate of $50 or more an hour may be high for a particular type of writing or may be quite reasonable depending on your level of experience, the perceived value of your work, the going rate for your geographical area, and the prevailing rates available to the client. In determining the prices you will charge for various types of work you must first conduct research. This includes talking to other writers about what they charge.

When calculating the hours you invest in your work you also need to consider the time spent writing queries and making calls to find jobs, billing, filing tax returns, driving to the post office, shopping for office supplies, and maintaining your computer. To be successful, at least one-fifth of your time should be spent marketing yourself. Your hourly rate for all these activities needs to be recouped somewhere—either in higher fees or additional hours that you bill your clients.

None of the above calculations includes reimbursement for expenses for specific jobs, such as travel, overnight mail, or long-distance telephone calls. These should be added to the bill and paid by the client. It's best to have a written contract spelling out what work you are expected to do at what rate.

PROJECT RATE CALCULATION

An alternative way of pricing is to charge by the project. The advantage of project pricing is that if you work quickly, you can earn a high hourly rate. If you quote a price of three hundred dollars for a piece and manage to turn it around in three hours, well, you do the math. If you decide to work more slowly, that's your option, too. But with a project rate, you've set your ceiling and a client probably won't pay you more.

The disadvantage of accepting a project price is that if you estimate too low, you may discover you could have earned better wages elsewhere. You can always try negotiating for more, but you'll have to convince your client why your original estimate was wrong, which is difficult and, if it's your fault, embarrassing.

Some clients will tell you the pay rate up front. Others may ask what you charge. If asked, don't be evasive. It's not very professional to show uncertainty about something as basic and important as your price. Since they're asking, feel free to quote your full fee. Remember, you can always adjust downward, but it's hard to negotiate upward after you have already quoted a price.

Seasoned writers have an easier time figuring out an acceptable price for a project. Almost by instinct they can discern the amount of time and effort that will go into a project. Beginners typically fare better by focusing on an hourly fee. This way they not only learn which types of projects are best suited for them, but they also can keep better track of the gains they make in skill and efficiency. Unfortunately, most clients want a fixed price, especially if they are not familiar with your work. The solution is to negotiate a set price based on the number of hours you expect to spend on the project. If you are going to earn a set fee, it is important to detail up front precisely what the work will entail. Once you have talked this over with the client or editor, estimate how many hours you expect to spend on the project including research, interviews, editing, and proofreading. (It helps to look at similar projects completed for the client in the past.) Then multiply the number of hours by your hourly rate to get the amount of money you expect to earn.

When starting out as a freelance writer, you won't be able to command the same fee as someone with several years of experience. This does not mean, however, that you are at the mercy of the client. If you are qualified as a writer, you are producing a professional product and should be compensated fairly. Decide early on the lowest figure you will accept and stick to it.

Early in your career, you might not make out as well charging by the project. But as you gain experience—enabling you to work faster and to estimate your time better—you will do quite well. Publications and most other businesses are time sensitive. To your pleasant surprise, clients and editors will be willing to pay you more for getting work done more quickly. As your proficiency and efficiency improve you will, in effect, earn more money for less work.

KEEP TRACK OF TIME

Keeping track of how long it takes to finish a project might feel as if you're attaching a meter to your mind. But it is vitally important, whether you are charging by the hour or by the project. By keeping good records for specific types of projects, you will eventually discern patterns. You can use the insight you gain to improve your work flow, cut out unnecessary steps, and set fees that maximize your income while still keeping you competitive. Even so, many writers do not closely track how much time they spend on a project. Even if they know how much time they spend at the keyboard, they often underestimate the hours spent researching, interviewing, billing, and corresponding with their clients.

It need not be this way. Keeping track of your time doesn't take as much effort as you might think. And the payoff far outweighs the investment of time you put into it. The insight you gain into your work habits can help you better use your time in the future—giving you more free time down the road. You will also improve your ability to accurately bid your services.

One easy method is to watch the clock and keep a log book by your computer or in your briefcase. Some people even use a stopwatch. They simply start the watch when they begin work, turn it off whenever they step away, and turn it on again when they resume work. The watch keeps an accurate tally of their cumulative time.

Ironically, it's sometimes the small projects that reveal the most about our work habits. Bigger projects get spread over weeks or even months, making it harder to get a clear picture of all the work involved. A small project that lasts just a couple days is easier to track and analyze. You might be surprised by what you learn.

NEGOTIATING FOR MORE

Few of us like to haggle over the price of goods or services. When you land a writing job, however, you are in a good negotiating position: You have something your client wants.

A good rule to consider in wrangling over fees is to imagine a triangle with three points: good, fast, and inexpensive. Most people want things done well, inexpensively, and fast. But most times, they will only get two of the three. For example, you might be able to write something cheaply and fast, but you probably won't be able to do it well. Or you can do it fast and make it good, but it won't be inexpensive. By this reasoning, if a client asks for a quick turnaround time, you should expect to be paid extra for it.

Once you work with a client or editor and prove you can deliver, it will be easier to negotiate for more money. While many editors are understandably reluctant to invest large amounts in unknown writers, they may be able to find more in their budgets for someone they have come to know and trust.

It may be easier for beginning writers to quote a range of pay they would like to earn. You could tell the client the job would cost between one and two hundred dollars, for example, depending on how much time it involves. If you can do it for less, they may be grateful for a smaller bill and be more willing to give you another assignment. But never undervalue your work, for if you do, you can be sure that others will, too.

Negotiation doesn't have to be confrontational. After all, an editor often doesn't hold the purse strings and may be sympathetic to polite requests for more money. Before you ask for more (or ask to retain certain rights to resell your work), decide which things you sincerely want and which you can give up. First, state everything you would like. Then be prepared to adopt a position that gets you most of what you want. If you've kept a log of how long previous projects have taken and what types of work they entailed, your arguments will be more persuasive. Be realistic, however. A publication that pays ten cents a word is hardly likely to increase that tenfold.

Keep in mind that business people talk money all the time, and writing is a business. If you ask for more, usually the worst that could happen is you'll be told no. At that point, it's up to you to decide whether you'll take the job or move on.

RAISING YOUR RATES

A freelancer, like any business person, eventually faces the day when he needs to raise prices. Maybe it is because inflation has cut into your profit margin or your living standard. Perhaps you feel the value of your services has increased. Or maybe you have discovered that you have been pricing your services below the market value. In any of these cases, don't be reluctant to ask for what you think is fair and justified.

Other businesses consistently raise their rates. Price increases are a fact of life. So don't keep your prices artificially low when an increase is justified. Underpricing your services can produce an image that you lack the skill and experience to command professional fees. It can also suggest that your work is of lower quality.

If you do decide to raise your rates, avoid being erratic. If you change prices often—whether raising or lowering them—you may create the impression that you have no basis for your fee. When you do raise your price, make the increases small and base the change on a sound business decision you can justify. Keep in mind that an increase of just a few percent in your overall price can raise your profit margin substantially.

Of course, you don't always have to raise your rates to bring in extra income. If you really can't justify a rate increase, examine your work for instances where you give services to clients for free. While you don't want to nickel-and-dime your clients with petty fees, neither do you want to give away vital services, especially when the client receives a direct benefit. If you keep good track of your time, you can also look for ways that you may be wasting time. Improving your work habits can have the same effect as raising your rates. You can increase your earning potential by being more efficient.

You can also base your price on speed of delivery. If you are asked to turn a project around in half the time, charge 10 to 20 percent extra for this value-added service. Chances are you have to put other projects on hold and work extra hard to accomplish a last-minute request. Be fair, but charge extra for the added effort. Most businesses and consumers realize the added value of convenience, which is why we pay more for quick oil changes, overnight shipments, and eyeglasses that are ready "in about an hour."

If you are questioned about a price change, explain how you have incorporated extra value into your services and how your work has helped the client win business or helped a publication gain readership. Explain how your fee is a bargain given the benefits provided or the service received.

As a final word, consider this: A client who does not want you to earn a fair wage is not a client worth having. Is it worth losing some low-profit clients in return for earning extra income from your more profitable clients? Raising your prices may be a way to do a profitable business in a forty-hour week—to work smarter instead of working longer hours.

SAMPLE FEES

The following prices are culled from the 2010 Writer's Market survey and represent a range of prices charged by freelance writers across North America. Use the prices only as general guidelines because the fees writers charge can vary greatly depending on location, size, complexity of the project, and the writer's own experience or expertise. The prices do not include additional expenses that are typically paid by the client. You can learn more about the going rates charged in your area by networking with other writers or by joining professional writers' organizations near you. The benefits you receive will likely be more than offset the annual fees charged by most groups.

Advertising, Copywriting, and PR

Ad copywriting: $40 to $125 per hour, avg. $1.59 per word
News release: $40 to $100 per hour, avg. $440 per page
Speechwriting: $43 to $150 per hour, $2,700 to $10,000 per 30-minute speech

Audiovisual

Copyediting: $35 to $90 per hour
Film script for business: $50 to $150 per hour

Radio editorials: $50 to $70 per hour

Screenplay: $56,500 to $106,070 per screenplay

TV commercial/PSA: $60 to $85 per hour

TV movie: $100 to $500 per run minute

TV news feature: $70 to $100 per hour

TV scripts (teleplay): $100 to $500 per run minute

Book Publishing

Abstracting and abridging: $30 to $125 per hour

Book proposal consultation/writing: $30 to $125 per hour

Book query critique: $50 to $100 per hour

Book query writing: $120 to $500 per project, $200 average per project

Content editing: $29 to $100 per hour

Copyediting: $25 to $100 per hour

Ghostwriting, uncredited: $30 to $100 per hour

Indexing: $2.75 to $6 per page

Manuscript evaluation and critique: $23 to $100 per hour

Proofreading: $19 to $55 per hour, $2 to $5 per page

Research: $20 to $100 per hour, avg. $53 per hour

Rewriting: $30 to $100 per hour

Translation: 6¢ to 12¢ per target word, $7,000 to $10,000 per book

Business and Government

Annual reports: $45 to $150 per hour, $1,000 to $15,000 per project

Brochures/fliers: $50 to $200 per hour, avg. $2,777 per project

Business plan: $35 to $125 per hour

Catalogs: $50 to $80 per hour, avg. $5,000 per project

Corporate periodicals, writing: $35 to $125 per hour, $83 average per hour; $1.75 per word

Grant proposal: $30 to $125 per hour

Computer and Technical

Computer manual writing: $43 to $125 per hour

Online editing: $25 to $100 per hour; avg. $38 per hour

Technical writing: $40 to $125 per hour; avg. $65 per hour

Web page writing/editing: $40 to $125 per hour

Magazines and Trade Journals

Book/arts reviews: $25 to $900 per project

Content editing: $30 to $100 per hour, avg. $3,167 per issue

Copyediting: $20 to $60 per hour, $39 average per hour

Fact checking: $25 to $100 per hour

Feature articles: $100 to $10,000 per project; avg. $3,597

Proofreading: $17 to $60 per hour

Newspapers

Book/art reviews: $15 to $200 high per review

Copyediting: $15 to $35 per hour; $26 per hour avg.

Feature story: $125 to $1,040 per project; $350 avg.

Local column: avg. $171 per column

Obituary: $35 to $225 per story; avg. $112 per story

Proofreading: $15 to $25 per hour; avg. $19 per hour

Stringing: $50 to $1,000 high per story; avg. $290 per story

RESOURCES

These books and websites can help you as you determine your rates.

WEBSITES

Anne Wallingford, WordSmith (www.aw-wrdsmth.com). Anne Wallingford's Freelancer's FAQs offers useful information about setting fees, taxes, and other aspects of finance.

National Writers Union (www.nwu.org). In a section for members, includes a database of magazine rates paid to NWU members.

Society for Technical Communication (www.stc.org). The STC publishes a survey for members detailing salaries and benefits in the U.S. and Canada. For technical writers and editors.

WritersMarket.com (www.writersmarket.com). Offers members a link to the detailed results of its annual rate survey.

BOOKS

The Wealthy Writer **by Michael Meanwell** (Writer's Digest Books). Includes suggested pricing for high-paying freelance writing work.

Writer's Market (Writer's Digest Books). Includes typical pay rates, updated annually, for a variety of writing and publishing work. Writer's Market Deluxe Edition includes access to WritersMarket.com, the regularly updated online component of the book.

APPENDIX B: GLOSSARY OF PUBLISHING TERMS

Advance: A sum of money a publisher pays a writer prior to the publication of a book. It is usually paid in installments, such as one-half on signing the contract; one-half on delivery of a complete and satisfactory manuscript. The advance is paid against the royalty money that will be earned by the book.

Agent: A liaison between a writer and editor or publisher. An agent shops a manuscript around, receiving a commission when the manuscript is accepted. Agents usually take a 15 percent fee from the advance and royalties, and an additional percentage if a co-agent is involved, such as in the sale of dramatic rights.

Anthology: A collection of selected writings by various authors or a gathering of works by one author.

Assignment: Editor asks a writer to produce a specific article for an agreed-upon fee.

Auction: Publishers sometimes bid for the acquisition of a book manuscript that has excellent sales prospects. The bids are for the amount of the author's advance, advertising and promotional expenses, royalty percentage, etc. Auctions are conducted by agents.

Avant-garde: Writing that is innovative in form, style, or subject, often considered difficult and challenging.

B&W: Abbreviation for black-and-white illustrations or photographs.

Backlist: A publisher's list of its books that were not published during the current season, but are still in print.

Bin: A sentence or brief paragraph about the writer. It can appear at the bottom of the first or last page of a writer's article or short story or on a contributor's page.

Blog: Short for weblog. An online journal, diary, or hub in which the blogger uses writing, images, videos, and links to state opinions and interact with others online.

Boilerplate: A standardized contract. When an editor says "our standard contract," he means the boilerplate with no changes. Writers should be aware that most authors and/or agents make many changes to the boilerplate.

Book packager: Draws all elements of a book together, from the initial concept to writing and marketing strategies, then sells the book package to a book publisher. Also known as a book producer or book developer.

Byline: Name of the author appearing with the published piece.

Category fiction: A term used to include all various labels attached to types of fiction. See also genre.

Circulation: The number of subscribers to a magazine.

Clean copy: A manuscript free of errors, cross-outs, wrinkles, or smudges.

Clips: Samples, usually from newspapers or magazines, of your published work.

Coffee-table book: An oversized, heavily illustrated book.

Column inch: The amount of space contained in one inch of a typeset column.

Commercial novels: Novels designed to appeal to a broad audience. These are often broken down into categories such as Western, mystery, and romance. See also genre.

Concept: A statement that summarizes a screenplay or teleplay before the outline or treatment is written.

Confessional: Genre of essay in which the author or first-person narrator confesses something shocking or embarrassing.

Contributor's copies: Copies of the issues of magazines sent to the author in which the author's work appears.

Co-publishing: Arrangement where author and publisher share publication costs and profits of a book. Also known as cooperative publishing. See also subsidy publisher.

Copyediting: Editing a manuscript for grammar, punctuation, and printing style, not subject content.

Copyright: A means to protect an author's work.

Cover letter: A brief letter, accompanying a complete manuscript, especially useful if responding to an editor's request for a manuscript. A cover letter also may accompany a book proposal. A cover letter is not a query letter.

Creative nonfiction: Nonfiction writing that uses an innovative approach to the subject and creative language.

CV: Curriculum vita. A brief listing of qualifications and career accomplishments, like a resume.

Derivative works: A work that has been translated, adapted, abridged, condensed, annotated, or otherwise produced by altering a previously created work. Before producing a derivative work, it is necessary to secure the written permission of the copyright owner of the original piece.

Desktop publishing: A publishing system designed for a personal computer. The system is capable of typesetting, some illustration, layout, design, and printing so the final piece can be distributed and/or sold.

Docudrama: A fictional film rendition of recent newsmaking events and people.

Dramatic poetry: Poetry written for performance as a play. It is one of the three main genres of poetry (the others being lyric poetry and narrative poetry).

Eclectic: Publication features a variety of different writing styles or genres.

Electronic submission: A submission made by e-mail or on computer disk/CD.

E-mail: Electronic mail. Mail generated on a computer and delivered over a computer network to a specific individual or group of individuals.

Erotica: Fiction or art that is sexually oriented.

Facebook: A popular social networking site where individuals can "friend" one another, discuss what they are doing, and share opinions on culture.

Fair use: A provision of the copyright law that says short passages from copyrighted material may be used without infringing on the owner's rights.

Feature: An article giving the reader information of human interest rather than news. Also used by magazines to indicate a lead article or distinctive department.

Filler: A short item used by an editor to "fill" out a newspaper column or magazine page. It could be a timeless news item, a joke, an anecdote, some light verse or short humor, puzzle, etc.

First-person point of view: In nonfiction, the author reports from his own perspective; in fiction, the narrator tells the story from her point of view. This viewpoint makes frequent use of "I," or occasionally, "we."

Formula story: Familiar theme treated in a predictable plot structure—such as boy meets girl, boy loses girl, boy gets girl back.

Frontlist: A publisher's list of its books that are new to the current season.

Galleys: The first typeset version of a manuscript that has not yet been divided into pages.

Genre: Refers either to a general classification of writing, such as the novel or the poem, or to the categories within those classifications, such as the problem novel or the sonnet. Genre fiction describes commercial novels, such as mysteries, romances, and science fiction. Also called category fiction.

Ghostwriter: A writer who puts into literary form an article, speech, story, or book based on another person's ideas or knowledge.

Gift book: A book designed as a gift item. Often small in size with few illustrations and placed close to a bookstore's checkout as an "impulse" buy, gift books tend to be written to a specific niche, such as golfers, mothers, etc.

Glossy: A photograph with a shiny surface as opposed to one with a matte finish.

Google: The primary search engine on the Internet. In addition to organizing information through precision searching, Google also provides more specialized kinds of information through Google Earth, Google Maps, Google Groups, Google Translate, and others.

Gothic novel: A fiction category or genre in which the central character is usually a beautiful young girl, the setting an old mansion or castle, and there is a handsome hero and a real menace, either natural or supernatural.

Graphic novel: An adaptation of a novel in graphic form, long comic strip, or heavily illustrated story, of forty pages or more, produced in paperback form.

Hard copy: The printed copy of a computer's output.

High-lo: Material written for newer readers, generally adults, with a high interest level and low reading ability.

Honorarium: Token payment—small amount of money, or a byline and copies of the publication.

How-to: Books and magazine articles offering a combination of information and advice in describing how something can be accomplished. Subjects range widely from hobbies to psychology.

Hypertext: Words or groups of words in an electronic document that are linked to other text, such as a definition or a related document. Hypertext can also be linked to illustrations.

Illustrations: May be photographs, old engravings, or artwork. Usually paid for separately from the manuscript. See also package sale.

Imprint: Name applied to a publisher's specific line or lines of books (e.g., Avon is an imprint of HarperCollins).

Interactive fiction: Works of fiction in book or computer software format in which the reader determines the path the story will take. The reader chooses from several alternatives at the end of a "chapter," and thus determines the structure of the story. Interactive fiction features multiple plots and endings.

Internet: A worldwide network of computers that offers access to a wide variety of electronic resources.

Kill fee: Fee for a complete article that was assigned but which was subsequently cancelled.

Lead time: The time between the acquisition of a manuscript by an editor and its actual publication.

Libel: A false accusation or any published statement or presentation that tends to expose another to public contempt, ridicule, etc.

List royalty: A royalty payment based on a percentage of a book's retail (or "list") price.

Literary fiction: The general category of serious, nonformulaic, intelligent fiction.

Little magazine: Publications of limited circulation, usually on literary or political subject matter.

Lyric poetry: Poetry in which music predominates over story or drama. It is one of the three main genres of poetry (the others being dramatic poetry and narrative poetry).

Mainstream fiction: Fiction that transcends popular novel categories such as mystery, romance, and science fiction. Using conventional methods, this kind of fiction tells stories about people and their conflicts with greater depth of characterization, background, etc., than the more narrowly focused genre novels.

Mass market: Nonspecialized books of wide appeal directed toward a large audience. Smaller and more cheaply produced than trade paperbacks, they are found in nonbookstore outlets, such as supermarkets.

Memoir: A narrative recounting a writer's (or fictional narrator's) personal or family history.

Midlist: Those titles on a publisher's list that are not expected to be big sellers, but are expected to have limited sales. They are usually written by new or unknown writers.

Monograph: A detailed and documented scholarly study concerning a single subject.

Multimedia: Computers and software capable of integrating text, sound, photographic-quality images, animation, and video.

Multiple submissions: Sending more than one poem, story, or greeting card idea at the same time.

Narrative nonfiction: A narrative presentation of actual events.

Narrative poem: Poetry that tells a story. One of the three main genres of poetry (the others being dramatic poetry and lyric poetry).

Net royalty: A royalty payment based on the amount of money a book publisher receives on the sale of a book after booksellers' discounts, special sales discounts, and returns.

Network: A group of computers electronically linked to share information and resources.

Novelization: A novel created from the script of a popular movie, usually called a movie "tie-in" and published in paperback.

Novella: A short novel, or a long short story; approximately 7,000 to 15,000 words. Also known as a novelette.

On spec: An editor expresses an interest in a proposed article idea and agrees to consider the finished piece for publication "on speculation." The editor is under no obligation to buy the finished manuscript.

One-time rights: Grants a publication a single-use, nonexclusive right to your material.

Outline: A summary of a book's contents in five to fifteen double-spaced pages; often in the form of chapter headings with a descriptive sentence or two under each one to show the scope of the book. A screenplay's or teleplay's outline is a scene-by-scene narrative description of the story (10 to 15 pages for a 1/2-hour teleplay; 15 to 25 pages for a 1-hour teleplay; 25 to 40 pages for a 90-minute teleplay; 40 to 60 pages for a 2-hour feature film or teleplay).

Over-the-transom: Describes the submission of unsolicited material by a freelance writer.

Package sale: The editor buys manuscript and photos as a "package" and pays for them with one check.

Page rate: Some magazines pay for material at a fixed rate per published page, rather than per word.

Parody: The conscious imitation of a work, usually with the intent to ridicule or make fun of the work.

Payment on acceptance: The editor sends you a check for your article, story, or poem as soon as he decides to publish it.

Payment on publication: The editor doesn't send you a check for your material until it is published.

Photo feature: Feature in which the emphasis is on the photographs rather than on accompanying written material.

Plagiarism: Passing off as one's own the expression of ideas and words of another writer.

Platform: An author's influence over her core audience, and that author's ability to sell a book. Platforms may include speaking engagements, blogs, regular columns, conference appearances, and social media profiles, among other things.

POD: Print on demand. Digital technology that enables authors and publishers to order only as many copies of a book as they actually need.

Podcast: An Internet radio program.

Proofreading: Close reading and correction of a manuscript's typographical errors.

Proposal: A summary of a proposed book submitted to a publisher, particularly used for nonfiction manuscripts. A proposal often contains an individualized cover letter, one-page overview of the book, marketing information, competitive books, author information, chapter-by-chapter outline, two to three sample chapters, and attachments (if relevant) such as magazine articles about the topic and articles you have written (particularly on the proposed topic).

Prospectus: A preliminary written description of a book or article, usually one page in length.

Pseudonym: A pen name.

Public domain: Material that was either never copyrighted or whose copyright term has expired.

Query: A letter that sells an idea to an editor. Usually a query is brief (no more than one page) and uses attention-getting prose.

Release: A statement that your idea is original, has never been sold to anyone else, and you are selling the negotiated rights to the idea upon payment.

Remainders: Copies of a book that are slow to sell and can be purchased from the publisher at a reduced price. Depending on the author's book contract, a reduced royalty or no royalty is paid on remainders.

Roundup article: Comments from, or interviews with, a number of celebrities or experts on a single theme.

Royalties: The author's share of a publisher's sales of the book, after earning out any advance paid before publication. Traditionally, royalties were paid on the list price of the book, but many publishers have moved to a less lucrative pay schedule based on the net price of the book.

Screenplay: Script for a film intended to be shown in theaters.

Self-publishing: In this arrangement, the author keeps all income derived from the book, but he pays for its manufacturing, production, and marketing.

Serial: Published periodically, such as a newspaper or magazine.

Serial fiction: Fiction published in a magazine in installments, often broken off at a suspenseful spot.

Series fiction: A sequence of novels featuring the same characters.

Short-short: A complete short story of 1,500 words maximum, and around 250 words minimum.

Sidebar: A feature presented as a companion to a straight news report (or main magazine article) giving sidelights on human-interest aspects or sometimes elucidating just one aspect of the story.

Simultaneous submissions: Sending the same article, story, or poem to several publishers at the same time. Some publishers refuse to consider such submissions.

Slant: The approach or style of a story or article that will appeal to readers of a specific magazine. For example, a magazine may always use stories with an upbeat ending.

Slice-of-life vignette: A short fiction piece intended to realistically depict an interesting moment of everyday living.

Slush pile: The stack of unsolicited or misdirected manuscripts received by an editor or book publisher.

Social networking: Also called social media. Online, interactive tools for creating communities around a book, author, or common interest.

Subsidiary rights: All rights other than book publishing rights included in a book contract, such as paperback, book club, movie rights, etc.

Subsidy publisher: A book publisher who charges the author for the cost to typeset and print a book, the jacket, etc., as opposed to a royalty publisher who pays the author.

Synopsis: A brief summary of a story, novel, or play. As part of a book proposal, it is a comprehensive summary condensed in a page or page and a half, single-spaced.

Tabloid: Newspaper format publication on about half the size of the regular newspaper page, such as the National Enquirer. These are not usually considered hard journalism.

Tagline: A caption for a photo or a comment added to a filler.

Teleplay: A play written for or performed on television.

TOC: Table of contents.

Trade: Either a hardcover or paperback book; subject matter frequently concerns a special interest. Books are directed toward the layperson rather than the professional.

Treatment: Synopsis of a TV or film script (forty to sixty pages for a two-hour feature film or teleplay).

Twitter: A microblogging website that is sometimes part of an author's social media presence.

Unsolicited manuscript: A story, article, poem, or book that an editor did not specifically ask to see.

Vanity publisher: See subsidy publisher.

Work-for-hire: Author surrenders creative rights to the work in exchange for a flat, one-time fee.

World Wide Web (WWW): An Internet resource that utilizes hypertext to access information. It also supports formatted text, illustrations, and sounds, depending on the user's computer capabilities.

YA: Young adult books.

INDEX